RENEGADE MONK

RENEGADE MONK

Hōnen and Japanese
Pure Land Buddhism

SOHO MACHIDA

TRANSLATED AND EDITED BY

IOANNIS MENTZAS

University of California Press
Berkeley · Los Angeles · London

University of California Press
Berkeley and Los Angeles, California

University of California Press, Ltd.
London, England

© 1999 by
The Regents of the University of California

Library of Congress Cataloging-in-Publication Data

Machida, Sōhō, 1950–
    Renegade Monk : Hōnen and Japanese Pure Land Buddhism /
Soho Machida ; translated and edited by Ioannis Mentzas.
       p. cm.
    Includes bibliographic references and index.
    ISBN 0-520-21179-0 (alk. paper)
    1. Hōnen, 1133–1212.   2. Jōdoshū—Doctrines.   3. Pure Land Buddhism—
Japan—History.   I. Mentzas, Ioannis.   II. Title.
BQ8649.H667M23   1999
294.3'926—dc21   98-22139
[B]   CIP

Printed in the United States of America

9 8 7 6 5 4 3 2 1

Contents

Acknowledgments

In 1992, I submitted a doctoral dissertation to the Department of Asian and Middle Eastern Studies at the University of Pennsylvania. I called my work *The Specificity of Hōnen*. In a few years, my views on the subject changed drastically; in the course of substantial revision, I decided to produce a totally new book in my own language. The result, *Hōnen: Seikimatsu no kakumeisha* (Hōnen: Revolutionary in an Eschatological Era), was published by Hōzōkan in 1997 and was reviewed very generously by both specialists and nonspecialists. This English version expands further on that Japanese volume.

I owe much to Ioannis Mentzas, a doctoral candidate at Columbia University, who not only translated my work into superb English but also suggested new insights due to his strong background in critical theory. Together we inserted additional points of reference. Rather than seeking refuge in the ideal of word-for-word fidelity to the original, we preferred to recast the book so as to see it newly buoyant in a new context. Professional guidance from Laura Driussi and Rachel Berchten, editors at the University of California Press, and from David Severtson, who copyedited the manuscript, must also be mentioned here. I am thankful too for the support offered me over the years by Professor Martin Collcutt, my colleague at Princeton University.

Finally, I would like to express my huge debt to Machiko Machida, my wife, whose enduring support lies beneath every sentence.

Abbreviations

HSZ   Ishii Kyōdō, ed. *Shōwa shinshū Hōnen Shōnin zenshū.*

JZ   Jōdoshū kaishū happyakunen kinen keisan junbikyoku, ed. *Jōdoshū zensho.*

NKT   Iwanami Shoten, ed. *Nihon koten bungaku taikei.*

NSI   Risshō Daigaku Nichiren Kyōgaku Kenkyūsho, ed. *Shōwa teihon Nichiren Shōnin ibun.*

NST   Iwanami Shoten, ed. *Nihon shisō taikei.*

SZ   Ishida Mizumaro, ed. *Shinran zenshū.*

Z   Ōhashi Shunyū, ed. *Hōnen zenshū.*

Introduction

Give up your professionally rigorous asceticism. Not even an ethically regulated life will save you. Simply chant *namu Amida butsu*—the *nembutsu*—and you will be delivered from your sins and to the Pure Land.

With this message of exclusive-*nembutsu* (*senju-nembutsu*), Hōnenbō Genkū (1133–1212), known as Hōnen, founded the Pure Land sect of Japanese Buddhism. Today the Pure Land or Jōdo sect, with approximately seven thousand temples and three-and-a-half million followers, comprises one of the strongest currents of sectarian Buddhism in Japan. Hōnen's name is associated, on the one hand, with the far-reaching initial dissemination of *nembutsu* belief in the medieval era and, on the other hand, with that of his famous disciple Shinran (1173–1262), whose *Tan'nishō* (Notes Lamenting Deviations) is read by a wide generational spectrum of what may be termed a Japanese "general public."

Its tenets were at once simple and revolutionary. Exclusive-*nembutsu* immediately aroused popular response so sympathetic and abundant as to threaten the religious order. In the *Gukanshō* (an interpretive history of Japan written in 1219), Jien (1155–1225), younger brother of Regent Kujō Kanezane and a highly regarded abbot of the Tendai school, casts a cold eye on Hōnen's popularity: "During the Ken'ei reign, a holy priest called Hōnen, residing in Kyoto, founded a *nembutsu* school that he called exclusive-*nembutsu*. He preached 'simply to recite *namu Amida butsu*, for all other practices are not among one's duties.' The mysterious inanities pleased the ignorant nuns and monks. It became popular and spread through the world" (*NKT*, 86:294). The masses were not alone in extolling Hōnen, for the regent himself, Jien's brother, also acquired a profound inclination toward *nembutsu*. We can imagine the chagrin of traditional Buddhism's highest authority, Jien.

Myōzen Hōin, another Tendai scholar-priest, reported that "many have advanced the Pure Land and preached *nembutsu* in our country, but this saint has surpassed all others in both fame and infamy" (*JZ*, 16:490). Hōnen's extraordinary power of influence may be fathomed from the first impressions of Myōe (1171–1232), Hōnen's most important contemporary critic, of the *Senchaku hongan nembutsushū* (Collection of Passages Concerning the Nembutsu of the Selected Original Vow): "Now I know in minute detail how the various heresies of innumerable *zaike* (laypeople) and *shukke* (priests) spring from this tome" (*NST*, 15:44–45). And of Hōnen himself, Myōe bemoaned, "The noble and the vulgar join in venerating him" (*JZ*, 8:128).

Likewise, Nichiren (1222–82), who clambered onto the stage of history half a century after Hōnen made his exit, noted in a calamitous tone the immense influence of exclusive-*nembutsu*:

> Thanks to Hōnen's tome, people have turned away from Shākyamuni toward Amida in the faraway West, away from Shākyamuni's Bodhisattvas, Bhaiṣajyaguru, away from all scriptures but the Pure Land Triad Sūtras, away from all temples other than Amida's. They turn away monks unless they are Pure Land sectarians. Temples are disintegrating: their moss-grown roofs resemble pine trees, and only the thinnest strands of smoke are to be seen; the cells are dilapidated, and in the wild grass the dew is deep. And yet people have reconstructed neither the temples nor their faith; thus neither holy monks nor benevolent gods have returned to the temples. Hōnen is to blame. Alas, for the past few decades, hundreds, thousands, ten thousands have been waylaid by the demonic phantasmagoria and have lost sight of the sacred laws. If they have turned away from the central Lotus Sūtra toward the marginal *nembutsu*, is it any surprise that the gods rage while demons take courage? A thousand prayers will not avert disaster—may we instead seal this one evil. (*NSI*, 1:216–17)

Of course, one of Nichiren's master tropes is hyperbole, and we need not take his words at face value;[1] nevertheless, we may surmise that Hōnen's influence did not entirely fade after his death.

In addition to eliciting criticism from contemporary antagonists, the Jōdo priest was also the rare religious persona to appear by name in literary works such as *The Tale of the Heike*, *Azuma kagami*, and *Essays in Idleness* (*Tsurezure gusa*).[2] In early medieval Japan, Hōnen had a presence that was already, in a historical sense, auratic.

THE POLEMIC IN EXCLUSIVE-*NEMBUTSU*

Hōnen had not intended to initiate a religious movement by preaching exclusive-*nembutsu*; rather, in the course of an existential self-questioning, he had finally settled upon a ruling paradox: salvation comes only in death, through Amida's Vow to save all. Thus one could be saved only by affirming death. The core of *senju-nembutsu* was non-conditional, egalitarian salvation in the moment of death. Hōnen challenged the religious establishment's threatening dogma that people were in danger of falling to hell unless they showed their dedication to the buddhas and the *kami*, as well as the priesthood. It was taking death rather than life as its point of origin that forced Hōnen to depart from the prevailing religious system. To him, quasi-professional asceticism was a waste of time and effort in a social context of crisis, and he took a distinctly negative stance toward all pursuits other than the vocalization of *nembutsu*. Hōnen asserts, "*Nembutsu* is a superior practice selected from the twenty-one billion lands of Buddha; other practices, opted against, are inferior. Thus we say, 'They do not compare.' *Nembutsu* was vowed by the Amida—not so the other practices" (Z, 2:229). To posit a one-in-twenty-one-billion choice is consciously revolutionary.

Earlier Pure Land Buddhists in Japan had always thought of vocal-*nembutsu* as an inferior practice suited for those incapable of contemplative-*nembutsu*. Hōnen's message, therefore, was an about-face. The physiognomy of Hōnen presented in biographies is that of a man flexible and tolerant enough to receive, heartily, people of all classes, but on the *nembutsu* issue he was trenchantly exclusive.[3] Hōnen insists, "Exclusive-*nembutsu*, which guarantees salvation for a hundred out of a hundred, must not be relinquished for practices that save only one out of a thousand. Focus on *nembutsu*, and forget the others" (Z, 2:157). Hōnen justified *nembutsu* not by appealing to personal conviction but by invoking none other than the ultimate authorities. "Only about *nembutsu* can it be said that Shākyamuni, Amida, and all other buddhas have chosen the practice in unison" (Z, 2:309). *Nembutsu* was defined as the most orthodox of Buddhistic practices; it was not simply a component of Pure Land dogma but the proper, consecrated choice of the omniscient and all other buddhas.

Since vocal-*nembutsu* was thus the one and only Buddhism, Hōnen never considered it to be a merely smooth path fit only for those lacking opportunities and perseverance. It is not surprising, then, that he writes in his "Reply to Kita-no-Mandokoro, Regent Kujō's Wife": "When those who are ignorant of the paths to salvation say that *nembutsu* is an easy practice for those incapable of better ones, the ignorant are also terrible slanderers" (*HSZ*, 533). It amounts to an assertion that practices other than vocal-*nembutsu* are being rejected not because of their difficulty but for their utter pointlessness. Hōnen's "Correspondence with Hōjō Masako" bespeaks an even more self-righteous view: "Those who do not believe in *nembutsu* are those who have committed serious sins in their past lives and who will promptly return to hell" (*HSZ*, 532). That last word was one he seldom used: his dogmatic and obsessive faith in *nembutsu* had pushed him so far.[4]

As the creative expression of a transcendental truth, *nembutsu* could have coexisted with other practices, but for Hōnen it necessitated a fundamental denial of the value of all other traditional pursuits of salvation. His attitude toward other Buddhist leaders reveals a belligerent hostility. Can this hostility be solely motivated by dogmatic confrontation?

LIBERATION THEOLOGY IN JAPAN

We shall make a detour through the Latin America of our own century to flesh out the polemical edge of exclusive-*nembutsu*. For many Latin American Catholic missionaries who worked in villages and slums, a serious engagement with popular suffering under perennial tyranny was added to the tasks of the Christian. During the 1960s, the Council of Latin American Bishops, held in Colombia, as well as the second Vatican Council, adopted a manifesto: Catholic ecclesiastics must act to abolish oppression and discrimination against Latin American believers: the liberation theology.

In 1971, the Peruvian priest Gustavo Gutiérrez wrote *Teología de la liberación* and established the theory and practice of the liberation of the masses as a form of Christian theology. In the Old Testament, Jehovah liberated the Jews from Egyptian rule; in the New Testament, Christ expounded the good news mostly to the poor; thus it follows, in Gutiérrez's argument, that true belief must always be accompanied by practice and that, upon hearing the voices of the oppressed, a Christian must stand up in alliance and fight structural injustice.

According to Gutiérrez, the kingdom of God is to be realized not in another world but in and through our own, through struggles for freedom.

> The universality of Christian love is only an abstraction unless it becomes concrete history, process, conflict; it is arrived at only through particularity. To love all men does not mean avoiding confrontations; it does not mean preserving a fictitious harmony. Universal love is that which in solidarity with the oppressed seeks also to liberate the oppressors from their own power, from their ambition, and from their selfishness. . . . But this cannot be achieved except by resolutely opting for the oppressed, that is, by combatting the oppressive class.[5]

Such a liberation of the Bible from metaphysical interpretation founded a rock on which to confront the temporal world and its endemic exploitation of the masses.[6]

When this religious movement against institutional violence joined hands with the Marxist movement against dictatorial politics, the amalgam of extremism provoked the Papal District to denounce liberation theology (1984) and to impose a gag rule on one of its leaders, the Brazilian Father Boff (1985).

Despite the radical difference in time and place, Hōnen's exclusive-*nembutsu* might be thought of as the "liberation theology" of medieval Japan, for the presence of dual vectors, secular and religious, generated a liberating potential against the hierarchic nature of the Old Buddhism (the traditional schools of Nara and Mount Hiei) and the otherworldly orientation of ancient Jōdo belief. By the end of the Heian period, the temples had become religious landlords of sacred and inviolable estates, whose lands were Buddha's lands and whose peasants were Buddha's slaves; the ancient system had turned medieval. For the peasants, taxes and labor on religious land were obligatory offerings to the buddhas and the *kami*, while for the landlords, other temples were rivals to be cursed ritually, along with any unfaithful taxpayers.[7] Just as the major temples transformed not only the mechanism of land-rule and tax-rule but, through those measures, themselves, the faces of the buddhas and the *kami* were refigured for the peasants: divinities did not at all lose their appearances as objects of worship but were thenceforth also looked upon as physical and financial oppressors.[8]

Hōnen was well acquainted with the power structure of Buddhist organizations. He himself experienced discrimination, being a "mere" *nembutsu* preacher of "mere" provincial warrior-class origin. Hence it is difficult to imagine that Hōnen was interested only in the theoretical dimensions of *nembutsu* and not in the dissolution of the reactionary social regime. Exclusive-*nembutsu* in and of itself, without the resolute negation of all other practices and of the gargantuan and oppressive Buddhist machine, would be a flower in a mirror. Was that not perhaps Hōnen's *absolute choice?*

Indeed, if Hōnen had followed his Jōdo predecessors and had characterized *nembutsu* as an inferior practice for inferior spirits, and had shown respect for other routes to salvation, he would not have been seen as the rather aged *enfant terrible* that he came to be. On the contrary, Hōnen's teachings denied the importance of the traditional religious hierarchy and, moreover, rasped against the grain of the estate system that supported and permeated the feudal order. As such, his teachings were no longer a petty dogmatic quibble for the powerful, in whose eyes an organized insurgency was reflected instead. The practitioners of exclusive-*nembutsu* were declared persona non grata status by the established temples—just as the Vatican relegated the liberation theologians to a time-honored brand of exclusion— because exclusive-*nembutsu* exceeded its bounds as a revolutionary religious doctrine and grew into a social movement with politico-economic impact.

The insolence of *nembutsu* practitioners has been recorded in the *Shasekishū*, written by Mujū (1226–1312) after Hōnen's death. For instance, in the episode "A Pure Land Buddhist Blasphemes the Gods and Incurs Punishment," a certain believer in Kyūshū takes over part of the rice paddies owned by a Shinto shrine. When the angry priests threaten to curse him, he simply retorts, "I have nothing to fear. Go ahead and curse me. We Pure Land Buddhists think nothing of divinity. The *kami* cannot punish those of us who do not bask in their light" (*NKT*, 85:83). Despite his mother's frenetic pleas, he refuses to repent, and the priests place a curse upon him. Madness overtakes him, and he dies. Hence, the moral goes, by all means refrain from taunting the gods. Probably such boisterous acts actually occurred, not only on paper. In the *Senjishō*, Nichiren has also recorded such disturbances of the social order by *nembutsu* fanatics. "Those who hope for the Pure Land curtail their faith in Enryakuji, Tōji, Onjyōji, the seven major temples of Nara, and others all over Japan. They rob the temples' lands in order to replenish *nembutsu* halls" (*NSI*, 2:320).

Prior to the dissemination of exclusive-*nembutsu*, practitioners of *nembutsu* were not known for appropriating the precincts of powerful temples, at least according to extant texts; the tenets of exclusive-*nembutsu* were always seen as the aegis for the newfound defiance.

Exclusive-*nembutsu* exhibited a tendency to remove moral obstacles and to outgrow Hōnen; it walked on its own, proceeded to extremes, and turned into a political movement, just like liberation theology. To allow exclusive-*nembutsu* to run amok amongst the masses posed the danger of economic upheaval to the powerful temples that required peasant labor to till their soil. In addition, the temples could repeatedly dispatch troops of warrior monks to dissenting aristocrats in the capital only because the ecclesiastics were backed by divine authority, whose authenticity, when questioned, destabilized the temples' political might.

Hōnen himself, however, was probably aware from the very inception of exclusive-*nembutsu* that its cliché-wracking doctrines could easily lead to antisocial behavior. Thus the final words of the *Senchakushū* warn, "Once you have finished reading this book, do not leave it by a window but bury it under a wall, so that it may not corrupt those who would readily challenge Buddhist law" (Z, 2:320). But it was improbable for the first expression of a Japanese liberation theology to remain solely in the hands of trustworthy disciples. Its content resonated all too urgently with the religious and social demands of a people under oppression. The *Senchakushū* eluded the grasp of the coterie and was born unto the world, and, as Hōnen had feared, its public life begged for the organized overthrow of the religious establishment that had originated it.

EXCLUSIVE-*NEMBUTSU*
AND PEASANTS' REBELLIONS

Exclusive-*nembutsu* was persecuted because it surpassed the bounds of mere doctrinal heresy and acquired subversive force, politically and economically. Of the countless peasant rebellions (*ikki*) that occurred later in the fourteenth and fifteenth centuries, a good number—a series later called *ikkō ikki*—were caused by followers of Shin Buddhism, founded by Shinran. It is true that accounts dating from Hōnen's own days tell only of the recalcitrance of this or that *nembutsu* practitioner; there are no records of organized uprisings against feudal lords. It is also the case that, after Hōnen's death, his successors chose to blunt the heretical edge of exclusive-*nembutsu* as much as possible, to divert attacks from the imperial court and the Old Buddhism. Hence we cannot directly relate the peasant rebellions to exclusive-*nembutsu*, but denying any connection whatsoever would be naive.

In an attempt to elucidate the relationship between Hōnen and his disciples, Yamaori Tetsuo has analyzed the structure of the handful of testaments that Hōnen authored. The structure consists of two parts—an oath plus a penalty—such that those of shared faith swear an oath that is broken on pain of a preset penalty. For instance, the *Ichimai kishōmon* (One-Page Testament) demands the followers to make an oath—I believe in salvation by *nembutsu*—and warns, "If there be further thought, you will leak out of the True Vow and remove yourself from the pity of the two Buddhas (Shākyamuni and Amida)" (*HSZ*, 416). In short, there is no salvation for anyone who doubts *nembutsu*. In the *Shichikajō seikai* (sometime called *kishōmon*), seven oaths not to foment disorder in the sect are followed by this punitive codicil: "Those who still disobey are no longer my own. Such demonic minions shall not visit my abode. From now on, may each on one's own follow those rules" (*HSZ*, 789). In other words, Hōnen used the testament as a kind of contract in order to force his followers to choose between faith and perdition, cohesion and expulsion.

What interests us is that the same notion appeared among the members of Ishiyama Honganji, Shin Buddhists' headquarters at Osaka, when they rebelled against the conqueror Oda Nobunaga (1534–82) in the bloody siege of Ishiyama (1570–80).[9] On the flags that these believers carried into battle, there flapped the slogan "Advance to salvation, Retreat to hell"—either camaraderie and salvation, or betrayal and hell.[10]

Should we not say that the coterism of exclusive-*nembutsu* seeped into *nembutsu* practitioners and, four centuries after Hōnen's death, burst into flames in the extreme form of the siege of Ishiyama? Although Shinran contributed to the spread of *nembutsu* worship and Ren'nyo (1415–99) fortified the Shin Buddhist sect, it is hard to maintain that incidents like *ikkō ikki* could have arisen out of Japanese Pure Land belief without Hōnen's formulation of *nembutsu* worship as a pure and radical negation of authorities both religious and secular. The rulers of Hōnen's Japan were not mistaken, in this sense, when they vigorously persecuted the liberation theology called exclusive-*nembutsu*.[11]

BOTTOM-UP EQUALITY

The antisociality of exclusive-*nembutsu*, which negated the validity of traditional pursuits of salvation as well as the estate system that supported the religious order, may be surmised from the sixth article of *Kōfukuji sōjō*, the official request by Kōfukuji monks to the court, issued in 1205.

> On the day when an august emperor designates, at the court where he conducts affairs of state, the officials to act in his behalf, he requests service from the wise and the foolish, each according to their abilities, and from families both of high and low status. But to the foolish he does not entrust a position which would not be within their capacity even if they were to apply themselves from morning till night; and a person of low social status cannot advance to the rank of the nobility even if he is diligent in public affairs. In his own country the Great King of Enlightenment dispenses his ranks of Nine Stages at the gate where the wise and the foolish come to his court. His principle of selection is surely that one receives in accord with his performance in observing virtuous behavior in former lives. It would be an excess of stupidity for one to rely entirely on the Buddha's power without taking into account his own condition in life.[12]

In other words, just as the momentary successes—and even the sustained diligence—of a low-status person cannot propel him through customary boundaries into augmented prestige in the temporal world, so, in the realm of the spirit, is he reincarnated only in accordance with his lowly birth; the followers of exclusive-*nembutsu*, however, foolishly believe that they can attain salvation through the power of Amida Buddha, despite their meanness. On the one hand, such a view betrays the arrogance of these particular establishment monks who came from aristocratic origins, but, on the other hand, strict correlations between temporal and religious class were in general an unquestioned fact.[13]

Due to the perspicacity of early Buddhism, which over a few centuries had ravenously ingested continental religious thought, Japanese Buddhism was able to construct a sufficiently variegated system. But only an elite few who could pass the national entrance examination could pass through the pillars of Buddhism proper; others could become private monks and practice outside its gates but could not participate in the political and economic privileges of the institution. We can manage not to be surprised by the intrusion of a bureaucratic procedure if we observe with Karl Marx that "the *examination* is nothing but the *bureaucratic baptism of knowledge,* the official recognition of the transubstantiation of profane knowledge into sacred knowledge (it is plain that in every examination the examiner is omniscient)."[14] For those who were not officially "in," the gates of temples, which housed abbot-landlords, did not invite free access. "The bureaucracy is the religious republic," Marx says.[15] We can add conversely that at least one religious republic was a bureaucracy. The gears of the Buddhism machine repelled impurities. In short, a deep gulf divided the temples from everyday life.

In Hōnen's case, however, the core of his values was the transcendence of death through untainted faith in rebirth in the Pure Land. By the transcendence of death we do not mean that Hōnen attempted to transcend death; rather, it was for him death and its absolute inevitability that transcended all else. He thus disregarded the intellectual framework, the horizon of the thought system of his contemporaries—that is, the estate system in both its secular and religious forms. In the *Senchakushū,* he sweeps away *ropparamitsu* (the six *pāramitās*)—charity, the observance of precepts, perseverance, motivation, meditation, and wisdom—and instead sheds light on the darker, lower rungs of the ladder of salvation:

> If financing towers and statues are a condition for salvation, then hopeless are the poor; if wisdom and ability are a condition, hopeless are the foolish; if vast learning is a condition, hopeless the unschooled; if observation of precepts is a condition, hopeless are the disobedient. The list goes on; however, few are the rich, the wise, the learned, and the observant, while many the poor, the foolish, the unschooled, and the disobedient. . . . Thus Amida vowed vocal-*nembutsu,* a practice open to all. (Z, 2:198–99)

The temples of the Old Buddhist establishment craved ties to court nobles and other aristocrats precisely because the temples hoped for generous donations of statues and towers.[16] For Hōnen to deny any causality between such generosity and salvation was a deliberate challenge, and the order of temples could not ignore it—nor the absolute valuation of *nembutsu* that launched it.

The truism is that Hōnen presented a flat egalitarianism in which everyone, regardless of birth, ability, knowledge, and conduct, would be saved. On the contrary: just as he capsized the prevalent ethic, he reversed the order of salvation, in an ideological carnival not confined in the usual manner to momentary, tension-releasing festivities. "Supposedly, the Pure Land has nine categories [*kuhon*]. So be it. What matters is that a terrible sinner can be reincarnated into a higher life just as faithful students of sacred texts can be reborn as lowlife" (Z, 2:270). Thus Hōnen did not deny the traditional concept of *kuhon* but interpreted it in his own manner. If he had preached that both knowledgeable, high-ranking monks and those lesser souls who broke or lacked precepts were equally guaranteed salvation, exclusive-*nembutsu* would probably not have won such a vast following so rapidly. Hōnen clearly handed out the one-digit tickets of salvation to those who had been less prioritized and sent the envied elite monks at the summit of the religious estate system to the very end of the line. The masses' acute feeling of political, economic, and moral oppression made them ingest, with particular relief and relish, the mirror-image derangement of the order of estates.

WOMEN'S INFLUENCE

Hōnen made another major contribution to Buddhist thought; namely, he rectified its persistent misogyny. Before the absoluteness of death which he found in the nonconditional salvific power of Amida, the asymmetric gender distinction was shaken, as was social status. Hōnen won many female followers. In the *Nembutsu ōjōyōgishō*, he says:

> Amida's Vow was made so that we who live in the latter days of the law may attain *ōjō*. Do not despair that, because you are women, you are corrupt and sinful. Amida made his vow in the first place because he took to heart the sinful, sentient folk that were abandoned by the buddhas of three generations and the *tathāgatas* of the ten directions. If you believe deeply in your salvation and chant *namu Amida butsu*, *namu Amida butsu*, then good or not, man or not, ten out of ten, a hundred out of a hundred, all will be saved eventually. (*HSZ*, 682)

Hōnen, it is true, did not completely elude the prejudices of his epoch and repeated clichés such as *henjō-nanshi* (transforming a woman into a man to be saved). He did not treat the sexes with full equality.[17]

Nor did he have the revolutionary intent of liberating women from religious sexism—the fact is that his reversal of salvation, which prioritized "evil" people, implicated women as such lesser beings.

Nonetheless, his dialogues with women suggest that he was one of the few monks who interacted with women by fully accepting their humanity. For instance, in the *Ippyaku shijūgo kajō mondō* (The Hundred Forty-five Questions and Answers), we find one of Hōnen's responses to a woman's question:

> Q: What is your opinion on women reading scripture during their menstruation?
> A: I do not see any problem in it. (*HSZ*, 658)

No religious leaders before Hōnen had such practical conversations with women. Let us also quote Hōnen's well-known lecture to a prostitute in Muronotsu, one of the many mean and vulgar people he saves in his hagiographies:

> What you are doing is indeed sinful. The retribution for your acts will be immeasurable; your present fate is due to past karma, and your present evils will surely bring you an evil future. If you can do something else for a living, quit your present means right now. Even if you do not have any other means, if you have courage, then go ahead and quit. If you have neither other means nor courage, then keep reciting *nembutsu* just as you are. . . . In fact, women like you are the most welcome guests of Amida's Vow. (*HSZ*, 718)

These are supposedly the words Hōnen uttered to a prostitute who lamented that the nature of her profession drastically reduced, to say the least, her chances for salvation. Of course, the historical veracity of the episode itself is moot, but this legendary story illustrates, symbolically, how Hōnen's believers might have appreciated his radical teachings.

Further, we might ask: Was it not in fact the women of the capital who enlightened the renegade monk, who had previously spent four decades in the single-gendered community of Mount Hiei? It is quite possible that Hōnen's attitude toward women was profoundly altered by the strong-willed, opinionated ladies, akin to those who produced Heian literature, who surrounded him. Had not Hōnen found so many women in his audience, his religious teaching could have remained closer to the traditional one. It was not Hōnen who liberated women, then, but women who liberated Hōnen from the prejudices of Buddhism.

Exclusive-*nembutsu* prioritized the salvation of the denigrated, including women, through an egalitarianism that was not uniform but complex and compensatory. Hence it exerted the immense social impact that previous *nembutsu* doctrines had lacked. Hagiographies represent Hōnen in free, direct, unprejudiced discourse with various personages, ranging from court nobles, aristocrats, and warriors to merchants, peasants, fishermen, and prostitutes. We would do well to doubt the veracity of these fables, but we would do better to imagine that Hōnen's disregard for the rigid estate system did embody a freshness that attracted such various characters to him. If we took too lightly the principle of salvation as equality in death, which Hōnen discovered in a strictly categorized society from which neither ecclesiastics nor commoners could easily slip away, we would miss the entire meaning and function of exclusive-*nembutsu*.

DANGEROUS ELEMENTS

The forces of the Old Buddhism quickly launched a counterattack against exclusive-*nembutsu*, which was clearly a deranged theory in the medieval context. Although the high priests admitted the value of *nembutsu* as one of many practices, they emphasized, to the imperial court, that Hōnen's assertions blasphemed the Buddhist order that shielded the state spiritually and thus by extension jeopardized state sovereignty itself. In the first year of the Genkyū era (1204), the monks of Enryakuji appealed to their abbot, Shinshō, to condemn exclusive-*nembutsu*. A year later, the imperial court received the *Kōfukuji sōjō* excerpted earlier; Gedatsubō Jōkei (1155–1213), it has been said, wrote up this appeal on behalf of eight orthodox Buddhist schools. The nine vigorously denounced wrongdoings of exclusive-*nembutsu* were as follows:

1. Founding a new school.
   "Court permission should have been requested. It was improper to found a school privately." Since, under the statute system, the state was in charge of religious affairs, it was unforgivable for Hōnen to proceed in disregard of Buddhist tradition—that is, without the formal authorization of a master.

2. Depicting a new image.

The followers of exclusive-*nembutsu* created a *sesshu-fusha* (all-embraced) maṇḍala in which the light of Amida shines upon lay *nembutsu* practitioners but eschewed the scholars and monks of other schools, leaving them in the dark. The eight powerful schools feared that the masses would hence be "brainwashed" visually as well as verbally.

3. Making light of Shākyamuni Buddha.

Namely, "They do not pay their respects to all the buddhas." Amida was treated as the only buddha; indeed, Hōnen writes in the *Senchakushū* that "By the marginal practices is meant the worship of any buddhas other than Amida" (Z, 2:178), and he rejects the traditional multiplicity of Buddhism.

4. Preventing good deeds.

The followers of exclusive-*nembutsu* were criticized for asserting that "Those who read the Lotus Sūtra are bound for hell" or that "Those who seek the Pure Land through the Lotus Sūtra slander Mahāyāna Buddhism." They were also criticized for rejecting the good deeds of financing religious edifices and drawing holy images. In the *Senchakushū*, Hōnen says that donations, the observation of precepts, aspiration for enlightenment, almsgiving to monks, and reverence for one's parents have all been ruled out by Amida as routes to salvation (Z, 2:194–95).

5. Betraying the divine spirits.

"The *nembutsu* cult has long ignored the virtues of *kami*, has failed to respect shrines, and has refused to distinguish the sacred manifestations of the Buddha and *bodhisattvas* [*gonge*] from the spirits of animals and men [*jitsurui*]. They say that believers in the *kami* plunge themselves into the realm of demons." Needless to say, the establishment Buddhist's claim—not submitting to the spiritual avatars is equal to not submitting to the Buddha himself—was supported by the traditions of *shinbutsu shūgō* (Shinto-Buddhist amalgamation) and *honji-suijaku* (the manifestations of the original nature of the Buddha in the *kami*).

6. Misunderstanding Pure Land thought.

Hōnen was attacked for dismissing multiple practice, for misunderstanding Pure Land thought, and for misleading the people. Also criticized here was Hōnen's view that absolutely everyone is saved equally through *nembutsu*, with no causal connection to degrees of goodness, wisdom, behavior, or merit, whereas the Buddhist establishment had set up ranks in salvation.

7. Misinterpreting *nembutsu*.

Until then, Pure Land belief had ranked the contemplation of *nembutsu* above its vocalization, but Hōnen raised the latter from the bottom to the pinnacle of paths to salvation. Jōkei points out that there is no basis to Hōnen's claim that, out of Amida's forty-eight vows, only the eighteenth is authentic.

8. Insulting the ecclesiastics.

Namely, assertions of exclusive-*nembutsu* followers like this: "Gambling does not conflict with our faith. Neither adultery nor eating meat prevent salvation. The observers of the precepts of another world are tigers in our own world to be feared and hated. The fear of sin and the hatred of evil belong to those who do not have faith in Amida." For Jōkei, who hoped to reintroduce precepts into Buddhist organizations, *nembutsu* believers who flaunted their transgressions were virtually criminals.

9. Disturbing the national order.

"Religious law and secular law," this final article begins, "are as mind and body. Their health and fortunes reflect each other." The article in turn reflects the situation of the eight schools as the spiritual guardian of the state. They point to the political menace of a doctrine that called for an end to all state-ordained rituals and that could easily produce anti-Buddhas such as King Puṣyamitra of India and the Chinese Emperor Hui-Ch'ang (*NST*, 15:32–42).[18]

Like Myōe, Jōkei was striving to reinstitute the precepts. He held a belief in Shākyamuni Buddha that could be called absolute, a veneration for the gods based in *honji-suijaku* that made him write the *Kasuga daimyōjin hotsuganmon*, and in general a value system that exemplified the Old Buddhism; he held, also, that the aspiration for enlightenment was crucial in exiting the cycle of transmigration. He did not give vent, however, to the murderous rage toward exclusive-

nembutsu that we might impute to him, for the appeal is logical and cogent. It is uncertain whether or not Hōnen and his direct disciples had committed the acts listed, but among the followers of Hōnen many doubtlessly took their master's teachings to extremes. Jōkei's appeal, in fact, contains a passage that sympathizes with Hōnen: "The priest is a wise man. He himself probably does not mean to slander the precepts. . . . We are not so sure about his disciples. Misdeeds have been perpetrated by the foolish sort amongst them, and in the future, all of them may well prove to be of that sort" (*NST,* 15:42). The fact that Jōkei is said to have written the appeal without ever having read the *Senchakushū* suggests that the antisocial conduct of exclusive-*nembutsu* believers was indeed rife, and ripe for criticism.

Hōnen was not the only leader among the New Buddhism of the Kamakura period to be persecuted for his radical teachings. Eisai (1141–1215) and Nichiren (1222–82) also provoked violent backlash; however, national consciousness played a central role in the teachings of the authors of the *Kōzen gokokuron* (Promulgation of Zen as a Defense of the Nation) and the *Risshō ankokuron* (On Securing the Peace of the Land through the Propagation of True Buddhism), whereas the idea of the nation was entirely absent in Hōnen's exclusive-*nembutsu.* In this sense, Nichiren and his opponents shared a common ground despite their disagreements. It was Hōnen who formulated, through his silence regarding the state, the perturbing dictum that Marx would express centuries later: "Man emancipates himself *politically* from religion by banishing it from the province of public law to that of private law."[19] This did not mean ignoring religion as a political force, nor leaving the state untouched, but rather using faith to negate: "when man liberates himself *politically* he does so in a *devious way,* through a *medium,* even though the medium is a *necessary* one."[20] Hōnen's silence did not elude the administrators, and the persecution of exclusive-*nembutsu,* the foremost dangerous element of the medieval era, surpassed all precedents in Japan's religious history. The faith in *nembutsu,* for which *sesshu-fusha* (all-inclusive salvation) was a first principle, and from which national consciousness was excluded, could easily tap the potential energy of a people wishing to resist power. Such a historical necessity, as Jōkei had foreseen, did arise in the fifteenth and sixteenth centuries, when riots of *nembutsu* followers erupted again and again and all over Japan.[21]

HŌNEN'S AGONY

The imperial court could no longer neglect the proliferation of appeals that blew in from the Buddhist establishment. Two years after Jōkei wrote his, the Ken'ei Persecution of 1205 took place: Hōnen, Shinran, and six others were condemned to exile; four, including Anraku and Jūren, were sentenced to death. Shinran protested with these words, in the *Kyōgyōshinshō:*

> Lords and vassals who opposed the Law and justice bore indignation and resentment against the *nembutsu* teaching. Thus, the great promulgator of the True Teaching Master Genkū and his disciples were, without proper investigation, indiscriminately sentenced to death, deprived of their priesthood, and exiled under criminal nomenclatures. I was one of them. I am neither a priest nor a layman; hence, I surnamed myself "*Toku* (bold)." Master Genkū and his disciples spent five years in exile in remote lands.[22]

While Shinran, by no means Hōnen's closest disciple, fumed against the violent persecution, his master, curiously enough, not only did not organize a frontal resistance but adopted an attitude that appeared conciliatory. For Hōnen was no longer a lone seeker of the way but the leader of a rapidly expanding network of *nembutsu* practitioners. He could no longer voice his first-order principles without hesitation.

For example, in 1204, when the monks of Enryakuji clamored to the abbot of Tendai for the cessation of *nembutsu*, Hōnen penned a request of prudence to his followers, namely the *Shichikajō seikai (HSZ,* 787–93), and submitted it to the abbot with the co-signatures of two hundred disciples. In its first article, Hōnen cautions against slandering other sects: "Self-righteous slander is external to Amida's vow. The certain punishment is the abyss." Although he claims in the *Senchakushū* that only exclusive-*nembutsu* is the doctrine of right, here he effects, or affects, an about-face. In the fourth article, he cautions against misdeeds and the breaking of precepts, going so far as to declare, "Precepts are the ground of Buddhism." We can sense the extent of Hōnen's compromise if we recall that one of the main tenets of exclusive-*nembutsu* was the elimination of precepts. The man who urged, in the *Ichimai kishōmon*, to practice *nembutsu* "as if one were a dim-witted illiterate or an ignorant nun or monk, that is, without a pedantic air" (*HSZ*, 416), says here instead, "In the last decade or so, there have been more and more bad, ignorant folk, who not only do injustice to Amida's vow, but pollute the teachings of the omniscient Buddha. They must and will be chastised." It manifestly contradicts Hōnen's customary affirmation of sinners.[23]

What loomed before Hōnen was a compendium of authoritative temples referred to today as the *kenmitsu* alliance. Compared to an organization that could and did manipulate the will of the imperial court, the exclusive-*nembutsu* collective was feeble. Hōnen's posture of submission attests to the anguished position of a man who was, on the one hand, an individual with an immovable religious experience and, on the other hand, a leader responsible for the destiny of a new-born association of faith. Of course, although Hōnen showed an out-ward face of humility, his principles probably had not wavered; for even after the *Shichikajō* incident, he transmitted the *Senchakushū* to disciples such as Ryūkan and Shinran. The *Kōfukuji sōjō* had criticized Hōnen's followers for never truly reforming their attitudes and for assuring mutually that "The Shōnin's words are all two-sided and don't go to the heart of the matter. Don't be influenced by what you hear from outsiders!"[24] Amongst them, an official proclamation like the *Shichikajō seikai* quite lacked any significance, except perhaps a parodic one. As George Tanabe writes, "Hōnen the radical was also a master of secrecy."[25]

The persecution, however, continued after Hōnen's death. Thirteen years hence, in 1224, Enryakuji submitted its report to the throne, which moved to ban exclusive-*nembutsu*. In 1227 (third year of Ka-roku), Hōnen's tomb in Ōtani of Higashiyama was destroyed, and, in response to an appeal from warrior monks, the imperial court reis-sued its ban. Ryūkan, Kūa, and Kōsai were sentenced to exile, and forty-four others were chased out of Kyoto. Before the grand audito-rium of Enryakuji, copies of the *Senchakushū* rose up in flames along with the woodcuts.

Thus it was that vocal-*nembutsu*, with its tenet of salvation in death, and as an expression of the consciousness of this salvation, originally a solution to Hōnen's personal agony, constructed a value system at odds with a religious tradition and at blows with the templar and secular authorities. Because the agonies of the thirteenth-century Japanese had their cause not only in the fear of karmic retribution af-ter life but, finally, in the political and economic system that enclosed them, the new movement that attempted to liberate the people from such agony had to encapsulate a destructive kernel that could explode the twinned church and state. In a sense, a faith that did not beckon persecution could not have helped a people to cope with the unbearable heaviness of living in time.

HŌNEN STUDIES

The end of the twelfth century and the beginning of the thirteenth century undeniably constitute, in Japanese history, a *knot:* a certain bulbous thickening in which social structures as well as religious traditions undergo drastic change; a maddeningly overdetermined thickening, which, unlike the Gordian one, must not simply be cut. These were Hōnen's times. The forces of change that intertwined in him, his thought, and his surroundings cannot be approached through a single framework; the knot cannot even be untied, and its center cannot be seen; the lines must be traced, merely, by the scholar's grubby and awkward but loving fingers and the kernel imagined by his or her slightly nimbler mind. But this difficulty guarantees the fecundity of Hōnen studies, whose knot we might untie into four main twines as they exist in Japan.

The first is sectarian research. More publications on Hōnen belong to this category than to any other. Their purpose: to bolden the contour of Hōnen's role as a saint of the masses in whom the Pure Land tradition culminates. We are speaking not only of the sect's official chronicles of institutional and doctrinal progress but also of the immense effort that has been exerted (Tamura Enchō, Ōhashi Toshio, etc.) to explicate the character of exclusive-*nembutsu*, in a maximally accessible language, to an unconverted audience. Since these works are conducted with at least a modicum of academic method, their sectarianism must not mislead us into underestimating their utility; the comparisons of Hōnen's works with anterior Chinese and Japanese scriptures and their commentaries, as well as the meticulous combing of biographies and contemporary accounts, are of substantial philological merit. The approach as a whole, of course, tends to idolize Hōnen and to pepper reality with myth. We cannot expect sectarian researchers to distance themselves from Pure Land dogma: neither a strategic severance of Hōnen and *nembutsu* nor a demystification of concepts like true vow (*hongan*) and salvation (*ōjō*), let alone

points of view that would defamiliarize the entire Pure Land existential weltanschauung.

The second strand comes from historians of Japanese Buddhism,
whose systematic accounts include comments on Hōnen. The products of this field, in which the unavoidable vicissitudes of sectarian
research are carefully weeded out, might be, academically speaking,
the most reliable. Laboring here are those who attempt to examine
the history of the sect from as objective a standpoint as humanly feasible (Inoue Mitsusada, Shigematsu Akihisa, etc.) and those who theorize Pure Land belief on the grounds of intellectual history (Ienaga
Saburō). Recently, Kuroda Toshio's theory of the *kenmitsu* alliance
has stirred up theoretical debate regarding the relationship between
religion and society and Hōnen's role therein. Hence the historicist
field encompasses a wide variety of figures, but their differences do
not exceed a common horizon—in other words, the history of Japanese Buddhism or, even more specifically, of its Kamakura varieties—
within which they invariably situate Pure Land belief. To comprehend the intricate contingencies and necessities that gave birth to
exclusive-*nembutsu* in late-twelfth-century Japan, however, one must
bow to the diagnostic potential of a more comparative approach.

The third line of investigation attempts to elude the objectivist
grounds of historicism and to grasp the a priori of subjective religious phenomena—we mean the philosophical "take." No philosopher has tackled Hōnen head-on, but our thinkers of sin and enlightenment have indeed contemplated salvation free of asceticism
as it is expressed in the *Senchakushū* and the *Ichimai kishōmon.* Their
insights are sharp; however, they sever Hōnen the thinker from
exclusive-*nembutsu's* irreducible aspect as an organized social movement. Hōnen's physiognomy is not only that of a thinker but also that
of a wily, experienced man, and philosophy has not always excelled
at capturing such complexities. Moreover, philosophical purists tend
to cast Hōnen as a mere step along the way to his disciple Shinran,
who focused on his damnation with the coolest gaze and took a determined plunge into carnality; in imagining such progress toward
consummation, the philosopher takes an unreflexive plunge into history without historicity. For example, Nishida Kitarō and Watsuji
Tetsurō have given us brilliant essays on Shinran's thought but have
avoided a full engagement with Hōnen. Granted, master and disciple
were roughly contemporary, but the former had to grope through the

immense chaos of the late Heian, as the statute system liquefied, while the latter lived in the early Kamakura, as warrior rule solidified; the disciple's self-appointed task was to extend and to deepen the basis of the exclusive-*nembutsu* already formulated, in the dark, by his master. To discuss the two in a tabular space—the condition of possibility of philosophical insight—without sounding the differences of their temporally nuanced worldviews is a familiar form of violence.

The fourth strand is literary. Hōnen overcomes one difficulty after another and acquires human warmth (Nakazato Kaizan, Satō Haruo, etc.). The narrative or (melo)dramatic approach to Hōnen has been practiced by present-day writers as well. The Hōnen who swallowed his violent emotions and mixed with people from various classes indeed supplies an expansive character and a plethora of literary motifs. Depicting Hōnen the man allows for a kind of rejuvenation not always experienced via academic debate and indubitably remains an effective method, among others, in probing Hōnen's inner world. But the adventure of interiority, aside from its probable anachronism as such, relies too much on the subjectivity of the writer, not to speak of his or her talents. A small writer gives us a small Hōnen.

In spite of the proliferation of books on Hōnen in Japan, the only anglophone publication to this day is Coates and Ishizuka's volume from almost half a century ago. A translation of a biography of Hōnen fills most of this book, edited with the missionary intent of spreading the words and deeds of the master. Its value is open to question. Although Buddhologists outside of Japan have touched upon Hōnen in the heated debate over Kamakura Buddhism, it is surprising that, as of yet, there is not a single full-length work of academic quality on Hōnen in the English language. It might be that Western scholarship, with its strongly empiricist leanings, has eschewed a figure to whom only a handful of works can be attributed with confidence. However, it is finally nothing but puzzling that the deserved attention has not been paid to the major religious personality about whom a noted Japanese critic has written, "From the fifteen hundred years of the intellectual history of Japanese Buddhism, if I were to choose one thinker, it would have to be Hōnen."[26]

The purpose of this book is not so much to fill this gap but to indicate its size. If we were forced to place the book in one of the four categories outlined above, then the second one, intellectual history, would be most apt. But we would also like to partake in the loving understanding of the first, the icy ecstasies of the third, and the unfounded, unbounded insights of the fourth. Nor are we averse to the use of Western theory.

Our objective is decidedly not to decide whether or not Hōnen was a great religious character but rather to conduct a rigorous investigation into what the nucleus of a certain religious worldview might have been. To achieve this goal, we will struggle not to forget—we will reiterate—the importance of the starting block that Hōnen kicked. If we may paraphrase the young Marx, then the question is not, "Which religion gives us the most freedom?" but rather, "The negation of which religion liberates us most?"[27]

1

Constructed Death

Earthquakes, typhoons, floods, chills, droughts, conflagrations—in short, a concatenation of disasters sowed the seeds of lack, of blights, famines, and epidemics, from the middle Heian up to the early Kamakura.

The natural disasters were compounded with catastrophes of human provenance. The death of Emperor Shirakawa, who had reigned in fact as much as in name for close to half a century, shook the foundations of the ancient statute system. He left the political arena open for the turmoil that we associate with late Heian society. The emperor died in 1129; Hōnen was born four years later. When, in his mid-twenties, Hōnen lived as a hermit in Kurodani Valley of Mount Hiei, the imperial and the regent families realized their conflicts, abandoned their tenuous partnership, and entered into full confrontation over succession and land; the split was replicated in the warrior class as the Minamoto; and Taira clans agreed upon mutual destruction and the glory of one to the exclusion of the other. Kyoto turned into a battlefield in civil wars (1156 and 1159) that contradicted the hopes embedded in the *kanji* characters of the reigns, namely Hōgen (the secured origin) and Heiji (the peacefully ruled).[1] With these two insurrections, Taira-no-Kiyomori (1118–81) subdued the Minamotos and seized power, a moment the *Tale of Heike* celebrates thus: "Those who do not belong to the clan are no longer human." Hōnen is said to have descended from Mount Hiei to Kyoto in 1175—there in the same city, then, a dictator surnamed Taira was wielding unbridled power.

In 1177 the "great fire of Angen" burned down the Sujaku Gate and the Daigoku Palace, a scene described in the *Hōjōki* of Kamo-no-Chōmei (1152–1216), the man of letters who resided in Mount Hino in the suburbs of Kyoto:

They say it broke out in Higuchi Tomi's alley, from an inn for dancers. The billowing winds fanned the fire, which itself assumed, with its wide ends, the shape of a fan. Faraway houses were choked

23

with smoke, and the closer ones blew flames onto the ground tire-lessly. . . . Smoke suffocated some people, who soon collapsed, and flames engulfed others, who immediately died. Those who escaped did so bare-handed, unable to rescue their belongings, and treasures turned to ash. The loss in property cannot be assessed. Sixteen impe-rial abodes burned down; as for others, our count fails. The fire con-sumed a third of the city. Dozens died, and innumerable horses and cows disappeared. (*NKT*, 30:24)

Before Kyoto could recover from the great fire and the "gale of Jishō" that followed immediately, Kiyomori moved the capital temporarily to Fukuhara. That was in 1180. Kyoto fell to shambles.

Panic beset the city when Minamoto Yoritomo (1147–99), who had mobilized in Izu that year, threatened to assault Kyoto to eradicate it of Heike influence. Meanwhile, Taira-no-Shigehira and his troops em-barked on a punitive mission against the Nara temples, an anti-Taira bastion, and burned down Tōdaiji and Kōfukuji, the power nodes of the Buddhist forces. According to the *Tale of Heike*, "The galloping riders chased the defenders in all directions, hitting every one of them in fast and furious barrages of arrows. The battle began with a cere-monial arrow exchange during the Hour of the Hare and raged throughout the day. After nightfall, the two positions at Narazaka and Hannyaji both went down to defeat."[2] The *Tale of Heike* is a tale initially told and sung by *biwa* (lute) priests for popular consumption and no doubt tends toward exaggeration; however, since the great statue of Tōdaiji was constructed in the Nara period as a national project and as a symbol of the reign of Buddhist law, the mere fact of its having burned down must have been enough to arouse immense anxiety.

The "famine of Yōwa" followed shortly after. The *Hōjōki* records this misfortune as well:

A year later, when recovery seemed imminent, a pestilence struck what still stood. All were starving—more acutely with each new day, just as in the adage about fish in a diminishing pool. Eventually, noble figures in costly headgear and footgear were also begging from door to door. Just when one would be wondering how some of the emaciated people could walk at all, they collapsed to the ground. Countless were those who starved to death in front of roofed mud-walls and by the roadside. Since there was no means to remove them, a stink filled the world, and the changes the shapes underwent made one look away. (*NKT*, 30:30)

Kamo-no-Chōmei continues with descriptions of people who demolish not only their own homes but temples, people who steal sacred statues to splinter all wood as firewood; of babies who obstinately suck on the teats of dead mothers; not only of the profusion of corpses left by the roadside but of monks who stoop over them, to draw the first vowel on the corpses' foreheads—minimalist memorial services. It was six years after Hōnen descended from the mount that he witnessed the dire famine and the putrefaction that filled Kyoto. Death was not a concept but a reality.

The Genji and the Heike were further augmenting the visibility of death. In 1183, Kiso Yoshinaka and his cohorts, who had triumphed in the battle of Kurikara Peak, stormed through Kyoto to subdue the Heike legions. Opportunistic robbers and murderers exacerbated the chaos, as Fujiwara (Kujō) Kanezane (1149–1207) noted in his diary, *Gyokuyō*: "The thieves of Kyoto have multiplied, and they even steal crumbs. At this point, no one in Kyoto has the least chance of surviving" (ninth month, Juei 2 [1183]).[3] Hōnen is said to have recalled these days as follows: "There was not a single day that I did not read the holy scriptures—the only exception was when Kiso's troops bumbled into the capital" (*HSZ*, 486). Moreover, in July 1185, as the history of the Heike clan was terminated in the battles of Ichinotani and Dan'noura, an immense earthquake shook Kyoto. The *Hōjōki* once again:

> The world was not as we had known it. Mountains crumbled into rivers and filled them, and the sea tilted and flooded the land. The ground split and spewed out water; cliffs cracked and tumbled down valleys. Off-shore, ships wandered with the waves, and on the road, horses knew not where to stand. None of the towers and the halls in the outskirts of the capital stood untouched; they were either falling or had fallen. Ash and dust rose swirling, like thick smoke. The shaking of the earth, and the houses coming down, were as thunder. Indoors, the house threatened to fold itself. Run out, and the ground gaped. Wingless, one could not fly; a dragon would have mounted a cloud. Nothing is more frightful than an earthquake: that seems to be the lesson. (*NKT*, 30:32)

In diaries such as the *Gyokuyō* and the *Sankaiki* of Fujiwara Tadachika, aristocrats also mention this seismic catastrophe. Aftershocks dragged on for three months, and the crumbled edifices never lacked pillars of dust.

In the midst of social disorder, Minamoto Yoritomo steadily consolidated his power base and in 1192 finally founded the Shogunate in Kamakura; however, it was not until Emperor Gotoba's countercoup, the Jōkyū insurrection (which ironically quickened the demise of the imperial front), that warrior rule was firmly established. This was in 1221, and Hōnen was eight years dead. In Hōnen's times, in short, death suspended its good manners and did not hesitate to saunter into everyday life. It was not a time for abstract religion but one of crisis. High on the popular agenda was the viability of lines of escape from the forked and flicking tongue of death.

EVIL SPIRITS AND AMBITION

It does not surprise us that they who suffered began to desire meanings and causes as misery grew repetitive. Images of death multiplied, but its perpetual threat was ubiquitous—a fact that only fed fears. The imagination turned toward the figures of otherworldly spirits, who henceforth wore the mask of death. Vindictive spirits grew in stature.

The belief in *mono* (spirits), curseful gods and souls, dates back to the era of the mythical chronicles. It was in order to elude the malice of vindictive spirits that the capital was shifted from the Heijōkyō to the Nagaokakyō to the Heiankyō. The fear of vindictive spirits, however, did not hold full sway until the ninth century and after. In the *Shoku nihon kōki*, for example, we find passages such as this: "On July 5, 840, sixty monks were summoned to the palace and seated in Halls Shishin and Jōnei to incantate excerpts from the great *Prajñā-pāramitā-sūtra*."[4] Monks were solicited in fact almost every day in the palaces, where they declaimed Shingon scriptures and the *Prajñā-pāramitā-sūtra* to appease the *mononoke* (the spirits of entities, things). The Yasaka Shrine in Kyoto, famous for the Gion Festival, was built to appease vindictive spirits itching to cause epidemics. Such monuments, monumental requiems so to speak, proliferated in the late ninth century.

The fear of vindictive spirits was systematized in the *onmyōdō*. This popular form of belief, which mixed Confucian and Buddhistic tenets with the principle of the two polarities (*ying* and *yang*) and the five natural elements (fire, water, wood, metal, earth), dictated the everyday practices of the Nara and Heian court nobles. In the bowels of the palaces, experts of the *onmyōdō* presided in designated chambers to foretell, with the assistance of the calendar and the stars, the destined outcome of every maneuver in the nobles' daily existence. Ignoring the advice of the fortune-tellers could result in the deaths or maladies of the emperor and his ministers, social chaos, conflagrations, epidemics, famines, and droughts; thus the aristocrats avoided traveling in the ominous directions of the day, if they did not entirely shut themselves up in their mansions because the day boded irremediable ill. The rule of the polarities began to extend not only to high politics such as succession and war but also to the mundane affairs of the entire population: marriages and funerals, recuperation and construction, outings, plantings, bathing, and clothing. Life decelerated.

In the *Konjaku monogatari* (Tales of Times Now Past), compiled in the early twelfth century, we find an episode that suggests the extent to which the prophetic reputation of *onmyōdō* enabled its practitioners not only to divine but to appease vindictive spirits. In "An *Onmyōshi* [a Master] Removes the Ills Caused by a Wife Turned Evil Spirit," a woman abandoned by her husband wastes away and dies nursing vengeful sentiments against him. Because she has no close relatives, her corpse lies in her house unheeded; even as a skeleton, she does not cease to grow ample hair. A neighbor happens across the fearsome situation and witnesses a bizarre fluorescence, not to speak of the uncanny noises. Rumors reach the ex-husband, who begins to fear that the spirit of his dead wife might cause him much unpleasantness; he visits an *onmyōshi*, who is skeptical about the man's chances of escaping harm. There is, however, one way. They go to the house; the ex-husband is told to mount the skeleton *à cheval* and to pull its hair vigorously; he must not let go, no matter what happens, until the return of the *onmyōshi*, who summarily leaves the frightened man to himself. Deep night: the skeleton moans, "Ah, how heavy," as it stands up and adds, "I shall seek him out." It runs rattling all over the city, followed by a man dutifully grasping its hair, but after a while it comes back home and grows quiet. Day breaks. The *onmyōshi* returns, and asks a question that is answered in the affirmative: "Something fearsome must have happened last night, but did you maintain your firm grasp?" The exorcist assures the man that he need no longer worry. He is proved right (*NKT*, 25:305–7).

The popular beliefs of Heian society are probably reflected quite accurately in this and several other tales in the *Konjaku* that feature vindictive spirits in conjunction with the *onmyōdō*. As this body of knowledge grew increasingly esoteric and occult, it absorbed elements of Tantric Buddhism. The fact that occult services were rendered to Heian aristocrats by Tantric monks has been observed from tapestries (*Kitano tenjin engi, Nenchū gyōji emaki*). Their background, then, was *onmyōdō* and the theory of vindictive spirits. Tantric monks were in high demand in the capital in the ninth and tenth centuries because political figures who perished under various unfortunate circumstances were feared to return, quite literally, with a vengeance; magical rituals for the appeasement of such spirits were held publicly in the interests of national security. The bureaucratic *gojisō* system, through which "defensive" monks, with incantations and prayers, served the emperor and the state night and day, was instituted in times like these—splendid ones for Buddhist monks for feeling out the lymph nodes of the body politic.

In the *Tale of Genji*, the spirit of the Shining Genji's first lover, Rokujō Miyasu-dokoro, enters the prince's three wives (Aoi-no-ue, Murasaki-no-ue, Onna Sannomiya) one after another, rendering them ill or killing them. When Aoi-no-ue is entranced, Genji calls in an incantatory monk, who delivers a prayer called the *godan mizuho* in order to exorcise the spirit. The monk attempts to save the princess by transposing Rokujō's spirit onto a medium, but finally to no avail: Aoi-no-ue dies. It was Motoori Norinaga who opined that the essence of the *Tale of Genji* is *monono aware* (pity). But does not the aesthetic quality of the *monogatari* arise also, if not to the same degree, from the eerie "presence" of spirits, which put in relief the deep-rooted human capacity, transcending even life and death, for attachment—in short, from the presence of *mononoke?*

Medieval texts, like the aforementioned *Konjaku monogatari* and *Tale of Heike* but also *The Pillow Book, Eiga monogatari*, and *Ōkagami*, are rich in ghosts and spectral curses. Established in the early thirteenth century, the *Hōgen monogatari* depicts the power struggles between the imperial and the regent families—a struggle that also enticed warrior clans to shed fraternal blood—and describes the rage beyond death of Emperor Sutoku. Defeated in the Hōgen Rebellion and exiled to Sanuki, Sutoku transcribes scriptures for three years to ensure his future salvation; he sends them to Kyoto hoping that they will be presented to the Iwashimizu Hachiman Shrine. When his request is denied, he vows to become a vindictive spirit in order to avenge himself against the imperial court:

With his scriptures piled up before him, he prayed, "I am devastated
that they have plunged me into sinfulness. Moreover, they have rejected my attempt to save them through the merit of my scriptures.
So be it. Instead, I shall use the power of the scriptures to become
the great demon of Japan. I shall turn the emperor into the common
masses and make imperial the common masses." Thus speaking,
he bit off the tip of his tongue, and, with the flowing blood, wrote at
the end of his sūtras: "May all, from the king of Brahma Heaven
high above to the god of the firm earth here below, assist me in this
endeavor." He then had his scriptures sunk to the bottom of the sea.
(*NKT*, 31:181)

Despair makes Sutoku resemble a *tengu*, or long-nosed goblin, since
he no longer attends to his hair or his nails. His funeral pyre sends off
a column of smoke that bends longingly toward the capital. Although
the story is clearly fictional, the repetition of the motif of vengeance
in other Heian and Kamakura narratives testifies to what was, for the
medieval Japanese, a virtual reality of vindictive spirits.

In the *Gukanshō*, Jien gives the following definition of vindictive
spirits: "They bear deep grudges against some specific person in this
world and scheme to ensnare the begrudged, from the level of the
family to that of the state. Because they circulate false rumors, they
create confusion in society and hurt people. If they cannot be avenged
in this world, they will simply continue their efforts in the other"
(*NKT*, 86:339). And this from Jien, the abbot of Tendai and one of the
foremost scholars of his generation. He writes elsewhere that harm
comes not only through the vindictive spirits of human beings but
also through long-nosed goblins, subterranean monsters, and the
spirits of foxes and badgers. We can only imagine the invisible but pal-
pable ontological existence and menace that vindictive spirits must
have embodied for the less erudite. Thus it was that the bitter dead,
who were mobilized to specify the causes of the various disasters
and the losses that ensued, gradually divorced themselves from the
images of visible death, to declare independence as organic "things,"
to stand, to walk, and to injure their imaginative godfathers.

The dead owed their new lives to that familiar surrender and oblivion of one's own agency that arise from the all-too-human tendency
to project the negative of mortal finitude outward—in other words,
to construct an unlimited exterior power, a "second nature" that is
initially made by humans. Marx investigates this mechanism in his
early *Economic and Philosophic Manuscripts* (1844). "The externaliza-

tion [*Entäusserung*] of the worker in his product means not only that his labour becomes an object, an *external* existence, but that it exists *outside him*, independently of him and alien to him, and begins to confront him as an autonomous power; that the life which he has bestowed on the object confronts him as hostile and alien."[5] Marx's theory of economic alienation performs such a fitting gloss on spectral self-projection partly because economic estrangement is modeled on religious externalization in the first place—if not in reality, then at least in the analogies that Marx liked to use. Suggestively too: "Just as in religion the spontaneous activity of the human imagination, the human brain and the human heart [let us say *kokoro*] detaches itself from the individual and reappears as the alien activity of a god or of a devil, so the activity of the worker is not his own spontaneous activity. It belongs to another, it is a loss of his self."[6] Marx's analogies between religion and political economy are valuable because they point out, quite persistently, that the philosophical critique of alienation should always involve an analysis of power relations. The platitude that self-objectification is a necessary condition of human consciousness should not deter us from analyzing how it also functions as a locus of exploitation.[7]

Philosophy deals with abstract, phantasmal entities called concepts; indeed, philosophy itself is quickly becoming a kind of phantom. But we assume that our readers are not afraid of ghosts. Far from leading to psychologistic guesswork about some *mono*-in-itself, the phenomenological stance, for example, helps us think through effects and interests in a community. A "hauntology" trains us to deal with the intangible, and given a shift in attitude, phenomenology allows us to ask the contextual, or better, the detective question, "Whom does it benefit most?"[8] In the Kamakura context, those who benefited the most from the generally unavoidable, but in this case too flamboyant and opportunistic, cosmetics of human death—the development of vindictive spirits—were none other than the esoteric and other Buddhist ecclesiastics. By becoming the proprietors in the economy of ghosts, they firmly secured their raison d'être in the central political arena and in high society. Every spate of deaths caused by the cataclysms brought the state and the temples (which respectively demanded and supplied ritual appeasement) into a lucrative business partnership and a political alliance.

According to Shigematsu Nobuhiro, in the *Tale of Genji* alone, prayers for public purposes and those for private exorcisms together number as many as 102.[9] The priests of the Buddhist establishment conducted these prayers—a major source of income as we can surmise from a passage in the "Wakana" chapter: "Back at Rokujō towards the end of the year, Akikonomu arranged the final jubilee observances, readings at the seven great Nara temples and forty temples in and near the capital. To the former she sent forty bolts of cotton and to the latter four hundred double bolts of silk."[10] The fear of vindictive spirits, which originated in the ancients' belief in angry gods, could no longer elude the ambitious religious professionals after the middle Heian; the index of manipulation was proportionate to that of social misery.

STAGED HELL

Having attracted the figure of organic, self-willed vindictive spirits, physiological death gained a surplus of effect, but the mise-en-scène of death was not complete without the concept of hell. In Japan, it is in the *Nihon ryōiki*, finalized in the early Heian, that we can identify hell's conception—at least for the first time with philological certainty—but this baby hell still lies "merely" beyond the horizon, in horizontal but contiguous displacement. The Buddhist vision of hell had not yet fully occupied the Japanese. Horizontality implies the possibility of going there and coming back again, unlike the irrevocable passage of time. On the contrary, the hell of Indian Buddhism, as pictured for instance in the *Kusharon* (*Abhidharmakośa-śāstra*), always exists down under or up above—that is to say, as a vertical, radical break.[11]

But Japan's Buddhist hell had matured, so to speak, by the time the *Konjaku monogatari* was edited in the late Heian. It presents hell as a vertical beyond. The title of a well-known episode bears out this fact: "The Wife of a Student in Ecchū Dies and Falls to the Tateyama Hell"; Tateyama, or "standing mount," is a mountain in present-day Toyama. In this anecdote, three brothers are climbing Tateyama when they hear the anguished cries of their dead mother, suffering in hell for her sins. They hold memorial services for her, and, although she does not return to earth (she does not try, for this is now, as a rule, a forbidden move), she is reborn in heaven. The *Konjaku* relates other stories about the Tateyama hell; the idea that the sinful live in an alpine inferno probably derives from a fusion between Buddhistic hell-fire and the ancient Japanese belief in other worlds folded into mountains. The archipelago is famously volcanic.

During the Heian period, the motif of hell was played out not only verbally but visually, in *rokudōe,* or pictures of the six ways—the extreme, the demonic, the animal, the *shura* (carnage), the human, and the heavenly. Especially common were "hell screens." Derived from the modalities of hell described in the *Butsumyō* (naming of the buddhas) scriptures, these screens were set up during *Butsumyō* congregations held in the innards of the imperial court the last three days of the year. In a hermetic enclosure formed by the screen, priests led the nobles in all-night chants of the names of the buddhas. *The Pillow Book* refers to these observances: "On the day after the Naming of the Buddhas the screens with the paintings of Hell were carried into the Empress's apartments for her to see. They were terrifying beyond words. 'Look!' said Her Majesty. But I replied that I had no desire to see them; I was so frightened that I went and lay down in my room next door where I could hide myself from the screens." [12] The screen must have been truly fearsome if it had such an effect on Sei Shōnagon, who immortalized herself as anything but a frail creature.

In the *Monshoshū,* the monk-poet Saigyō (1118–90) writes as many as twenty-seven compositions under the single heading, "On Having Seen a Hell Screen." Here are some samples:

> Depressing to see—
> That there are sins which deserve
> such retribution!
> How shall I arrange my life,
> how compose my mind and heart?

> Sinners resemble
> lumber, chopped down and lying
> at the foot of mounts:
> already dead, awaiting
> the axe that would split them crack.

> But the saddest pain
> must be to suffer your tongue
> yanked out of your mouth.
> Not to be able to speak,
> not even your proper thoughts. [13]

It is generally agreed that the hell screen Saigyō had seen was the famous one mentioned in the thirty-first volume of *Konjaku* and drawn up by Kose Hirotaka, who withdrew into Chōrakuji in Higashiyama for the task. Saigyō probably composed these poems because the hell screens, which existed in abundance, instilled a general fear that death would lead directly to hell. The monk-poet, who left scarcely any prose, unwontedly inserts four long notes in this sequence to remind us that salvation was possible through Jizō (Kṣitigarbha) and Amida Buddha. One could avoid verifying the truth of his descriptions.

It was traditional practice during the Heian and Kamakura periods to paint the wall space behind a Buddhist statue in ways that inflicted "forepain" on the sinful. Although texts such as the *Kokin chomonshū* and the *Izumi Shikibushū* allude to the horrifying pictures, very few samples from the Heian period remain. It is only through the hell and demon pamphlets dating from the early Kamakura that we can intimate their intimidation; through these imposed images, death became imposing. It no longer tiptoed in the dark, for, through a process of particularization, life after death, which used to sleep in a monotonous, undifferentiated world of eternal darkness, saw dawn; preceded by deafening screams, extreme temperatures, and tingling anticipations, hell made its grand reopening as a theme park of eternal physical pain, for sinners only.

The cruelty of death was a roughly collective impression shared by all those who experienced the dense and richly variegated series of natural and human disasters. Meanwhile, we must not forget that amongst the fellow victims one group was more enthusiastic than any other in grafting a detailed, dazzlingly colored image of hell onto the "real" death that was apparently too bland: this group was the priesthood. Before Buddhist monks injected hell, through parables and pictures, into the minds of the populace, there had been no concept in Japan—or at least there are no traces in the surviving records—of a retributive space for sinners. In the mythical chronicles, the boisterous god Susano'o, exiled to the land of roots, does not undergo cruel punishment. In the *Nihon shoki*, the corpse of Izanami (who died when she gave birth to the fire-god Kagutsuchi) is run over by maggots and worms. Izanagi sees it when he visits the land of night, but this is a realistic portrayal of putrefaction rather than an image of punition.

Why did the priests become the directors of hell? We believe the simplest explanation suffices—to wit, that the fear of death amongst the masses was directly proportionate to their dependence on divinities. The temples propagated the concept of hell in a manner reminiscent of hunting in groups: on one side of the forest, a line of pursuers shouted, banged, raised hell as it were, while at the other end a second party awaited the fleeing prey. The religious establishment discovered that the concept of hell was an effective technique for capturing minds and, through them, bodies. The trap worked only because the priests could make the masses *themselves* imagine and fear hell; the whole operation would have been meaningless for the priests if this were not the case. More important, the priests also succeeded in systematically appropriating the fear generated by the masses. The priests provided the means of production—the concept of hell— while the actual production of the fear of hell was forced upon, then turned against, the masses themselves. To make the curious structural similarity with economic exploitation clearer, let us quote another passage from the early Marx: "Just as he [the worker, the Heian layman] creates his own production as a loss, a product which does not belong to him, so he creates the domination of the non-producer over production and its product. Just as he estranges from himself his own activity, so he confers upon the stranger an activity which does not belong to him." [14] In this economy of images and affects, it is not so much a question of denied consumption, for the workers indeed consume their own product, fear, at their own detriment of course; the problem, rather, is that the priests gain a crucial surplus value in status through the infernal and phantasmal transactions. This intersubjective surplus value produces real differences in levels of consumption in the material economy.

During the transition from the ancient statute system to the feudal order of estates, the religious establishment schemed to maintain its influence by requiring the peasants to enter into servitude on parishes as a necessary condition for salvation through the gods and buddhas. With divine light shining from behind them, the temples could justify their exploitation: the parishes were Buddha's land, labor on it was for the Buddha, and the fruits of labor were a gift to the same. But finally the peasants were serfs, whom the templar authority threatened to curse and deliver to hell if they abandoned their lots. According to Kuroda Toshio, "Buddhist monks and Shinto priests appeared before the superstitious peasants, making demonic expres-

sions, wringing beads, and uttering curses (*juso*); low-ranking followers sometimes exercised violence, including executions in the name
of the Buddha."[15] Such misdeeds could be perpetrated partly because
powerful temples were designated by the imperial court to be its
servitors; their privileges as landlords were protected by nothing less
than state authority.

It was not only to secure a labor force for their lands but also to
gain new land in skirmishes with the court and the aristocracy that
the quasi-occultic arbitration of an either-or, hell or the Pure Land,
became a condition sine qua non of religious authority. The superstitious, many of whom harbored a naive awe and fear for the gods
and the buddhas, were helpless against the privileged few's double
maneuver: on the one hand present the holy presences and on the
other hand stage the stages of hell. The catastrophes and the wars
that had shaken the earth had ironically packed the soil for a stage,
but death's appearance thereupon, in the form of vindictive spirits
and in a hellscape, was provided for by the ecclesiastics. As the ex-
ecutive producers, they reserved the right to dispatch the accursed
invitations. The French dramatist Antonin Artaud dreamed of a theater that would be as contagious as the plague.[16] Here was one, with
audience participation, and epidemics as the backdrop. It was not
only the masses but also the secular lords who wished to be liberated
from the spell of the temples. They did not dare, however, to extin-
guish the divine lighting that illuminated the edifices.

THE AGENTS OF THE "LATTER DAYS"

As long as only vindictive spirits and hell colored death, the fear it
occasioned hovered at a personal level; the socialization of this fear
into a component of the *epistêmê* required the apocalyptic theory of
mappō, or the latter days of the law. The theory trumpets a graduated
fall in which Buddhist law deteriorates in stages, according to the
lapse of time since Shākyamuni's life on earth. It was in sixth-century
China that Buddhist time assumed the following tripartite schema:
the era of the true law (*shōbō*) when teaching, practice, and evidence
coexist; that of the counterfeit law (*zōbō*), when evidence has faded
away; and finally the latter days, when only the teachings remain.
The epoch of the counterfeit law was agreed to last exactly a millennium, but learned opinion diverged on whether the true law had en-

dured the same amount of time or only half—that is, five centuries. Kyōkai, the author of the *Nihon ryōiki,* believed that the first era lasted only half a millennium, and thus announced that his own days were the latter days: "Those who practice goodness are as fresh flowers on crags; the doers of evil, hair on a heap of soil" (*NKT,* 70:303). But since the influential Saichō (767–822), who had returned from China in the early ninth century, believed that the first two epochs lasted a millennium each, the general consensus was that the latter days began in the seventh year of Eishō, or 1052. The conflagration of Hasedera temple in that same year confirmed the hypothesis. Fujiwara Sukefusa wrote in his diary, *Shunki,* that "Hasedera has burned down and is no more. . . . Fear that the latter days have come." [17]

The aristocrats, whose politico-economic foundations faltered in unison with the statute system, felt the *mappo* earlier than all others. For them, it was an urgent reality not reducible to idle catastrophism. Kujō Kanezane, for example, who, as the pater familias of the Fujiwaras, helplessly witnessed the decline of his once-glorious regent family, employs pessimistic terms throughout his diary *Gyokuyō*— end of the world, last generations, impure times, chaos. When Tairano-Shigehira's army assailed Nara in 1180, Kanezane lamented that both royal and Buddhist laws, secular and religious authorities, were about to disintegrate: "Have Buddhist and royal law—meant for the good of society and of the people—perished? The situation is beyond words and cannot be described in writing. . . . There are many Buddhist temples in Japan, but Tōdai, Kōfuku, Enryaku, and Onjō are central. In the past, disasters have beset the Tendai temples [the latter two], but never before those of Nara. Is this then the era of misfortune? Are these signs that the end is near?" [18] It was perhaps when the constellation of Nara's great temples stopped burning and only darkness remained in the heart of Japanese Buddhism that Kanezane decided to approach Hōnen in order to receive confirmation. The fleshly symbol of the drowning aristocratic class flailed his arms for spiritual straw.

Because Buddhism was introduced into Japan by the ruling class in expectation of shamanistic benefits, and because the religion turned into an aegis for the state after the establishment of the statute system, secular and religious law had developed in mutual dependence over a few centuries. When the statute system began to waver, Buddhist law was feared to follow royal law into oblivion, and in the late

Heian the questionable doctrine of the latter days gained immense currency. Just as with the spirits and hell, a search for the counterfeiters once again leads us to the ecclesiastic class. The degeneration of social conditions may indeed have elicited pessimism in a kind of spontaneous generation; however, the pessimism was given the lucid contour of an irreversible temporal plunge by the Buddhist literati. The motive for such teachings, once again, was to lure the people into servitude. Religion's relationship to state power, one of mutual dependence, had to be augmented with another relationship: the masses' unilateral dependence on religion. The doctrine of the latter days was the final touch, the ominous background music, as it were, of the staging of death.

For the religious powers that were, the *mappō* theory provided a means for controlling the damage done to their political and economic influence. With the impending rise of the warrior class, the rule of transparent and stable might was being craved and affirmed. This cultural atmosphere threatened the joint reign of monarchic and Buddhist law—the form the latter days took for the high priests. In the *Gukanshō,* Jien frequently uses words that refer to "ending (*sue*)," or "the latter days (*masse*)." "Truly, we are living in the latter days, in a bad world where warriors rule. It is to be hoped that the emperor and his advisors will acquire at least some idea of what is going on; that they will be surprised by what evil spirits have been able to do" (*NKT,* 86:340). Jien, who himself belonged to the Fujiwara clan, could not have remained indifferent to the clanging ascendance of the warriors over the court nobles. He understood the misfortunes caused by vindictive spirits to be a consequence of warriors tampering with social order. Evidently, he did not take the onset of the latter days as a cue to problematizing the growing laxity of Buddhist organizations as well as his own possible insufficiency as a man of faith.

Hōnen, Shinran, Eisai, and others often referred to the *Mappō tōmyōki,* reputedly authored by Saichō, as a telling sign of the coming of the latter days. The text supports the stance of nominal monks who do not engage in ascetic practices. "In the latter days, monks are monks in name only. It is pointless to look for any other sort. Hence, we must treasure nominal monks. In fact, if, in these latter days, there is a monk who observes precepts, he is simply as bizarre as a tiger in the city streets. Who would believe such a thing?" [19] The attribution of the text to Saichō is dubious; it was probably fabricated during the period of the cloister reign. Although the above passage defends monks-in-name, another applies the phrase "locusts that destroy the nation" to monks who accost aristocrats. In general, the text is full of the animosity that an anonymous, low-ranking monk in tutelage in a powerful temple would have nurtured against its high priests. Since the lower echelons consisted of warrior monks drafted from the peasantry, we may surmise that the text—produced sometime during the cloister reign when warrior monks were most active—was a ruse on their part to break precepts in the name of Saichō. The text epitomizes the breathtaking ingenuity of the *mappō* doctrine, which not only heightened the feeling of crisis in secular society but also allowed the monks to rationalize their own decadence. It was in this way that the text heralded the latter days.

It was theoretically possible for the men of faith to supply optimistic religious ideologies in such a way as to offset the primitive accumulation of corpses in a chaotic social reality; it was perhaps ethically imperative for them to provide such a value system in order to facilitate life under nearly desperate circumstances. The monks, however, gleefully added layer upon layer of pessimistic concepts to death and toiled to make them stick. In the turbulent moment of transition from ancient to feudal society, the material images of death acquired one gloating, menacing death mask after another. Death was no longer a physiological end to particularity but rather, loaded with ethical, religious, and political meanings, a complex event. Large-scale disasters create fertile ground for destructive rumors, which circulate as if they were terrestrial sustenance. That is not uncommon. During the miseries of the late Heian, however, deathly demagogy was willfully supervised by the doorkeepers of spiritual solace.

THE MECHANISM OF POWER

Let us briefly review the institutional structure of Buddhism that operated the mechanism of power in Hōnen's times. The conceptual binarism between Kamakura Old Buddhism, or the traditional *nantohokurei*, and Kamakura New Buddhism, or the Zen, Jōdo, Nichiren, and other sects, has recently been put to task in and out of Japan. Robert E. Morrell, for example, questions the facile categorization:

> In speaking of the innovations of Kamakura Buddhism, we need not overstate the case, leaving the impression that Eisai, Dōgen, Hōnen,

Shinran, and Nichiren instantly swept away not only Tendai and
Shingon, but the vestiges of the old six Nara sects as well. Nor need
all of the changes, justified today as the "popularization" of Buddhism, necessarily be seen as improvements. It is only from our
vantage point in light of the subsequent success of certain select
movements and with our own current biases, that we are able to
reconstruct this fluid time with such empathetic clarity. But if we
painstakingly try to place ourselves in that time and place as it was
experienced by the participants, the hard black lines become shad-
ows, and the caricatures dissolve into something more amorphous,
more complex.[20]

Such skepticism is indeed well founded, given that Eisai practiced
both Zen Buddhism and esoteric, or Shingon and Tendai, Buddhism;
or that Myōe Kōben (1171–1232) spent his life trying to reform Buddhist practice from a suprasectarian perspective although he belonged to the traditional Kegon sect. There is no doubt that the gargantuan *nanto-hokurei* system encompassed precept-observing and
precept-neglecting monks and that dichotomizing the New and Old
Kamakura Buddhisms into the "good guys" and the "bad guys" is
questionable.[21] The followers of the new sects were persecuted because they were characterized simplistically as dangerous antisocial
elements lacking common sense. We who live several centuries after
the emergence of the new sects should be able to remember and respect the relativity of value judgments with far more success.

With that in mind, however, we insist on the "bad guy" character
of Old Buddhism. A sustained examination cannot help revealing the
profound social problems generated and perpetuated by the Old Buddhism's politico-economic might. What was occurring in Enryakuji—
for the Heian period one of Japanese Buddhism's holiest locales—was
a tireless and harrowing struggle for power amongst fellow monks
whose machinations surpassed, in nastiness, most of what was hap-
pening in the secular world. The foreswearers of temporal meanness
maneuvered according to their factions and grabbed at each other's
throats in order to grab the seat of Tendai abbot. Only monks of the
loftiest aristocratic origins, such as those of the regent families capable
of financing lavish additions to Mount Hiei's estates, could occupy
important positions in Enryakuji.[22]

The Hiei tradition, which Saichō had established under strict ordi-
nance, had been torn apart by power plays that polarized, at the end
of the tenth century, into two divisive factions, Sanmon and Jimon.
They gathered respectively behind Ennin (794–864) and Enchin (814–

91), in temples Enryaku and Onjyō, and sent sabotage corps of monks against each other. In the era of the cloister government, such powerful temples drafted low-ranking monks and peasants and organized them into regular armies. It is well known how they clashed with the cloister government, whose supporters and beneficiaries wished for the expansion of their own estates; the soldier-monks also petitioned repeatedly, carrying the sacred trees and palanquins of the Kasuga and Hie shrines into the capital. Neil McMullin elucidates the mechanism of power in the monastery-shrine complexes of Nara and Kyoto.

> On their estates the monastery-shrine complexes collected taxes and
> corvée from the people, and in some cases they even had juridical
> authority, that is, the right to police their lands and punish offenders
> of the law. There is much evidence of the economic and political
> power of those complexes through the early and medieval periods.
> For example, the Kōfukuji/Kasuga complex was the de facto master
> of Yamato province for centuries. Similarly, the Mt. Hiei/Hie com-
> plex, which owned over 350 estates scattered throughout dozens of
> provinces, was the de facto master of most of Ōmi province where
> many of its estates were located, and it was also a powerful force
> in the commercial world in the medieval world.[23]

According to *Ōkagami,* the early twelfth-century historical narrative, "People let alone misdeeds of the worst sort if the deeds related to Temple Yamashina [i.e., Kōfukuji], simply calling them examples of *Yamashina dōri* [method]" (*NKT,* 21:235). It appears that Kōfukuji provided a proper adjective to self-righteous self-justification.[24] The exasperation and resignation of others is also expressed in the middle Kamakura *Genpei seisuiki:* "The cloister Emperor Shirakawa, it has been told, always lamented that three things defied him: the water of Kamogawa, dice, and mountain monks."[25] Even the imperial court had to give up on the warrior monks of Hiei, who were often tantamount to an unruly mob.

In order to suppress the unruly behavior of religious characters, Emperor Goshirakawa (1127–92) issued a seven-article edict in 1156. We shall paraphrase three:

1. The Ise, Iwashimizu, Kamigamo, Shimogamo, Kasuga, Sumiyoshi, Hie, and Gion shrines must no longer receive bribes or
   increase their numbers without the permission of the imperial
   court.

2. The followers of temples Kōfuku, Enryaku and Onjyō and mounts Kumano and Kinpu must not pocket the payment they receive for their services, or appropriate public and private funds.

3. Some of the provincial temples and shrines claim ties to central ones and house several thousand followers and warriors. They must not disturb bureaucratic procedures, wreak havoc in villages, or harass the administrators of national estates.[26]

Goshirakawa was no less than the prime instigator of the Hōgen rebellion, through which he dislodged his brother Sutoku; we are talking about a seasoned and bold politician who did not hesitate to confront the warrior clans when he had to do so to maintain imperial authority. He was not prone to appease, but he too found the religious forces hopelessly nerve wracking.

The temples warred not only against the imperial court but amongst themselves. To extend their dominions, the major temples dispatched monks, who might be better termed mercenaries, who skirmished, plundered, set fire, and killed. More than a hundred riots spanning the Heian and Kamakura periods are on record; because they are too numerous, we shall limit ourselves to listing those that occurred in the six years between Hōnen's entry into the Hiei priesthood and the beginning of his hermitage in Kurodani.

14 March 1145	Kōfukuji's monks fight those of Tōdaiji.
12 July	Kōfukuji's monks attack Mount Kinpu.
13 September	Kōfukuji's monks fight those of Mount Kinpu.
March 1146	Onjyōji's monks burn down Enryakuji's hall, Enmyōin.
18 March	Great fire in Kyoto.
15 April	Kiyomizudera's monks set the mansion of Bettō Chōen on fire.
25 April	Kōfukuji's monks fight those of Mount Kinpu again.
14 April 1147	Retired emperor Toba mobilizes against Enryaku.
28 June	Enryaku's monks carry a palanquin to the capital to petition for the exile of Tadamori and Kiyomori of the Tairas.

12 August	Enryaku's monks banish Gyōgen, their abbot.
8 October	Imperial forces capture Enryaku's new leader, Jūun, but his followers retrieve him.
26 August 1148	Kōfuku's monks enter the capital to make a direct petition.
February 1149	The monks of Tōdaiji and Yakushiji fight.
7 July 1150	The monks of Kiyomizu fight amongst themselves.
5 August	Kōfukuji and Kasuga shrine send a holy tree to the capital to make a petition.
16 September	The court rules that Enryaku's monks must not fight.

It was in September 1150, supposedly, that Hōnen secluded himself. The Hōgen and Heiji rebellions followed shortly after, and Heian society skidded off into the chaotic late-twelfth century. The rioting of monks continued to increase in frequency and in degree and never completely subsided until many years later, when the warlord Oda Nobunaga finally quelled them during his saga to unify Japan under himself.

No matter how subtly a handful of studious monks may have honed their respectable Buddhist philosophies, it is difficult to imagine that their wisdom ever reached ears other than their own. To begin with, scholarship itself was first and foremost a means for institutional success for most monks, as is clear from the *Shasekishū*, written by the Rinzai-sect priest Mujū (1226–1312): "Monks who appear secular, but who have given up the world at heart, are the ones to be envied. The latter days are full of people who have shaved their head, dress in robes, and look like monks, but they study Buddhism as a means to profit, fame, and glory. Their aim is to be promoted, and their ambition is to become wealthy. They hope to work with the state and to win high posts. It is sad to see them present a modality of the latter days" (*NKT*, 85:135). Religious men behaved like Stendhal's Julien Sorel, in other words with insatiable ambition, thanks to the invincible principle of church–state cooperation forged by ancient Japanese Buddhism. Mujū's critique continues: "Those who would die poor and unknown if they remained in the world gain fame and wealth by forsaking it. The number of people who forsake the world—to succeed in it, not to seek the way—has increased steadily in recent years. Instead of *ton-se* we ought to say *ton-se* [the character 'ton' (forsaking) is replaced by another 'ton' that means 'devouring']" (*NKT,* 85:163). Like Dean Jonathan Swift, Mujū excelled at satire.

Here we must touch upon the theory of the *kenmitsu* alliance that Kuroda Toshio advocates: Enryakuji, Kōfukuji, Tōdaiji, and other powerful temples not only secured prominent economic roles for themselves, as landlords of huge estates, but also allied themselves with state authority, thereby exercising immense social and ideological influence.[27] The Kuroda thesis arose as a critique of the views held by Ienaga Saburō, Inoue Mitsusada, and others. The latters' seldom-questioned view was that, with the disintegration of the statute system, an aristocratic Buddhism that had professed spiritual guardianship of the nation declined in power, while a new popular Buddhism with ties to the emergent warrior class moved to center stage. Kuroda's critique has had an immense impact on medieval studies, but we shall not delve too deeply into the thriving *kenmitsu* debate. We do wish to emphasize here that in late Heian and Kamakura, the sheer bulk and might of *kenmitsu* Buddhism menaced outsiders no matter how piously and quietly individual monks may or may not have been practicing behind the gates. The religiosity of individual monks was hardly the issue.

ANALOGIES TO MEDIEVAL EUROPE

Late Heian society was overrun by a death given macabre rainbow stripes by the priesthood. Fourteenth-century Europe was ravaged by a death nicknamed black. Giovanni Boccaccio (1313–75) begins his *Decameron* with a description of its arrival:

> Let me say, then, that thirteen hundred and forty-eight years had already passed after the fruitful Incarnation of the Son of god when into the distinguished city of Florence, more noble than any other Italian city, there came a deadly pestilence. Either because of the influence of heavenly bodies or because of God's just wrath as a punishment to mortals for our wicked deeds, the pestilence, originating some years earlier in the East, killed an infinite number of people as it spread relentlessly from one place to another until finally it had stretched its miserable length all over the West.[28]

As Europe's commerce with the East grew, so did the tiny continent's cities; ironically, the same trade routes facilitated the exchange of microbes that caused the decimation of the burgeoning urban habitats. In England and France, the Hundred Years' War that broke out in 1337 already heavily tormented citizens and peasants in various ways; the epidemic that broke out shortly after taxed them further. The plague left 100,000 corpses in London, 50,000 in Paris, 60,000 in Avignon, the same amount in Florence, and 100,000 in Venice. In other words, roughly every other European succumbed to the disease.[29]

Once exposed to invisible terror, many people, in desperation, abandoned moral precepts and lived nihilistic series of ephemeral moments. The reliance on astrology regarding every facet of daily life reminds us of the Heian craze for the *onmyōdō*. Astrologists discovered that the plague could be traced back to the overlapping of Jupiter and Mars in 1345, and doctors accepted the discovery. Such were the Middle Ages.

In an age where death was an everyday reality, the masses began to clamor for a worry-free way of dying. What people wanted was a guarantee that their death would be mourned properly, administered in appropriate fashion, lived, and accompanied symbolically by the community they would leave behind. Most of all, they were eager to have access to a site where death would be formally inscribed. The Catholic church provided just such a site. As the Middle Ages matured, the church, in providing this site, ended up systematizing and even dramatizing death. It provided a stage and furthermore the mise-en-scène for a ritual mourning of the deceased.[30]

In this sense, the resemblance to the Japanese temples' reaction is striking; death was recruited and institutionalized much in the same way for Catholic purposes. Ingmar Bergman captures this blightful making flesh of death in his film *The Seventh Seal*. A disillusioned Crusader, who always felt Death by his side but never saw him, finally returns to his homeland, where a plague is raging. Death finally appears to him in anthropomorphic form, and they begin the legendary game of chess. In Bergman's film it is not war but the plague that makes death take shape (not only in grotesque frescoes featured in the film but as allegory incarnate), and it is not the warrior but priests who take advantage of the situation.

Medieval European preachers expounded the presence of two different deaths: on the one hand there was good death, with sacraments and confessions, loyal to Christian teachings, and under the auspices of a representative of the church; and on the other was the bad, plagued by devils and sudden and prayerless. The Black Death was the craved fertilizer for preachers who had long been planting seeds of traumatic obsession with mortality. Beginning circa the twelfth century, the dying had been required to leave written testaments in order to die good deaths. Those without letters approached those with them, for without a testament one was not guaranteed a place in the churchyard, not to speak of the other coveted location. Whatever else it might say, the testament also had to indicate that the dying desired to leave a tithe for the church. The testaments were the forerunners of the sixteenth-century indulgences.

It was against the implication of these testaments that François Villon wrote his famous testament. Although it is full of bawdy hostility toward those who are in the material and/or spiritual position to buy tickets to heaven, the poem's message, in the final analysis, is not hatred.

> Since popes, kings, and kings' sons
> Conceived in wombs of queens
> Lie dead and cold under the ground
>
> And their reigns pass into other hands
> I a poor packman out of Rennes
> Won't I also die? Yes, God willing
> But as long as I've sown my wild oats
> I won't mind an honest death.
>
> The world won't last forever
> Whatever the robber baron may think
> The mortal knife hangs over us all
> A thought which comforts the old-timer.[31]

Villon's message is positive: the equality of human beings in the face of death. For Villon, this equality does not breed pessimism; it leads instead to an affirmation of life. We will see that Hōnen was a kindred soul of Villon.

When famines, wars, and epidemics heightened social anxieties, it was the itinerant monks, mostly Franciscan and Dominican, who preached the end, characterized death as the wrath of God, and carried pictures of skulls and rotting corpses called the *danse macabre*. The parading of these images, produced from woodcuts, remind us of the hell and demon pamphlets carried around by the itinerant *kan-jin hijiri* of the late Heian. And just as hell was painted behind Buddhist statues, the figure with the scythe adorned this or that wall of the fourteenth-century church. As the pestilence mounted, there appeared manuals of death, or the *Artes Moriendi*, which offered advice regarding, for instance, devils lurking by one's deathbed—in general, on how to get to heaven.[32] With the help of the new printing technology, it became a bestseller, closely resembling the popularity of Genshin's *Ōjōyōshū* in Heian Japan.

Both in Europe and in Japan, it seems, the happiness of the general populace and the enthusiasm of men of faith were inversely proportionate. The fact of death was dressed up with various religious significances that would benefit the clergy; however, the colorations of death took place not as overtly opportunistic acts but rather under the guise of compassion, and they could not easily be rejected. The assuringly rhythmic incantations and the beautiful choral hymns muffled the gears of the mechanism of death. There are metaphors and metaphors.

2

This Side of Despair

The poet-philosopher Søren Kierkegaard (1813–55) tells us of an unhappy man. Ruthless skepticism toward ossified Christian practice prompts the man to break off his marriage engagement and to wander in a realm of despair. Given Kierkegaard's own relationship to his lover, we sniff autobiography in this tale where the narrator calls despair for oneself—devoid of all values and coordinates for life but nevertheless alive—a "sickness unto death."

> But in another sense despair is even more definitely the sickness unto death. Literally speaking, there is not the slightest possibility that anyone will die from this sickness or that it will end in physical death. On the contrary, the torment of despair is precisely this inability to die. Thus it has more in common with the situation of a mortally ill person when he lies struggling with death and yet cannot die. Thus to be sick *unto* death is to be unable to die, yet not as if there were hope of life; no, the hopelessness is that there is not even the ultimate hope, death. When death is the greatest danger, we hope for life; but when we learn to know the even greater danger, we hope for death. When the danger is so great that death becomes the hope, then despair is the hopelessness of not even being able to die.[1]

The Kierkegaard who on the yonderside of torment was "resurrected as a Christian" asserts, from then on, that the uncompromising examination of one's vanities and deceptions ends in the "absolute contradiction" of despairing over oneself. This despair can be transcended only if one confronts, in one's singularity, the "eternal One"—by making a leap of faith. Did not the young Hōnen, although ironically as witness to too many corporal deaths, also anguish over deferred death, the endless transmigration along the six ways (*rokudō*)? The sickness unto death afflicted not only Hōnen but his contemporaries, not only as separate individuals but collectively, since not even death as the sole object of nihilistic hope could be attained: the truly final death, salvation, was hopelessly deferred. As we shall see, Hōnen could overcome his sickness unto death only through a reinterpretation.

It is not necessary to turn Hōnen's life into an epic. At the same time, however, we must not neglect the character of his early anguish, for which some understanding on our part seems conducive to grasping his later religious views. Even during his Kurodani days, he must have learned of the deployment of infernal pictures in Kyoto, especially when he paid his respects to Saga Seiryōji, to those scholars of Nara from whom he wished to absorb Pure Land teachings. Since Kurodani itself was not merely a locale for hermetic *nembutsu hijiri* but also a corner of Mount Hiei, one of medieval Japan's politico-economic centers, information regarding the latest developments in the capital and the maneuvers of warrior monks probably reached Hōnen quite frequently and accurately. Moreover, after he descended from Hiei and set up residence in the capital, it was not as an outsider but as an insider of the secular world that he experienced the social chaos that could not have left unperturbed the imagination of a man who spent thirty years, ever since he was thirteen, as a monk deep in the folds of a mountain. Perhaps he had reached a certain stage of conviction regarding *nembutsu* worship before his descent; whatever stage that may have been, the spectacle that unfolded before him in the capital must have radically altered his religious worldview.

Exclusive-*nembutsu* developed out of a feeling of crisis lived by the masses, who were surrounded, confronted, and threatened by the abyss of death. In other words, exclusive-*nembutsu* was not some doctrinal progress in Pure Land thought. To cull exclusively from the discursive history of Pure Land thought (or for that matter Buddhism *tout court*) the seeds of the valorization of *nembutsu* that flowered in Hōnen would be grossly insufficient if not mystical. In reading the conceptual event, our inscription of time must take the form not of a smooth line stretching parallel to others but rather that of a point— the point not as the infinitesimal constituent of a line but as an intersection of multiple lines. To sense the historicity of an event often requires forgetting, for a while, history as anteriority and attending instead to history as contemporaneity—in our present context, the span of a life, and death.

From Hōnen's earliest days, death was neither ambiguous nor objectifiably distant. Seishi-maru, later renamed Hōnen, was born to Uruma Tokikuni—the head of a powerful provincial clan in Mimasaka, or present-day Okayama. Tokikuni was a police chief (*ōr-*

yōshi) responsible for the maintenance of order in the region. When Seishi-maru was nine years old, Akashi Gen'nai Musha Sadaaki, the administrator of a *shōen* estate in the vicinity, ambushed Uruma at home, at night; it was in Seishi-maru's presence that the police chief's lifeblood flowed out. This alone must have had an immense impact on the young boy, but we must extend our imagination to the general atmosphere in which he was raised and which precipitated such an incident: the various clans of the new warrior class were intensely and perennially at odds with one another over the expansion of their estates. In this case, in particular, the friction was between "the center and the margin": Tokikuni, the rural notable, had refused to pay due respect to Sadaaki, the representative from the capital. Because most of the biographies do not mention Seishi-maru's mother after describing this ambush, it is possible that she followed her husband by her own hand or that she was forced to serve her husband's enemy as a concubine. None of the early biographies support the alternative ending that she lived out her old age in a hut in Yoshimizu, in the loving care of her son.[2] According to Umehara Takeshi, Hōnen suffered a sense of discrimination throughout his life because his mother was originally from the Hata clan. The Hatas raised silkworms, and, as craftspeople whose livelihood involved the "unclean" animal world, they were ostracized.[3]

Thus Hōnen's eye-averting times took for him the tragic form of his parents' perdition and the demise of their clan. He was sent off to live with his maternal uncle, a Tendai priest who sent the boy to Mount Hiei four years later. But the all-too-secular power struggles of the religious world could only push him farther into the realm of despair. Hōnen probably experienced petty politics firsthand, for the young hopeful, who supposedly gobbled up Tendai teachings ravenously and whose wisdom marked him out, very early, as a future abbot, shook off the expectations heaped onto him and instead secluded himself in Kurodani *bessho* (separate place)—not one of Mount Hiei's hot spots—to become for the sect, at age eighteen, a stranger within. A *bessho* was a locale where temple-forsaking hermits gathered; there they practiced *Hinayāna*-type asceticism such as fasting, burning oneself, sitting under a waterfall, chanting *nembutsu* repeatedly, and using one's limbs as candlestands. Hōnen's decision to exile his young self to such a locale could not have been unrelated to the widespread decadence, paradoxically almost principled, of priests who delighted in political intrigue.

But the more time and effort Hōnen expended in Kurodani, the more nauseating must have been the impatience that besets the ascetic practitioner to whom spiritual enlightenment never seems to beckon. "Alas, alas, what was to be done? A man like myself was not even capable of the three fundamentals: precepts, meditation, and wisdom. Were there other teachings, suitable for someone like me? In search of a practice that I could endure, I visited numerous scholars and men of knowledge, but none of them could help me" (*HSZ*, 460). We have no means to ascertain the veracity of this statement, but we would not be widely off the mark if we asserted that a dedicated person is prone to experience frustration again and again in the course of his or her toils and that the passage accurately reflects Hōnen's mindset in more moments than one. Under the socially and personally desperate circumstances, there was therefore a reason for Hōnen— whose skepticism about life as such probably bordered on nihilism— to veer more and more toward Pure Land belief and its otherworldly orientation. Given his status as a disinvolved insider of the Tendai sect, it is unlikely that he did not see through the mechanism of death engineered deftly by the priesthood. As a critical faith—"critical" as the adjectival form of both "critique" and "crisis"—exclusive-*nembutsu* would owe its aggressive character not only to the masses' oppressed energy but also to the labyrinthian psychic convolutions of a man who spent the first half of his life in quiet despair. We can never reduce an entire thought system to the joys and sorrows of a single body or mind, but conversely, a biographical substratum, no matter how deep, is always also present.

As a young thinker, Hōnen had already experienced transience in the image of the Slain Father; he also encountered the elevation of death to a spirit of the times, in the grotesquely colored images of the vindictive, the infernal, and the apocalyptic. The purpose of this chapter is to trace Hōnen's engagement with death as an existential problem, but to do so we must first acknowledge, in Tendai Pure Land thought, the role of a predecessor, Genshin (942–1017).

GENSHIN'S ANXIETY

No man contributed more to the implantation of hell in Heian cosmology than the author of *Ōjōyōshū*. A contemporary of Fujiwara Michinaga and Lady Murasaki, Genshin has often been characterized as an elite scholar-monk with a firm foothold in aristocratic circles, but in reality the vulgarization of Mount Hiei disillusioned Genshin so much that he removed himself to Yokawa, far from the center of Enryakuji.[4] Unlike Hōnen and Shinran later, however, Genshin did not entirely leave Mount Hiei, and he deepened his markedly world-weary version of Pure Land thought within the Tendai sect as its resident theoretician. The *Ōjōyōshū*, finished in 985, describes heaven and hell in loving detail. The depiction of the eight great hells that opens the text is a marvel; let us peek into one of them, the *kyōkan jigoku*, or the hell of shrieks:

> The overseer's head is as yellow as gold, and flames shoot forth from his eyes. He dons a vermilion garment. With enormous limbs, he runs as fast as the wind. His fearful voice pierces the sinners, who, in abject fear, bang their own heads and beg for mercy: "Have mercy, give us respite, take a break!" The words only intensify the overseer's wrath. He clobbers their heads with an iron mace, making them scamper over grounds of heated iron; if not, he places them in hot trenches to scorch them again and again, or else, hurling them into steaming cauldrons, brews and boils them. He might also force them into blazing iron chambers, or force their mouths open with shears, to pour in molten copper that scalds the guts and exits promptly from the other end. (*NST*, 6:17)

Genshin's vivid imagery wells up from something other than creativity—from erudition, with which he weaves citations from various Buddhist texts. Perhaps precisely for that reason, it had the desired chilling effect on Heian aristocrats who would unroll the *Ōjōyōshū*.[5] The section called the "human way" delves at length into the ugliness of the human body, corpses exuding foul odors as they decompose, thousands of maggots feasting, birds and beasts scavenging, bones scattered about and returning to the soil. The work is structured so that, in contrast to the plethora of unpalatable images in the first chapter ("Eschewing the Impure Land" [*onri edo*]), the figure of Amida Buddha in heaven appears all the more incandescently divine in the second chapter ("Desiring the Pure Land" [*gongu jōdo*]). Whether for heaven or hell, the highly particular arrangements that Genshin offered had an immense impact and also influenced sculptural and architectural styles, specifically Pure Land art and Amida halls.

Genshin divides contemplative-*nembutsu* into three methodological categories according to the difficulty of the meditative modes: the first, *bessōkan*, is the mental observation, one by one, of parts of Amida's body; the second, *sōsōkan*, is the observation of the whole of Amida Buddha on a Lotus seat; and the last, *zōryakukan*, is the exclusive observation of one of Amida's thirty-two countenances, the *byakugōsō*. Genshin's advancement of contemplative-*nembutsu* takes for granted a formidable power of concentration. It is in this sense a *jiriki* practice (salvation must be attained through one's own efforts) quite heterogeneous to Hōnen and Shinran's *tariki* practice of vocal-*nembutsu* (salvation is to be attained through faithful dependence). Because Genshin was extremely anxious to fine-tune the methodology of salvation, he added circumstantial conditions "to assist contemplation," like arranging the environment of one's practices and having the right mindset.

Yet Genshin's ultimate interest was not in preaching Pure Land thought but in ensuring his own salvation upon death. "The Decorum of Death [*rinjū gyōgi*]" in the "Betsuji Nembutsu" section of *Ōjōyōshū* is a manual explicating how witnesses may assist, with ten steps, the salvation of the dying. He or she must be transposed to a special building, the *mujōin*, or hall of transience. There, the dying is laid down behind a statue of Amida to which he or she is connected, hand to hand, with five strings, all of different colors, while dreaming a vision of induction into the Pure Land. Alternatively, the expiring person may be laid down in such a manner as to face the statue of Amida, again in simulation of the moment of welcome. Citing Shantao (613–81), Genshin gives the following advice to the "expirant" and his or her witnesses:

> Practitioners, when you fall ill, or otherwise approach the end of your life, resort primarily to *nembutsu zanmai*, maintain correctly your body and mind, turn your fronts to the west, let your *kokoro* [mind/heart/spirit] concentrate on the contemplation of the Buddha Amida, correspond your *kokoro* and your mouth, let not your voice cease, steadfastly build your thoughts of salvation, of the welcome of the holy assembly on the flower seat. If the ailing person sees the above, let him speak of it to his nurses, and if the speech is made, let it be recorded. If he does not speak, let the nurse put questions to the ailing person so that he describes his visions. If he speaks of a sinful modality, then those present should immediately practice *nembutsu* in assistance, in common repentance. The sin must be annulled. If successful, if the holy assembly on the lotus seat appears in response to the solicitude, then make a record. (*NST*, 6:17)

Stimulated by "The Decorum of Death," twenty-five priests and aristocrats formed a Devotional Group of Twenty-Five (*Nijūgo Zanmaie*). Once a month in Yokawa, deep in Hiei, the members gathered to read the Lotus Sūtra during the day and practice *nembutsu* uninterruptedly all night. The members swore that, upon the malady of any one of them, all others will nurse the sick one in turn and, after the fatal outcome, hold funereal rites. In other words, the Devotional Group was a contract that allowed its members *not* to face death in one's own singularity. The *Ōjōyōshū* was not just a philosophical work but a morbid manual.

Of the twenty-five members, the death scenes of five, including Genshin, are recorded in the *Shuryōgon'in nijūgo zanmai kechien kakochō*. One of them, a grave monk by the name of Teikyū Daitoku, gravely sick and on the brink of death, enigmatically requests his fellow members to step out of the house and to stomp on the ground. He explains, "The ground upon which I lie is on fire. The flames are about to engulf me."[6] When the assistants of salvation learn that Teikyū is observing himself being scorched to death by a fire that envelopes the earth, their grief is deep. As they chant *nembutsu* with increased fervor, however, Teikyū regains his consciousness, announces that the chanting has extinguished the flames of hell, and breathes his last.

Genshin himself fell ill when he was seventy-one and spent five years as an invalid. On the day of his death, he takes his meal, pulls out his vibrissa, gargles his mouth as usual, and prepares for the passage. Grasping in his hand the five strings, all of different colors, tied to Amida's hand, and not forgetting to chant *nembutsu*, Genshin dies without undergoing physical pain. But according to the document, he repeats his lifelong assertion for the last time: even if he were to attain salvation, he would do so only at the low Lotus level of paradise.[7] The episode suggests how narrow, to use the Christian metaphor,[8] the gate was for Genshin and his circle, even though they hardly shirked on their contemplative-*nembutsu*. It is quite possible that very few experienced the "welcoming vision" on their death futons while many writhed in physical pain and gazed with horror at the "sinful modality."

In short, in the pellucid binarism of heaven and hell, there were successful deaths and failed deaths. In the *Yokawa shuryōgon'in nijūgo sanmai kishō*, where Genshin specifies the minutiae of the activities of the Devotional Group of Twenty-Five, he recommends a Shingon ritual called "Kōmyō Shingon Dosha Kaji" that Myōe too would practice many years later—that is to say, soil subjected to Kōmyō Shingon incantations are to be sprinkled on the corpse to purify it of its sins, to facilitate delivery to the Pure Land.[9] If *nembutsu* at the moment of death failed, or was insufficient, then such a ritual was deemed necessary to uplift the spirit hovering on the brink of hell. That is how difficult salvation by *nembutsu* was understood to be. If the fear for failed deaths, for deaths that lead to hell, seized priests and nobles to such a degree, we can only imagine the immense weight that the concept of hell exerted on a multitude who had to live and die under less privileged circumstances.

We must underscore our belief that Genshin himself was never entirely convinced about his own prospects for salvation. If he actually harbored a total faith in the salvational power of *nembutsu*, he would not have compiled the intricate methods detailed in the "Decorum of Death" to elude the "sinful modality" or a manual for death such as the *Yokawa Shuryōgon'in Nijūgo Zanmai Kishō*. In marked contrast with Hōnen, who would deny all customary rites surrounding death, Genshin remained a mannerist (to stretch this art-historical term a bit) to the very end. "And Genshin chanted, *namu saihō gokuraku sekai, mimyō jōdo daiji daihi, Amida, Kan'non, Seishi, shobosatsu, shōjō daikaishū*. Then he worshipped the Amida Buddha, and prepared strings of five colors to tie his fingers with those of the Buddha. . . . After a while, he asked his followers if his face were not exhibiting the fifteen bad modalities. They told him that he did not seem to be in pain, that his face looked the same as usual, and that, no, he did not exhibit the signs of bad death."[10] Thus, moments before his death, Genshin asked his disciples if his face had not acquired an unfavorable modality (*akusō*). So great was his anxiety. That such a man—who, during his life (and according to the records), practiced various Shingon mysteries as well as two billion chants of *nembutsu*, who read eight thousand volumes of Lotus sūtra, ten thousand of Amida sūtra, and fifty-five thousand and five of other Mahāyāna sūtras—that such a man felt compelled to pose such a question in his final seconds is pathetic in the French sense of the word. Salvation through *rinjū shōnen*, or *nembutsu* at the crucial hour of death, was, for Genshin, a desperately conscious aim-taking as if on a feeble bow for a faraway target.

THE *ŌJŌYŌSHŪ* VERSUS *LA DIVINA COMMEDIA*

Both Genshin's *Ōjōyōshū* and *La Divina Commedia* by Dante Alighieri (1265–1321) heavily influenced their contemporaries' view of the other world. The texts thus played no small historical role. Like Genshin, Dante was unusually erudite: born into an aristocratic family in Florence, one of medieval Europe's largest cities, he not only mastered philosophy, astronomy, and mathematics, but was a local politician of import. It is famously to an intrigue in which the vanquished Dante was forever banished from Florence that we owe the Catholic epic and in general the creativity that sprouted from the abrasion between politics and poetics. Just as the *Ōjōyōshū* is immaculately structured, the *Divina Commedia* proceeds as an orderly progression through a clear-cut schema of hell, purgatory, and paradise. That the vivid images in *Inferno* and *Purgatorio* were represented visually by artists who thus gave death a face—a human one in pain—resembles the inspiration that the *Ōjōyōshū* provided for hell pictures.

Nevertheless, while proper names and concomitant individuation are absent from the Buddhist text, the Italian poem involves the author himself as the narrating protagonist of a spiritual journey. It brings him face to face with historical figures and real-life political rivals. But in our context, the most notable feature of the Dantean cosmology is the prominence of the concept of purgatory in the soul's path. Let us look into the *topos* in summary:

> On each of the seven terraces of purgatory the pilgrim's imagination undergoes a different training in assimilating images of vice and virtue so that his mind will finally be ready for the vision of God. In hell he remained basically an observer, but in purgatory he is a participant in the unfolding drama. Dante staggers as he approaches the cornice of sloth, he cannot see in the place of blind anger, and he burns as he passes through the fiery wall of the terrace of lust. He is the sinner in need of reform and he is the purified soul who will drink the waters of Eunoe to be made whole again beyond confusion.[11]

Purgatory is by no means a land of despair. It is purgatory: sincere remorse and prayer transports the lost sheep of the lord to the terrestrial paradise whose fountain allows sinners to forget their sins. There the opportunity is provided for a ten-stage ascent through heaven, in which Dante, needless to say, reaches the highest level, there to see the three circles of light signifying the Trinity.

There is in Buddhism too a *chūu* or *chūin* (middle being/darkness), which functions as a mediating space between this world and the other. Genshin mentions it in his description of the *daishakunetsu ji-goku* or the great hell of flames. However, he does not treat it as a purgatory moment; in fact, from there the sinner must proceed to hell immediately. Why is Genshin, the master rhetorician regarding heaven and hell, so silent about the middle being? We believe the answer is that the impure land, this world, was precisely the middle being for Genshin; although he describes the six ways in his *Ōjōyōshū*, we may assert without unjust schematism that Genshin's view of the other world was a bipolar one of heaven and hell. In the tripartite structure of the *Divina Commedia* there is a buffer zone, namely purgatory, between heaven and hell, but according to the *Ōjōyōshū*, as soon as a person leaves the middle being of this world, he or she must immediately enter either heaven or hell and stay there. It was precisely because death was an unrepeatable trial without room for rehearsals, afterthoughts, and extenuating circumstances that it produced detailed regulations and unalloyed anxiety.

SALVATION CHRONICLES AS A REACTION

Genshin was not alone in dreading the indeterminacy of death, for *rinjū-shōnen* could easily fail and leave one to hell. The binarist teaching of heaven and hell was unsurprisingly accompanied by an anxiety that also infected laypeople who were at all familiar with Heian Pure Land worship. That the Pure Landists were inordinately interested in the manners of human death, from the middle to late Heian, explains why five chronicles of salvation appeared in rapid succession after Yoshishige-no-Yasutane (d. 997)—founder of *Kangakue*, the prototype of Genshin's group of twenty-five—compiled the *Nihon ōjō gokurakuki*. The chronicles of salvation include accounts of the happy ends of criminals in addition to those of nameless monks, laypeople, and other "unworthy" characters. The chronicles clearly fell outside the range of the imagination of the traditional, aristocratic Buddhism that formed an integral part of the statute system. The popularity of such chronicles was contemporary with the activity of itinerant monks, about whom Hayami Tasuku says, "The activity of itinerant monks that climaxed over the regent and cloister eras . . . was a stage in the development of individual-oriented worship that aimed to rescue, in this world and for the other, the 'individual,' thus departing from the basic drift of ancient Japanese Buddhism, in short state- and community-oriented worship."[12]

But the appearance of the various chronicles of salvation was also contemporaneous with the installation of the mechanism of death and its trinity of vindictive spirits, hell, and *mappō*. Such conflicting phenomena as the chronicles and the machine coexisted in the tenth century precisely because the negative images that accumulated onto death, by courtesy of a pessimistic mode of Buddhism, had to be alleviated by a more positive understanding. At the same time, we may guess that the chronicles were produced by low-ranking monks and some aristocrats as a reaction to the beams of religious elitism that radiated from the grand temples of Nara and Kyoto. Taken together, the chronicles state that being an important priest is not a necessary condition for salvation. Unfortunately, the actual examples are not just anecdotal and unconvincing; they fail in sum to probe, at any depth, the significance of death for faith. The following two examples are from the *Honchō shinsenden:*

> The abbot Kyōtai was from Shiga village in Ōmi. Although he was a few hundred years old, his age did not show. He always made love to young girls. He ate fish, and whenever he spitted out the flesh, it turned into a lotus leaf. One day, he met Chishō, the great master, and ceded Onjōji to him. Kyōtai said he had been guarding the superior lands until the arrival of Chishō, who should be able to spread Buddhist law. So saying, he passed away. (*NST,* 7:261)

> In the land of Minō, there was a man who lay by a stream, using a stone as his pillow and never taking to the streets. He had long ceased to eat or to drink, but his whole body remained warm. One day, Minamoto Shigezane came to this spot in the course of a hunting foray. Taking his bow, he poked the man's stomach: it was as soft as the skin of a living person. Shigetomo later tried to find out where he had been, but no one could tell him. (*NST,* 7:269)

These passages veil, mystify, and aestheticize death but do not attempt to comprehend the significance of death itself. The shrill and overly confident homages to salvation ironically imply a diametrically opposite attitude toward real-life death and its frightful outcome or, in other words, reveal the profound anxiety that the authors of the chronicles shared with Genshin.

In Japan, authentic confrontation with death could take place only after working through a kind of dialectic. In the first stage, confronting death meant communicating with *other* deaths; in the form of ancestral worship, death was externalized and delivered into the past (rituals for one's ancestors) and the future (making sure one's descendants will repeat the rituals for oneself). Far from being imbued with death, the present was the dominion of life. Death was community oriented and did not create conflict between the individual and the "society" of priests. In the second stage, death became a personal matter, in the form of individual salvation; however, it was caught in a web of codes and prescriptive advice. Salvation did not involve choice but rather a certain mastery of techniques, whose priestly custodians formed a caste of those in the know. Death became temporal, but mostly in the sense of secular, for it was indeed a locus of worldly power; in this form, death's temporal "being-in-the-world" merely stifled the experience of death as a limit. In the third stage, however, this very mannerism of death was sublimated: the mannerism was condensed into a formula that closed itself off from further priestly mediation. The extratemporal powers in whose *name* the priesthood had reigned—just as the regents had reigned in the name of the Emperor—left the gesturing hands of the priests when the *name itself* was chanted over and over by laypeople. Death was folded into life as a personal matter, as human temporality, as the limit of the future. "Let the dead bury the dead and mourn them," Marx wrote to a friend of his. "In contrast, it is enviable to be the first to enter upon a new life: this shall be our lot."[13] In Hōnen's case, it was by confronting the singular event of *death*—rather than the long faces of the *dead*—that he embraced a "new life." But the synthesis did not simply overcome the traumatic antithesis posed in some effort to revert back to the first, halcyon thetic existence; rather, the second stage was seized in its very contradictions and resolved into an "answer" through a radical reinterpretation of death. Religion might indeed be, as Marx says, "the table of contents of the theoretical struggles of mankind."[14]

THE DUBIOUS THEORY OF CONVERSION
AT AGE FORTY-THREE

Hōnen's conversion to vocal-*nembutsu* is habitually attributed to his forty-third year (1175) and to a textual encounter, namely with Shan-tao's injunction: "Concentrate on chanting the name of Amida, in all places and at all times, for adherence to *nembutsu* is the sanctioned practice aligned with his vow" (*Kuang ching shu*). The urge to pinpoint spiritual awakening chronologically is understandable but questionable. It is difficult to believe that Hōnen left Kurodani for Kyoto, the mountain for the multitude, immediately following some religious experience. We recall that even the Shākyamuni Buddha had to struggle—that he required an interval between his personal deliverance under the tree of enlightenment and his decision, in accordance with Brahmadeva's wish, to preach. The tree of enlightenment itself must of course be read symbolically, but there is a symbolic truth to a myth that insists on a time lag, insists, in other words, that a deep interior experience must be subjected to an extended process of conceptualization and verbalization before it can be expressed to others. The same applies to the legendary "Rousseau experience" had by Kant, the sage of Königsberg, who descended from the mount in his own way in order to theorize transcendence.

William James's *Varieties of Religious Experience* provides us with another reason to doubt the theory of instantaneous conversion: "To be converted, to be regenerated, to receive grace, to experience religion, to gain an assurance, are so many phrases which denote the *process, gradual or sudden,* by which a self hitherto divided, and consciously wrong inferior and unhappy, becomes unified and consciously right superior and happy, in consequence of its firmer hold upon religious realities [our italics]." [15]

"Gradual or sudden"—in James's view, there are two types of conversions, willful and coercive, pertaining respectively to "healthy" and "sick" souls. In the former case, one seeks out new ideals more or less autonomously and converts gradually, while in the latter case, a strong sense of guilt occasions a sudden conversion in response to an exterior force. Hōnen belongs to the former category because, despite his despair, he kept up a willed and uninterrupted practice of *nembutsu* for years. He slowly but surely solidified his faith. On the contrary, Shinran, who is said to have plunged into the world of vocal-

nembutsu in a state of emotional exhilaration upon meeting Hōnen, belongs to the latter category. The disciple's *zettai tariki* worship (absolute dependence on faith) indeed drips with a sense of guilt, by his own admission: he repeatedly characterized himself as *jigoku hitsujō* (bound for hell).

On Mount Hiei, which Hōnen ascended when he was thirteen, the mainstream practice was not contemplation à la Tendai but a mode En'nin had introduced earlier, namely *jōgyō zanmai*. It involved thinking about the Amida persistently and chanting his name while walking. In particular, they practiced the version associated with Fa-chao of Mount Wutai, the highly melodic *goe-nembutsu* designed to bring forth a vision of the Pure Land. This softly musical *nembutsu*, passed on to Genshin's times as uninterrupted- or mountain-*nembutsu*, eventually became the mainstream of Heian Pure Land practice, ramifying into the aristocratic class as well. In Kurodani *bessho*, where *nembutsu hijiri* gathered, *nembutsu* was observed in conjunction with reading from the Lotus Sūtra, exactly in the style of Genshin's group of twenty-five—"Kitadani and Kurodani valleys in Saitō, where *nijūgo zanmai* is practiced" (*Hōgen monogatari, NKT,* 31:56). Hōnen probably did not spend his quarter-century there in the purely scholarly lifestyle suggested by one of his biographies: "I read through the complete collection of scriptures five times" (*Shijū hakkanden, HSZ,* 733). At some point during his hermitage in Kurodani, probably following repeated, sustained sessions of *betsuji-nembutsu*, which requires intense concentration over a period of time, Hōnen achieved a state of equilibrium. At this saturation point, the particles of his despair solidified and could be removed with a sieve, after which renewed spiritual fervor meant religious intensity rather than an increased capacity for despair.

How else can we explain the vigorous faith he exhibits in his exchange with Eikū, his master?

> The master insisted that contemplative-*nembutsu* was superior to vocal-*nembutsu*, but the saint [Hōnen] argued that the latter was superior. Angered, Eikū took his wooden pillow and hit the saint on the back. Eikū said that his own master Ryōnin had also held that contemplative-*nembutsu* was superior. But the saint retorted that Ryōnen was born too early [to know the truth about *nembutsu*]. Enraged, Eikū reached for a wooden clog and hit his disciple with it. (*HSZ,* 727–28)

Hōnen must have been quite confident to try to discredit a view held by two generations of masters. There is no way to verify the occurrence of this conversation, but Hōnen's defiance toward Eikū is also recorded in other accounts of his life. Given the nature of hagiography, this may not mean much. Nevertheless, if there is a morsel of historical truth to the episode, then it means that already, in the middle of his Kurodani days, Hōnen had convinced himself of vocal-*nembutsu*'s effectiveness firmly enough to confront his master. It would contradict latter-day theories of his sudden conversion at forty-three.

Let us clarify the difference between contemplative- and vocal-*nembutsu*. While the former combines reading from the Lotus Sūtra with chanting and aims to contemplate Amida Buddha and the Pure Land, the latter may or may not involve reading the *Kanmuryōjukyō* (*Amitāyur-dhyāna Sūtra*) and other texts, may or may not involve contemplation, but mandates the repetition of a single phrase, *namu Amida butsu*. As in the motto *asa daimoku, yū nembutsu* (the name of the Lotus Sūtra in the morning, *nembutsu* in the evening), the Hiei tradition after Genshin considered the Lotus Sūtra and *nembutsu* to be part and parcel; Hōnen's new method of practicing only vocal-*nembutsu* was patently unheard of. Hōnen and his followers' vocal-*nembutsu*-without-Lotus-Sūtras was an anomaly, often criticized by contemporaries, as in the *Nomori kagami*: "The *nijūgo-zanmai* exclusivists of our days read the *Kanmuryōjukyō* and not the Lotus Sūtra. They disobey the intent of the True Vow and miss its real benefits."[16]

WHAT HŌNEN SAW

Whatever the nature of the experience that bestowed upon Hōnen such an unwavering faith in vocal-*nembutsu*, it allowed him to recuperate from the "sickness unto death" that overshadowed the first half of his life. Although Hōnen himself never described any religious experience that he might have had during his ascetic period on Mount Hiei, we can partially reconstruct his life as a *nembutsu hijiri* thanks to a document left behind by no less than his most renowned follower. The *Saihō shinanshō*, which Shinran copied from the original when he was eighty-four years old (1256), contains a text by the name of "Zanmai Hottoku-ki." There the visions Hōnen had during sessions of *nembutsu zanmai*—though well after the Kurodani days—are meticulously detailed.[17]

The exact kind of practice that Hōnen preferred was *jōzenkan*, or the observation of the Pure Land in thirteen steps, outlined in *Kanmuryōjukyō*. For the New Year's Day of 1198 (Kenkyū 9), the author makes the following entry: "After having visited the monk Kyōkei in Yamamomo, Hōnen commenced, at around three in the afternoon, his customary New Year practice of week-long *nembutsu*. On the first day, he said, the *myōsō* already began to present itself: his surroundings brightened naturally" (*HSZ*, 865). *Myōsō* refers to the first step of *jōzenkan*, namely *nissōkan* (*sōkan* means "contemplation," and the first character denotes the sun). Hōnen apparently succeeded in seeing bright light on the very first day of meditation. "On the second day," the author continues, "the *suisōkan* was achieved, smoothly. . . . During the week-long practice, he experienced the *chisōkan* [earth] and the first glimmerings of the crystal ground. On the morning of the fourth day of the second month, he saw the crystal earth very clearly" (ibid.). The second step, *suisōkan* (water), is the contemplation of water growing increasingly transparent and shimmering like ice or crystal. The third, *chisōkan*, is the observation (with eyes both open and closed) of the Pure Land as a glassy, crystalline earth supported by golden props glittering with gems. Thus, by the fourth day of meditation, Hōnen cleared the first two stages of *jōzenkan* and was halfway through the third.

Although he required a month to complete the third stage, the fourth through sixth stages followed promptly in the wake. In the fourth step, *jusōkan* (tree), he pictured a huge treasure tree shining with gold, scarlet, and green pearls, and also covered by a net of pearls, atop which rest fifty billion palaces; in the fifth *hakkudoku suisōkan* (eight virtuous waters), he envisioned eight kinds of lakes filled with water of the seven treasure-colors, atop which float lotus leaves; and in the sixth, *sōkansō* (whole), he peeped into the interiors of the fifty billion palaces, where sound the music of paradise, of various instruments suspended in mid-air. He thus completed the first six stages of *jōzenkan* in barely more than five weeks, chanting *nembutsu* approximately seventy thousand times a day for thirty-seven days, remaining in meditation well beyond his initial plan of just a week. The physical and spiritual constitution of this sexagenarian—for at this moment Hōnen was already sixty-six—must have been above average.

Two weeks later, Hōnen began to ascertain the fruits of his meditation.

On the twenty-fifth day of the second month, he opened his eyes in a
well-lit place. A red bag and a crystal pot emerged from the bottom
of his eyes, and he saw them. He had been able to see such things
with his eyes shut, but they used to disappear when he opened his
eyes. On the twenty-eighth day, he had to interrupt his *nembutsu* for
health reasons. After ten or twenty [instead of seventy] thousand
chants, he sensed light in his right eye. It was indigo. There was another light too, with red edges. He saw a crystalline color, in the form
of a glass vase—and in it, a red flower—that looked like some sort of
treasure. After sunset, he saw red and blue treasure trees of varying
heights in all directions. The trees' heights also varied according to
his mood, quadrupling sometimes. (*HSZ*, 866)

He either suffered a relapse of hemorrhoids or caught a cold and had
to decrease the rate of *nembutsu* per day, but continued: the red bag
and the crystal pot coagulated into a flower in a vase. Psychoanalysts
may have their field day regarding the treasure trees that elongated
and shrank. After this point, the diary entries become fragmentary:

Beginning on the first day of the eighth month, he returned to his
previous rate of sixty thousand chants per day. On the morning of
the twenty-second of the ninth month, he experienced the *chisōkan*
very clearly. His surroundings appeared seven or eight steps higher.
During the night and early morning of the next day, the same experience was repeated, again very clearly. (During a week-long session of
betsuji nembutsu in the eighth month of the first year of Shōji [1199],
the Pure Land presented itself to him on multiple occasions. His eyes
were radiating beams of light. His disciple Shinrenbō reported this to
him, but he did not express surprise.) During the second month of
the second year of Shōji, he could manifest the *chisōkan* and five other
contemplations at will, during meditation and also in everyday life.
On the night of [February 8, 1201 (Ken'nin 1)], he heard bird-calls
and the sound of flutes and *koto* harps. As the days went by, he could
hear *shō* flutes and other sounds by his own volition. (Ibid.)

It is stunning that the visual hallucinations that Hōnen experienced
were also accompanied by sounds. The hallucinations of schizo-
phrenics, for example, are at first entirely visual and become auditory only as their derangement proceeds. If this is a working analogy,
we can infer from the experience of auditory hallucinations that
Hōnen could enter into the most profound of meditative states.

The period of these spiritual exploits roughly coincided with the
landmark recording of the *Senchakushū*. But the capacity of Hōnen
the man is even more unfathomable in the first year of Genkyū (1204),

Hōnen's seventy-second. Political concerns—verbal missiles from a hostile Enryakuji—forced Hōnen to issue the painful public apology now famous as the *Shichikajō seikai*. Yet the tense circumstances did not obstruct his progression through circumstances of a less mundane nature:

> On the fifth day of the first year of Genkyū, an 11-foot face of bodhi-sattva Seishi (Mahāsthāmaprāpta) appeared thrice, behind a statue of himself. The same happened in the western hall of statues. Why did Seishi make the appearance? In order to prove the rightness of *nembutsu* to its practitioners. One must not doubt this. The next day, the area around the place Hōnen was sitting turned into a blue, crystalline earth. Now it is impossible to doubt the content of the scriptures; in fact, the section on *chisōkan* teaches us not to harbor doubts. Keep this in mind. (*HSZ*, 867)

The seventh step, *kezasō*, is the observation of the Buddha's lotus seat decked with gems and pearls, as well as a palatial curtain propped up by four columns of gems; the eighth, *zōkan*, involves picturing (eyes both open and closed) the buddhas on the lotus seats while looking at statues of the Buddhas in the triad form. That an 11-foot face appeared from a statue matches the corresponding passage in the *Kanmuryōjukyō*. The record continues:

> [On 28 December 1202], General Takahata came to visit and was shown to the hall of statues. That morning, Hōnen chanted *nembutsu* as usual. After he saw [the statue of] the Buddha Amida, the *shōji* screen grew transparent, and there appeared the face of the Buddha, about 11 feet long. The face gradually disappeared. It was around noon. On the fourth day of the third year of Genkyū (1206), the triad buddhas [Amida, Kan'non, and Seishi] appeared. This happened the following day as well, according to the record of the saint himself. (Ibid.)

The dates go back and forth, but Hōnen here attains the ninth *henkan issai shikishinsō*, or the vision of Amida's eighty-four thousand countenances and the light emanating from them, as well as the tenth *kan kan'non bosatsu shinjitsu shikishinsō* and the eleventh *kan daiseishi shikishinsō*, or the visions of the physical attributes of the Avalokiteśvara and Mahāsthāmaprāpta on both sides of Amida. The author did not put down the last two steps, but we shall for reference. In the penultimate *fukansō*, one must see the paradisal lotus from bud to full bloom, from within, while listening to the paradisal harmonies. In the last, *zōsōkan*, life-size and in golden splendor, Amida Buddha is placed on the shimmering lake surface.

Hōnen probably had similar experiences during his ascetic days and nights in Kurodani. Even after he reached the religious conviction of exclusive-*nembutsu*, in fact to his very last days, Hōnen repeated his sessions of concentrated *nembutsu*, seventy thousand chants per day. Discussing the nature of exclusive-*nembutsu* without taking Hōnen's experience of the Pure Land into account would be like discussing Dōgen without a knowledge of sitting in meditation.

What was this experience? *Jōzenkan* does not aim at originality of content, for its point is not "creativity" but *imagination*. Perhaps the purest practice of such imagination is to produce, as in *jōzenkan*, forms set out in so many words in a text. Rather than repeating an original image that exists in the same medium, Hōnen becomes the Pure Land itself, and the Pure Land the original that achieves evidence as the one afterworld. Although dreams, not visions, are the topic of Michel Foucault's "Dream, Imagination, and Existence," the dreaming subject that he describes is very similar to the contemplating Hōnen.

> The subject of the dream, the first person of the dream, is the dream itself, the whole dream. In the dream, everything says, "I", even the things and the animals, even the empty space, even objects distant and strange which populate the phantasmagoria. The dream is an existence carving itself out in barren space. . . . To dream is not another way of experiencing another world, it is for the dreaming subject the radical way of experiencing its own world. This way of experiencing is so radical, because existence does not pronounce itself world.[18]

For Foucault, the imagination does not posit another world in which one exists, of which one is a part, an agent among many others; rather, in the dream, one becomes the entire world where the imagined other is situated. This is the case for Hōnen, who becomes the Pure Land where Amida resides. In a given moment, one can finally *be* in "this" world only, since, during one's lifetime, one cannot be anywhere else but "here" in this world, and after death, the Pure Land is the one possible "here." Now is always here.[19]

THE FINAL HŌNEN

In contradistinction to the scholar Genshin—who in his *Ōjōyōshū* attempted to elucidate the significance of *nembutsu* worship by amass-

ing the discourses of various past preachers of the Pure Land and who
to his end maintained an obsession for mannerisms of contemplation
and death—Hōnen thought of the destination of salvation not simply as a fictitious world fantasized at the height of emotional exu-
berance in worship but rather as an existential reality that could be
imagined through the five senses. But why could Hōnen alone reach
that firm conviction when, within the Tendai sect, Genshin and others had applied themselves to contemplative-*nembutsu* diligently for
so many years? Could it have been that the abysmal profundity of
Hōnen's initial despair transformed his powers of imagination?

Despite his skepticism toward the salvific value of his immediate
predecessors' practice of contemplative-*nembutsu* (combined with
the reading of Lotus Sūtra), Hōnen did not underestimate the experience of contemplative-*nembutsu* as such, as he makes clear in the
Senchakushū: "Tao-ch'o was Shantao's master, but he did not experience *zanmai*. Thus he was never certain about salvation" (*HSZ*, 311).
He explicitly points to the lack of *zanmai* experience to discredit the
teachings of Tao-ch'o, who was none other than the master of the
man whom Hōnen respected so intensely, Shantao. As for Hōnen, his
mystical experiences were not confined to the designated time period of concentrated-*nembutsu* but were integrated into his daily life
over many years. There is, for instance, the following anecdote from
"What He Uttered to His Disciples When He Passed Away": "For
more than ten years, thanks to the merit of *nembutsu*, I have witnessed
daily the spectacular scenery of the Pure Land and the true body of
the Buddha and bodhisattvas. I kept the experience to myself and
never told others, but now that I am approaching the end of my life,
I have decided to tell" (*HSZ*, 724).

It is unlikely that such an experience did not influence his view of
nembutsu. As a rule, however, he kept the visions to himself because
making them public would have shaken the foundations of his
own teaching, exclusive-*nembutsu*. Hōnen surely practiced what he
preached, but he did not preach all that he practiced. As a peda-
gogue of salvation, his interest was in ending the pedagogy. To others
he recommended, unconditionally, the exclusive practice of vocal-
nembutsu.

The "Diary of Decease" indicates that Hōnen's supernatural tendencies only intensified as he lay dying: "[At around 8 P.M. on 3 Janu-
ary 1212 (Kenryaku 2)], the saint told the disciples who were nursing

him, 'I used to solicit alms with other ascetic monks in India. When I was reborn in Japan, I joined the Tendai sect, and encountered the teaching of *nembutsu*.' When one of his nurses asked him, 'Are you going to be saved and born in paradise?' he replied, 'That wouldn't be the right way to put it since I used to be there'" (*HSZ*, 871). The implication: the whole affair is not exactly the standoffish matter suggested by the lofty term "salvation"—he's "been there."

Genshin's last conversation with his disciples was fraught with anxiety. Hōnen's antipodal lack of anxiety regarding salvation is dauntless and resolute, reminding us more of the *Phaedo*—a climactic moment in the Platonic dialogues, the West's greatest hagiography with the sole exception of the New Testament. The apparently conflicting systems—Socrates's love of wisdom and Hōnen's principle of ignorance—turn out to be very similar, not so much because Socrates himself feigns ignorance but because the value of *philosophia* turns out to lie largely in learning how to die well. Just as, in his final moments, Socrates becomes uncharacteristically obscure to his disciples, Hōnen at the end appears foreign to his followers. "At one point, he asked his disciples, 'Did you worship bodhisattva Kan'non and Seishi when they appeared?' They answered that they had not seen anything. When the disciples carried a 3-foot statue of the Buddha Amida into his room and urged him to worship it in preparation of his death, the saint said, 'Apart from this Buddha, what other one is there?' He was pointing his finger at thin air" (*HSZ*, 871). At the end of his life, Hōnen's words and finger pointed toward phenomena of his consciousness that he had preferred not to discuss at length.

> For the last decade, by virtue of *nembutsu*, he was habitually seeing the Buddha, the bodhisattvas, and the Pure Land. But no one knew of this while he lived; for reasons of his own, he did not tell people about it. Probably, his visions of the Buddha were an everyday occurrence. When his disciples offered to connect his fingers to those of a statue of Amida, with strings of five colors, the holy man answered that such a practice was customary but not necessary. (*HSZ*, 872)

It seems that ever since Hōnen transcended his despair, his consciousness dipped into and merged with a domain that was either lower (psychoanalytically speaking) or higher (religiously speaking). No line could be drawn between ordinary cognition and visionary experience.

Thus Hōnen denied, in theory and in practice, prescriptive mannerisms of death akin to holding hands with the Buddha. For Hōnen, a world that he actually saw was real—as is the case for us. On the twenty-fifth of the first month, five days after the deictic incident, Hōnen died chanting *nembutsu* and as if he were taking a nap. It was in the afternoon.

3

Imagination and Experience

Impressions of Buddhist statues and pictures of entry into the Pure
Land were firmly established in Hōnen's image reservoir alongside
paradisal scenes visualized through scriptures. Without a doubt, they
conditioned Hōnen's mystical experiences. But if the images constituted a necessary condition for the experiences, they were not sufficient, for the psychological phenomena initiated by intense sessions
of *nembutsu* also involved no mean feat of concentration: the reproduction of perceptually received images and their alteration into—
as far as the five senses of the practitioner were concerned—a total
reality.

Ōe Kenzaburō, who as a novelist prizes the imagination more than
any other faculty, has written an interesting, concise essay on "*Ōjōyōshū* and the Imagination." Instead of merely applying present para-
digms to the past, Ōe also allows the past to elucidate the present, on
the level of language.

> The *kansō* [contemplation] in "contemplating the appearance of the
> Buddha and of the Pure Land" seems quite close to what we call
> imagination. I was taught that the word *kansatsu* has also been used
> to express the process. It would be mistaken to equate this *kansatsu*
> too hastily with our contemporary colloquial usage of *kansatsu* (ob-
> servation). However, when we reconsider experiences that involve
> our imagination, we begin to understand that the imaginative func-
> tion plays a fundamental, indispensable role in *kansatsu* (observation)
> in the ordinary sense. The same experiences seem to teach us that
> registering the eighty-four thousand veins of the lotus leaf and the
> rays of light that emanate from every one of them is a scientific—
> without scare quotes—feat; considering the sustained concentration
> required, it cannot be thought of as a properly human exercise of the
> imagination unless it involves an imaginative manipulation even
> more rigorous than the observation of reality.[1]

For Ōe, the imaginative faculty is the common ground of medieval
contemplation and modern observation. His general impression of

the *Ōjōyōshū* is that its descriptions of heaven and hell exhibit a scientific will to realism that has much in common with the novelistic imagination that supports his own creative activities. In fact, we might add that the way Genshin uses past texts to construct his own reminds us of techniques (montage, collage) and concepts (intertextuality) that have enjoyed self-conscious prominence in modern times. In this sense, Genshin was far closer to the modern novelist than Hōnen ever was.

This apparent "optical illusion" of cultural history is not simply illusory. Genshin appears to have a novelistic imagination because his images fill out, with extraordinary detail, a *text;* the fact that his imagination is immanent in the text is what likens the *Ōjōyōshū* to the modern novel, both of which, at least implicitly, operate on the assumption that only what is said, is. Genshin was unconsciously self-conscious about language (a consciousness that is thoroughly reflexive in the case of most modern novelists) because his realistic descriptions were not descriptions at all but, rather, transcriptions. In Hōnen's case, however, what we have are merely the texts that set out the method of *jōzenkan,* which Hōnen himself used, and which we can read today probably without visualizing a single passage. Hōnen's imagination does not appear in texts—our primary means of knowing the past— and therefore strikes us as transcendent. Put differently, if Genshin strikes us today as a medieval Japanese counterpart of the modern novelist, then Hōnen appeals to us as a superlative *reader*—a reader whose imagination could be stretched and summoned beyond the end of reading.

An imagination powerful enough to enfold a third dimension into the flattened images that rise to mind must be preceded by much training, persevered with joy or not. Mystical experiences do not arise without pious sentiment, certainly not without the human faculty to imagine, and the imagined object can become more real than reality. Even today, the ascetic monk about to seclude himself on Mount Hiei throws himself flat upon the ground in worship until he sees the figure of the Buddha, and the figure has an undeniable truth for him. We may be the materialists without reserve who point out factors, such as lack of sleep and the willful situation of the body at its limits that produce such visions, but we can also admit on a different plane that the phenomenological reality presents a kind of truth for the visionary that can be neither affirmed nor denied by others. Likewise, "the dark shadow of death that covered late ancient Japan" might seem an overblown metaphor, but for the people of that era, the product of their collective imagination had an inviolable truth content that we might begin to approximate only through overblown metaphors.

At this point, we realize that by imaginatively producing, through the practice of *jōzenkan*, the Pure Land scriptures' paradisal landscapes, Hōnen overcame the epochal fear of a death rooted in both reality and fiction. Hōnen ceaselessly, almost mindlessly chanted *nembutsu* until the negative figurations of death—vindictive spirits, hell, and the latter days of the law—were replaced by positive ones of infinite light, happiness, and many-splendored paradise. These images of death were "positive" not only because they were optimistic but because they were manifestly and variously *posited* until they became ineradicably true. In other words, unlike the Dantean tripartite structure in which purgatory mediates between heaven and hell, unlike Genshin's binarism in which one is destined to go to either the Pure Land or hell, Hōnen created the unipolar structure of the other world, consisting only of the Pure Land. Below is a passage from "Mondōhen" (The Collection of Questions and Answers).

> The demonic realm leads people astray. All duties and asceticism follow from relying on one's own efforts. On the contrary, practitioners of *nembutsu* think of themselves as sinful mediocrities and hope for salvation through Amida's Vow independent of their own efforts. Thus they have nothing to do with the demonic. Those who delve in contemplation are also said to have visions of demonic things, but those who rely on Amida will be free of them. (Z, 3:208)

It is highly significant that a man imaginative enough to experience *zanmai hottoku* repeatedly never spoke a word about visions of hell, characterizing them instead as the domain of *jiriki* practitioners. Negative visions of the sort Zen Buddhism refers to as *makyō* (demonic realm) almost certainly did occur to Hōnen as his *zanmai* experiences deepened, but he maintained a steadfast silence on the matter.

Through a conscious choice of what to imagine, Hōnen could transform for himself the epochal darkness of death into a death of immense light and happiness. ("Unquantifiable light/happiness" is the literal meaning of "Amida.") The fundamental tenet of the Pure Land sect is *senchaku hairyū* (option and exclusion), or the exclusive choice of vocal-*nembutsu* over all other practices. But there was a prior, original *senchaku hairyū* on the part of Hōnen regarding objects, and objectives, of imagination. Although he produced as many as four commentaries on the *Ōjōyōshū*, he chose not to treat the six ways depicted therein and instead focused exclusively on the Pure Land. The terms of Foucault's praise for Binswanger's theory of dreams applies closely to Hōnen's labor of imagination:

> What he brought to light regarding dreams [the imagination] is the fundamental moment where the movement of existence discovers the decisive point of bifurcation between those images in which it becomes alienated in a pathological subjectivity, and expressions in which it fulfills itself in an objective history. The imaginary is the milieu, the "element," of this choice. . . . [T]he unhappiness of existence is always writ in alienation, and happiness, in the empirical order, can only be the happiness of expression.[2]

This "expression," in our context, was finally *not* Hōnen's own visionary experiences but his exclusive advocation of vocal-*nembutsu* and the practice of chanting. "The moment of crisis is," according to Jacques Derrida, "always the moment of signs."[3]

Hōnen was fully cognizant that mystical experiences owing to a powerful imagination (and ample time) were not to be had by just anybody and therefore did not demand such experiences from his followers. "*Nembutsu* is not about viewing the Buddha either symbolically or in his particulars. The single-minded chanting of Amida's name is what we call *nembutsu*" (*HSZ*, 508). He thus explicitly negates both contemplative-*nembutsu* and *jissō-nembutsu*, which require meditating on the Buddha with or without definite features, respectively. Hōnen goes as far as to assert that no matter how exquisite, visions experienced during *nembutsu zanmai* do not compare favorably to well-crafted statues and the abundance of nature—that is to say, beauty of a sensual, material order, whether artificial or natural: "Do not follow the recent trend of contemplation. So you haven't seen the Buddha—well, the statues that Unkei and Kōkei sculpt are more vivid. You haven't seen the magnificence of the Pure Land—yet hardly ever is the sight as splendid as the flowers of cherries, plums, peaches, and pears" (*HSZ*, 494). It might be pointed out that by making such a comparison Hōnen indirectly attests to having had such visions. As the advocate of exclusive-*nembutsu* and faith in Amida's True Vow, Hōnen taught not to waste any time on contemplation. But this was partly a necessary public stance that did not reflect his private practice; we have already seen how much Hōnen valued the visionary experience of *zanmai hottoku* in confirming his unipolar view of the other world. We might criticize this bipolar act as self-contradiction or hypocrisy. But it was perhaps simply the case that the truth and ecstasy of the profound, fertile world of his imagination could be transmitted to others only as, if not most effectively as, the extremely simple practice of chanting in abandon: *gudon-nembutsu,* or ignorant-*nembutsu.*

THE ACTIVE IMAGINATION

In the *Ōjōyōshū,* Genshin suggests a kind of metalevel of contemplative-*nembutsu* in addition to *bessōkan, sōsōkan,* and *zōryakukan.* In *nyosōnen,* derived from the *Hanju zanmaikyō* (Pratyutpannasamādhi Sūtra), the practitioner learns to see the Amida Buddha at will, by virtue of past efforts at uninterrupted-*nembutsu:*

> In a dream, your family is rejoicing before a pile of treasure, but once awake, you do not know where the treasure is. Contemplate the Buddha in such a way. In the city, there is a woman and her name is Shumon. Hearing this you rejoice and you dream, you meet her time and again. The dream is over; you think, and she has not come to you, nor you to her. Yet your joy was extremely real. Contemplate the Buddha in such a way. You are walking through an immense valley, famished, and you dream of a sumptuous banquet. When you wake up, your stomach is empty. Contemplating possession always works like a dream, and you should contemplate the Buddha in such a way. Contemplate often, without rest, and you will be born in Amida Buddha's land. I call this *nyosōnen.* (*NST,* 6:203)

It is open to question whether Genshin himself had attained such a state of blissful asceticism. What is more certain is that the method of contemplative-*nembutsu* practiced by Genshin, Hōnen, and other Pure Land faithfuls was precisely the kind of experience that Carl Jung tries to elucidate in his concept of the "active imagination":

> In 1938, I had the opportunity, in the monastery of Bhutia Busty, near Darjeeling, of talking with a Lamaic *rimpoche,* Lingdam Gomchen by name, about the *khilkor* or maṇḍala. He explained it as a *dmigs-pa* (pronounced "migpa"), a mental image [*imago mentalis*] which can be built up only by a fully instructed lama through the power of imagi-

nation. He said that no maṇḍala is like any other, they are all individ-
ually different. Also, he said, the maṇḍalas to be found in monaster-
ies and temples were of no particular significance because they were
external representations only. The true maṇḍala is always an inner
image, which is gradually built up through (active) imagination, at
such times when psychic equilibrium is disturbed or when a thought
cannot be found and must be sought for, because it is not contained
in holy doctrine.[4]

The term *imago mentalis* provides us with a useful, anterior conceptualization of the similarly paradisal landscapes that arise in contem-
plative-*nembutsu* out of a practitioner's more or less personal imagination. As for Hōnen, he sought images of paradise in exclusion of
visions of hell and slowly but surely forged a positive view of the
other realm in himself. That was his maṇḍala.

For Jungians, the active imagination has also had a therapeutic potential: it helps reestablish a synthesis between ego and repressed
unconscious so that psychic totality is regained. As a form of therapy,
the ego, which by definition speaks in the first person, must maintain
an emotionally vivid dialogue with imagined characters who surface
from the deeper psychic regions. The world of images experienced
during the contact is then expressed directly in one artistic mode or
another, in the course of which communication occurs between ego
and unconscious. As a result, previously undiscovered talents and
traits are gained for the sake of a richer, happier life. It is typical of
Jungian thought that a dialogue that some of us would characterize
as an unmistakable sign of madness is in fact a route to recuperation;
it is perhaps typical of scholarship that we would advance the de-
scriptive but not the normative uses of "active imagination."

Descriptively speaking, whereas the conscious imagination creates images that are superficial and arbitrary, the active imagination,
by enlisting the unconscious, produces images that operate according
to their own logic. They evolve much like autonomous life systems.
That each step Hōnen attained was expressed and recorded at least
once also agrees with the Jungian system; the dialogue between Hōnen's particular conscious and unconscious—self and soul, to quote
Yeats—was expected to introduce idiosyncratic components worth
recording. In Hōnen's case, it was precisely by attempting to repro-
duce an original that was not present in picture form that he could

create significant alterations and shatter existing images, such as of hell.[5] Psychoanalytic concepts may indeed be of limited, albeit often overestimated, value in historical analysis. Yet, the bitter aftertaste of unruly conceptual overextensions should not immediately prompt us to carry those limits back onto psychoanalysis's firmer terrains— in other words, those that clearly encompass "immaterial," "fantastic," or "phantasmal" areas.

According to Jung, all human creativity entails, to varying degrees, the active imagination, and he pays particular attention to religious symbols, like the cross or the maṇḍala, that are born in the process of human efforts to entertain dialogues with the sacred. In "The Psychology of Eastern Meditation," he comments on the *Kanmuryōjukyō*, which is also a Yoga scripture, in order to explain how a yogist imagines paradise. The yogist's precaution—concentrating on a Buddhist statue while exercising the imagination in order not to indulge in "ungainly fantasies"—wins Jung's admiration. Hōnen observed the same method for *jōzenkan*. But Jung's most suggestive allusion might be to the suprasensual significance of Indian dances, statues, and temples.

What the European notices at first in India is the outward corporeality he sees everywhere. But that is not India as the Indian sees it; that is not *his* reality. Reality, as the German word *Wirklichkeit* implies, is that which *works*. For us the essence of that which works is the world of appearance; for the Indian it is the soul. The world for him is a mere show or façade, and his reality comes close to being what we would call a dream.[6]

Jung notes that the world that we recognize as real is false for Hindu believers, while the ones we consider illusionary are true for them. Hōnen probably faced much difficulty after sessions of *jōzenkan* in deciding which was true, the vivid landscapes of paradise or what his naked eyes cozened him to see.

Jungian psychoanalysis makes an important distinction between the personal unconscious and the collective unconscious. The latter is crucial in discussing varieties of religious experience. According to Jung, the collective unconscious transcends personal boundaries and is in fact a human universal whose primordial images, or archetypes, are expressed symbolically in myths, rituals, and religious thought.[7] These archetypes, in Jung's view, become fully conscious only through dreams and analysis. Deep, religious meditation may be another path, however, because the active imagination that constructs the figure of the Amida or the landscape of paradise during *jōzenkan* constitutes a channel for the psychic energy of the collective unconscious.[8] The scenery of the Pure Land that Hōnen witnessed in *jōzenkan* was not merely a train of images assembled on the superficies of his consciousness but rather a replay of the collective unconscious inherited from the long tradition of Pure Land thinkers. Jung's related theory of artistic activity may bear upon this case: "Whoever speaks in primordial images [*Urbild*] speaks with a thousand voices; he enthralls and overpowers, while at the same time he lifts the idea he is seeking to express out of the occasional and the transitory into the realm of the ever-enduring. He transmutes our personal destiny into the destiny of mankind, and evokes in us all those beneficent forces that ever and anon have enabled humanity to find a refuge from every peril and to outlive the longest night."[9]

"That is the secret of great art, and of its effect upon us." Carl Jung did not cease to appraise creative activity—nor did he cease to think of the essence of art as an attempt, "flowing forth naturally" from the realm of the unconscious, to perfect the symbol of our species' eternity. His use of concepts such as "essence," "perfect," and "naturally" is somewhat surprising; however, he also alerts us to the possibility that human creativity is an expression of our desire for immortality as a species. It is a crucial insight because such a desire would also bespeak its opposite: the lived recognition of mortality. Jung's homage to art is, in this sense, an expression of the mortality of art, its historical crisis.

In this vein, Hōnen's resurrection of a realistic image-cosmos, of another world full of light, was a kind of artistic act. As we have already seen, however, Hōnen's art was a readerly one that exists only as traces in the texts of others as much as in his own. We might say performer as an extension of "reader." Because the images that he made accessible to consciousness were not his personal possession, but rather an *Urbild* shared by many others in a collective unconscious, he could convince others—"with a thousand voices"—of the thought he preached, that one is guaranteed salvation in the Pure Land just by vocally expressing a collectively shared phrase of veneration, *namu Amida butsu, namu Amida butsu, namu Amida butsu.*

FAITH AND MYTH-POWER

Yoshida Kenkō (1283–1352), who belonged to a long genealogy of high priests of the Yoshida Shrine, was also a consummate intellectual familiar with Buddhist, Confucian, and Taoist thought. His thirty-ninth essay in idleness praises Hōnen anecdotally:

> A certain man once asked the High Priest Hōnen, "Sometimes as I am saying the *nembutsu* I am seized by drowsiness and I neglect my devotions. How can I overcome this obstacle?" Hōnen replied, "Say the *nembutsu* as long as you are awake." This was a most inspiring answer. Again, he said, "If you are certain you will go to heaven, you certainly will; if you are uncertain, it is uncertain." This too was a sage remark. Again, he said, "Even if you have doubts, you will go to heaven provided you say the *nembutsu*." This too was a holy utterance.[10]

It was probably Hōnen's composure that pleased the author of the *Essays in Idleness*, whose life was about being a "free spirit." We have quoted him because he quotes Hōnen: salvation is definite or indefinite according to what one believes.[11]

That *nembutsu* is a capacity open to all is stated in Hōnen's last work, the *Ichimai kishōmon*:

> The *nembutsu* I have taught is not the contemplative practice that has been discussed and proclaimed by the accomplished sages of China and Japan. Neither is it to recite the *nembutsu* after having grasped its meaning through scholarly study. It is simply to utter *namu Amida butsu*, realizing that if you just say it, you are certain to attain birth in the Land of Bliss. Nothing else is involved. . . .
> You may have carefully studied all the teachings that Shākyamuni taught during his lifetime, but if you entrust yourself to the *nembutsu*, then you should—by turning yourself into a foolish person ignorant of even a single written character, and becoming the same as the unlettered women and men who take religious orders while remaining at home—simply say the *nembutsu* with wholeness of heart, free of any pretensions to wisdom.[12]

If we take the short text—one of the very few that Hōnen wrote himself—as the conclusion of eighty years of thought, then we are immediately drawn to the injunction "to utter *namu Amida butsu*. . . . Nothing else is involved." This belief is not the difficult leap of faith of

Christianity but a vaguer attitude of trusting an event that took place within time but transcends it. In other words, the content of Hōnen's *nembutsu* worship is an almost simplistic teaching that tempts us to resort to symbolic notation. If you chant *nembutsu* believing that you will be saved, then you will be saved: if p and q' then q.

This is not a mannerism of salvation like the one Genshin elaborated; instead we have *the formula of salvation*. It also appears in "Nembutsu ōjōgi": "Amida vowed not to achieve enlightenment until all who would chant his name would be reborn in his country. That he has already achieved enlightenment is proof that all who chant his name will be saved. This is what we call salvation by *nembutsu*. All who believe in this vow and do not harbor a morsel of doubt will be reborn, ten out of ten, a hundred out of a hundred. Those who practice *nembutsu* but are still in doubt will not be saved" (*HSZ*, 688).

Amida's vow to defer enlightenment is the spine of Pure Land worship, the Hōzō myth. When Amida was still a bodhisattva called Hōzō, he vowed not to achieve the buddhahood unless all people could be saved through *nembutsu*. That he already has become Amida proves that everyone is guaranteed salvation.

If to worship is indeed to partake in a collective unconscious, then it is also to share myths. Pure Land believers participate in the Hōzō myth just as Jewish believers do in Yahweh's blessing of the people of Israel and the gift of the Law through Moses; Christians, in the resurrection of Jesus Christ three days after crucifixion; Muslims, in the last prophet Mohammed and his writing down of Allah's wisdom. Those who "harbor doubts" about the myths are not saved. The main difference is that Amida is neither omnipotent nor coextensive with the cosmos. Not believing in the Hōzō myth is not a rebellion against existence. But believing in it *is* the affirmation of this existence, an existence in which such an event took place.

Nakanishi Susumu has coined the term *shinwa-ryoku*, or myth-power, wherein are fused the power to make myths and the power of myths made already. In *Myth-Power*, Nakanishi theorizes myth as an atemporal concept in opposition to history, or motion along a temporal axis.

> God does not die, and lives on forever. This divine attribute of not-dying simply points to a characteristic: existence external to time.
> Since the fact that a human being lives and dies means that he or she

is within time, the not-dying of a god comes to mean that mythology has no time. For example, Susano'o is the great god of the land of death, and continues to live forever in this land of death. This atemporality of myth can be rephrased as the "mythical present." In short, myth always exists in the present and has no past or future.[13]

To worship is to choose to live in the "mythical present" (rather than "presence") of a religion. Hōnen demanded faith in the atemporal reach of the Hōzō myth. Surely, there were Pure Land thinkers before him who had also forbidden skepticism concerning this prerequisite. But Hōnen silently adds a myth of his own making to the Hōzō myth—or rather, he reads it with an unprecedented literal fidelity. In short, Hōnen asserts that human death as such (combined with faithful *nembutsu*) ensures rebirth in the Pure Land, and his formulation "ten out of ten, a hundred out of a hundred" expresses the statistical absolute of *one hundred percent,* which as a point of singularity transcends statistics, an equation he constructed as a myth of unipolarity. In negating the uncertainty of salvation, it was precisely not the case that Hōnen was afraid of the violence of chance. That is not the reason why he was predetermining the outcome of that ultimate event, death. Rather, the improbable event—guaranteed salvation for all— an event whose full implication had to be blunted, mediated by the temporal prowess of a quasi-secular priesthood and ordered into a hierarchy of probabilities, could, for the first time with Hōnen, happen as an event in all its mythical violence.

Hōnen's imagination established a simple myth, the identity of death and salvation, and withering faith was rejuvenated around this mythical present, the formula and the equation. Hōnen opted against demanding from nonspecialists the specialized faculty of imagination through which the Buddha is seen and instead chose to surround death with a new myth that the masses could own in common.

DIALECTIC APPROPRIATIONS

In the myth that came into being with Hōnen's imagination, anyone who chants *nembutsu* faithfully will reach the Pure Land. It is quite important, then, whether Hōnen believed salvation to be attainable during one's lifetime or only upon the moment of death. To begin with the conclusion, Hōnen held the latter view, as we see in "Tōdaiji Jū-mondō":

Q: It is said that ten chants, or even one chant, is enough for sal-
     vation. But does it happen during one's lifetime or upon one's
     death?

A: As I said last year, it is taught in the Holy Path that concentrating
     on a single practice can annul your sins immediately, after which
     you do not have to continue in order to attain salvation. . . .
     Amida Buddha has vowed to make all people shine golden, but
     then, how can anyone shine like that before dying? Instead of
     pretending to be so enlightened, you ought to wait for your
     death without ceasing to chant, since you decided to do so once.
     (*HSZ*, 646)

For Hōnen, who experienced the impersonal caesura between life and death in all its chaotic proliferation in the late Heian and Kamakura periods, the "Pure Landscape," which he glimpsed through *zanmai hottoku*, had to exist as a world beyond—beyond death as an end to this world.

We must now elaborate upon Hōnen's dialectic refiguration of the negative triad of vindictive spirits, hell, and *mappō*. According to Hō-nen, anyone who faithfully chants *namu Amida butsu* is guaranteed salvation but does not actually attain it until the moment of death. The chanter is thereby located in a conditional statement whose logic is *arrested*. Upon the satisfaction of the "if" (chanting faithfully), the "then" (salvation) becomes a given—but it does not happen yet. The seemingly atemporal truth of the statement cannot take place without time. When the *nembutsu* worshiper acquires a pending other-worldly existence in this world, he or she becomes, in a sense, a *phantasmal* being. Therefore it is not entirely a matter of Hōnen replacing "bad" images with "good" ones in order to dispel vindictive spirits from his followers' minds. Instead, the Pure Land imagination endows them with an egalitarian method of *becoming-spectral*—implicit in the other world, but being in this one. We must not confuse this phantasmal surplus with the Christian soul. The soul is immortal and subsists *regardless of* death (as opposed to Hōnen's future ante-rior "*through* death"). In addition, the soul has an indestructible on-tological existence that invariably places it in binary opposition with the body, whereas, with the phantasmal being, mortality is precisely its vector of transcendence. One might be inclined to point out that this limbo state is reminiscent of Amida's status in the Hōzō myth. This is not exactly the case because the gap posited in Amida's self-imposed conditional is collapsed, by definition, before any *nembutsu* worshiper can enter the analogous transitional state (Amida's buddhahood is its condition of possibility). We are therefore not dealing with a practice of *imitatio buddhi*. Recall that while Hōzō attains enlightenment the worshipers of Amida do not cultivate the "buddha within."

Instead, they chanted. Here let us turn to an exceptionally successful application of psychoanalysis to the workings of society—we mean the work of Slavoj Žižek.[14] According to Žižek, the "non-sense" of a pure signifier plays a crucial role in holding together an ideological field: "The element which represents, in the structure of the utterance, the immanence of its own process of enunciation is experienced as a kind of transcendent Guarantee, the element which only holds the place of a certain lack, which is in its bodily presence nothing but an embodiment of a certain lack, is perceived as a point of supreme plenitude."[15]

How was it that *nembutsu* functioned as such an embodiment of lack? We say "lack" because there is something dissatisfying about the usual explanation that the name of the Buddha was understood to be the Buddha himself. Although that was undoubtedly true on some level, one must grapple with the prevalence of *mappō* theory and priestly oppression in the Heian period if one is to offer a fuller explanation. After all, *nembutsu* worship suddenly swelled in influence then.

In the latter days, evidence and practice had supposedly faded away while only the teachings remained. This did not dissuade the priestly powers from making laypeople (as well as each other) obey this or that law *in the name of* the Buddha, in the name of the teachings attributed to his name. Because the repeated invocation of the name—in the avowed absence of evidence—still grounded the authority of the Heian ecclesiastic community, the name itself assumed a "supreme plenitude" in the symbolic order. The name seemed to be all they had—but they indeed seemed to have it! The name became a sort of evidence in itself. When a large number of people began to chant the name itself as *form,* as signifier, the effect was not the solidification of the symbolic order but its serious disturbance. Because the signifier was seen to suffice on its own, *nembutsu* worshipers freed themselves from the intersubjective economy run by the ecclesiastic order "in the name of."

ENDING THE "ETERNAL RETURN"

Nietzsche summarized late-nineteenth-century Europe—where as many traditional values were destroyed as technological advances were made—by announcing that "God is dead." In the decadent nihilism of the so-called progress that he assailed, however, he also smelled the residual presence of the Christian tradition whose latency made it all the more predominant, and he struggled to dismantle its value system. To annul the meaning of the religion that had supposedly poisoned most of Western civilization, Nietzsche opposed Christianity's twin pillars of "God with a will" and eschatological time with the concept or, rather, the challenge of the "Eternal Return." Only the strongest spirits can bear, let alone affirm, the idea that time runs quite viciously in a circle, whereby the Same is repeated infinitely; so strong must the spirits be that Nietzsche only presents the prophet Zarathustra, who announces the coming of such an "Overman."

The pertinence of Nietzsche's concept to our study is not exactly that circular time derives, at least in part and in form, from Eastern thought. Rather, we must heed the fact that in Heian society the concept of circular time was not a challenge indicated by a maverick philosopher but part of a predominant value system turning oppressive. In fact, it was precisely against the Buddhist idea of transmigration along the six ways that Hōnen hoisted the banner of salvation upon death as absolutely final. Hōnen's vision of the return was the point: while the religious establishment painted colorful images of suffering all along the circular path, Hōnen taught instead that *nembutsu* fills in the circle until it becomes a dot, becoming upon death and for eternity an infinitesimal particle of Amida's searing white light. If Hōnen trafficked in hollow circles at all, it was the circle of the Japanese full stop. No untimely meditation was more timely.

But in texts, Hōnen is habitually ambiguous. The issue of salvation is no exception. Contradictory statements are to be found in a single text, as in the tellingly titled "What He Always Used to Say": "While I live, the goodness of *nembutsu* accumulates, and when I die, I will go to the Pure Land. I therefore do not have to worry about anything, including life and death. Salvation is attained both during one's lifetime *and* upon death, for the texts of the True Vow do not make any distinction" (*HSZ*, 494–95).

We have seen how this "double session" of salvation gives rise to phantasmal being.[16] An alternative reading is to note that Hōnen uses the word *ōjō* (salvation) in two senses. On the one hand, *ōjō* is the end of life whereupon the flames of passion are extinguished, and on the other hand, *ōjō* is the conviction, while one is still alive, that death will bring such absolute repose.

Compared with Hōnen, however, his disciple Shinran is unwaveringly clear and requires no such philological resolution. In the *Mattōshō*, he writes, "Truly faithful practitioners will be saved according to the principle of acceptance without exception and become peers of the Buddha in this world. Thus they do not have to wait for death or for Amida's welcome. When faith is established, so is salvation" (*SZ*, 319). Because Shinran boldly asserts that salvation can be realized in *this* world, as *this* mediocre man, many students of religion have tended to characterize the ambiguous Hōnen, in contrast, as an immature thinker lacking in rigor. The significance of Hōnen's view of salvation, however, cannot be understood through such evolutionary schemata. In the hierarchic society in which he lived, the surest way to realize spiritual liberation and equality was not via bold verbal assertion; the only way was to confront the inevitable "way of all flesh" and to wrench new meanings from death and its beyond. Heidegger thought such meanings were fables; Hōnen thought such fables necessary. The existential dictum against attributing positive contents to death has simply given adolescents (of all age groups) an excuse to wallow in a well-known malaise.

An example from our times may illustrate that, under irremediably desperate circumstances, many people cannot but deposit their final hopes in another world. Jonathan Kozol, the author of *Amazing Grace: The Lives of Children and the Conscience of a Nation*, a report on Harlem's children, has said in an interview that many of the children who are forced to live in abject poverty in their corner of Manhattan hope intensely for life in heaven. It may be too risky to try to comprehend the situation of Hōnen's neighbors, the Heian residents of Kyoto, through such an analogy; the point is that we should not forget the amount of cultural capital that atheism, or science as opposed to utopia, takes for granted. The now-proverbial "opiate of the masses" may indeed be an ideology that stifles the will to worldly resistance; however, Marxism emerged in an era of unfaltering faith in progress, when rapid industrial growth suggested the possibility of providing for all human beings down here—perhaps the greatest event in the history of our imagination—a possibility not foreseen in twelfth-century Japan. We have already analyzed the intersubjective economy of fear that forced laypeople to sell their power of imagination to a caste that profited from the vicious circulation. If we could only recall that in Hōnen's times it simply appeared mendacious to assert the possibility of salvation in this world, we might start to fathom the immeasurable distance, as much historical as ideological, between Shinran's "Prior to death" and Hōnen's "Upon death."

Hōnen observes that anyone who meditates seriously upon salvation looks more melancholic than jubilant. "People who are always hoping for salvation and paradise usually appear unhappy about the world" (*HSZ*, 493). Here perhaps Hōnen is close to Genshin; the world that has to be seen askance may have been for him too a *chūu*, a middle and middling existence. But Hōnen found myth-power. He lived in a society too full of pain to define this world as the site of final salvation. "What joy could there be in flailing a dream-like wisdom in this dream-like world? True wisdom is to believe in Buddha's teachings, to forget about this world, and to hope for salvation. It is foolish to love one's ephemeral existence and thus suffer for a long time" (*HSZ*, 1104). Hōnen's fundamental conviction is repeated in the *Ippyaku shijūgokajō mondō*, when a somewhat disappointed questioner asks Hōnen if it is true that some of those who enter the Pure Land are delivered back to this world after a while. Hōnen answers that the thought is mistaken: once saved, no one ever returns to this world; upon death, one becomes a buddha. Even if the term *ōjō* could be applied, in principle, to the moment of faith in temporal existence, Hōnen probably thought of life, in the final analysis, as the realm of an Eternal Return, rife with suffering and contradiction. In fact, only where it ended could absolute repose and the immaculate equality of salvation begin. This knowledge allows one to make the present world one's own.

MERCY IN DEATH

No matter how passionately Genshin and other predecessors of Hōnen preached the salvational exit to the Pure Land, their doctrine relied on the almost bureaucratic procedure of *rinjū shōnen,* the intense chanting of *nembutsu* at the moment of death. On the contrary, Hō-nen preached that salvation was as necessary an outcome as death, notwithstanding fits of doubt or of pain at the moment of *rinjū.* In "Ōjō jōdo yōjinshū," Hōnen reassures that as long as one keeps up vocal-*nembutsu* in everyday life, the Welcome (*raigō*) is guaranteed regardless of one's *en* (karma), of where, when, and how one dies.

> The cause of human death is not affected by what one wishes. Your end can arrive while you are strolling down an avenue, or even while you are at the place for the greater and lesser excretions. Your link to past lives might dictate your death by fire, by water, by steel, or by countless other means. But you must believe this firmly: if you chant daily and hope for paradise, then Amida and his bodhisattvas will arrive in welcome when you stop breathing, regardless of the manner of your death. (*HSZ,* 564)

Traditional Pure Land worshipers believed that the stamp of *rinjū shōnen* was needed to pass into paradise. Hōnen astounded them by holding that accidental deaths are not to be feared, since death as such is salvation. We are far from Hamlet's hesitation before the pray-ing Claudius. Again, if Hōnen does muffle death's nature as an event, it is in order to clear out the space for Amida's Vow, which *could have* not happened but *did.* Pure Land faith is faith in this contingent event. For it is not simply the case that salvation is ensured by the event of the vow; conversely, the fruition of Amida's enlightenment depends on the endless repetition of a phantasmal series of salvation. Without this repetition, in a sense, the point of Amida's buddhahood is lost. Response and gratitude are one.

Let us examine Hōnen's attitude toward death and salvation from a different angle. In his works, he repeatedly uses the expression *shōji o hanaru,* or departing from (both) life and death. For example, in his correspondence with a local warrior's wife, the phrase *shōji o hanaru* is repeated five times.[17] It testifies to the prominent place it occupied in Hōnen's vocabulary, if not also his mind. For him, salvation was an act that transcended the relativity of life and death; and since for him salvation was coinstantaneous with death, he did not simply attribute positive images to death but cast it as an experience of transcendence, as a departure from both life *and* death. But this rationale for the ir-rational, our articulation that "death is an experience of transcen-dence," was not Hōnen's. As the advocate of an ignorant (*gudon*)-

nembutsu opposed to intellectualization, Hōnen never plagued his followers with *nembutsu*'s dialectical "foundations." He spoke instead in a dialect of resolute particularity. *"Hōni dōri:* the fact that flames rise toward the skies, that water flows downward, that there are sour candies and sweet candies. Thanks to Buddha Amida's Vow, to guide the sinful masses with his name, if you chant it determinedly, his welcome will occur *hōni dōri"* (*HSZ,* 462). Hōnen was the first Japanese thinker to discuss the certainty of salvation in plain words; the event of transcendence was an ordinary event to be explicated, unfolded, in the vernacular. Genshin's Pure Land, on which he tried so cautiously to alight, was not the Pure Land of Hōnen, onto which all the dead could fall with no margin of error, like the gentle fall of snow that closes James Joyce's "The Dead."

Another term that we often find in Hōnen's texts is "jihi," mercy or pity. Of its myriad occurrence we shall present only two: "The bulk of the various buddha's *kokoro* is mercy. Everyone can be saved according to the equality of this mercy, which benefits all and misses none" (*HSZ,* 71). As the scriptures say, to contemplate the figure of the Buddha is to see his *kokoro.* And Buddha's *kokoro* is nothing other than the greatest mercy. He saves people according to a mercy unrelated to karma (*HSZ,* 106).

"Amida Buddha's mercy" was the phrase uttered tirelessly by the man who neither told of his mystical experiences nor grounded salvation except in the True Vow. The more impotent and confused the masses seemed, the more he had to emphasize the absolute mercy of the Buddha. In fact, since salvation was the leap from life-and-death into transcendence, and since salvation was realized only in the moment of death, *death itself was Amida's mercy.* Hōnen's imagination transformed the dark, cold image of death into a mercy whose warmth and generosity convinced.

The interpretation of death as Amida's mercy gradually coalesced into the core of *tariki* worship among *nembutsu* practitioners. This is evident from the behavior of the numerous *myōkōnin* who appeared in the Shin sect in the modern period. For example, consider Asahara Saichi's (1850–1932) relaxed attitude toward death:

> Hey, Saichi, what's your happiness?
> Saichi's happiness is not to die
> Rather than die, to come to his parents' paradise

My salvation is with you
Your heart is with me
That's the joy, *namu Amida butsu*

Saichi, what if you stopped breathing now?
Yes, fine, I'll stop breathing, within you
namu Amida butsu, namu Amida butsu

Returning to the natural pure land day after day
How happy I am, *namu Amida butsu, namu Amida butsu*

Dying—let me have a taste of that
Not dying, but living
Living in the *namu Amida butsu*
namu Amida butsu, namu Amida butsu

Saichi, now, how will you spend your future?
I'll spend it in the mercy of Amida
namu Amida butsu, namu Amida butsu.[18]

A *myōkōnin* who had little to do with visionary experiences could attain such a seasoned state of equilibrium because the myth of salvation-upon-death graced *nembutsu* worship over several centuries. Suzuki Daisetz never ceased to admire *myōkōnin,* including Saichi.[19] The fact that, for missionary purposes, the Shin establishment has taken advantage of the existence of *myōkōnin* and their stance of absolute submission to Honganji and its abbots should be criticized. However, we would like to limit ourselves to pointing out that a tradition of affirming death seems to stretch from Hōnen in the thirteenth century to Asahara Saichi in ours.

IMAGINATION AND NATURE

As we claimed in our introduction, an exclusively intertextual approach to Hōnen—one that would examine his thought strictly within a scriptural realm whose hub would be the Pure Land tradition—is grossly insufficient. If we want to truly understand Hōnen, if we want to do justice to him, then we must commit the sin of positing an outside view transcending the textual field—transcendent because its signs are today *faux amis.* This will become clearer as we begin to analyze the workings of an imagination that transformed the prevalent death-of-darkness into a death-of-light.

According to the French thinker Gaston Bachelard, matter imagines. Less mystically put, it is possible to trace a certain unity amongst products of the human imagination because they deal with the four elements. It is this unity that makes it possible for superior works of the imagination to move us; they express unconsciously shared complexes determined by modalities of matter. The imagination is also the faculty that transforms perceptual images and therefore has the creative function of liberating human beings from typified images. The following passage captures our book's starting point so well that, in citing it, we feel as naked as a newborn babe.

> Studies of the imagination, like many inquiries into psychological problems, are confused by the deceptive light of etymology. We always think of the imagination as the faculty that *forms* images. On the contrary, it *deforms* what we perceive; it is, above all, the faculty that frees us from immediate images and *changes* them. If there is no change, or unexpected fusion of images, there is no imagination; there is no *imaginative act*. If the image that is *present* does not make us think of one that is *absent*, if an image does not determine an abundance—an explosion—of unusual images, then there is no imagination. There is only perception, the memory of a perception, a familiar memory, an habitual way of viewing form and color. The basic word in the lexicon of the imagination is not *image*, but *imaginary*. The value of an image is measured by the extent of its *imaginary* aura. Thanks to the *imaginary*, imagination is essentially *open* and *elusive*. It is the human psyche's experience of *openness* and *novelty*. More than any other power, it is what distinguishes the human psyche. As William Blake puts it: "The Imagination is not a State: it is the Human Existence itself." [20]

The formation of an image that both sings and transcends reality describes, quite accurately, the choice Hōnen made in a world of death: death precisely as the locus of salvation. As we have reiterated, what Hōnen accomplished through his imagination was to alter the image of the dark, painful deaths detailed in the *Ōjōyōshū* and the pictures of the six ways so as to liberate a people cowering before death.

Taking Bachelard's cue, however, we must acknowledge the materiality that, in one form or another, supported Hōnen's imagination from down under—that is to say unconsciously. We shall try to imagine his imagination from the object side. Specifically, given the fact that Hōnen spent as many as three decades on Hiei, we believe the materiality in question is of a highly mountainous nature. Mount Hiei has adapted admirably to tourist interests, and the newer, uglier structures on the precincts have yet to discontinue their occupation; in pre-modern times, however, only the tiniest huts dotted the dense woods of Hiei. Hōnen could not have been unaffected by his life as a hermit in deep Hiei, in that corner called Kurodani, which is tranquility itself even today.

Mountains, rivers, huge trees, bizarre rocks, and other natural objects with character and presence, as well as natural phenomena deemed unnatural, like floods and eclipses, have excited the human imagination everywhere it has existed, producing countless myths. This is beyond debate, and the inextricable relationship between nature and religion, evident in ancient animistic societies, extends beyond them. The fact that nature has almost always played a crucial role in religious experience also applies to Japan. A good example can be found in Dōgen, the founder of the Sōtō school:

> The hue of the peak,
> the echoes in the valley,
> all in unison
> they are the voice and figure
> of Shākyamuni Buddha.[21]

More examples come from Ippen, an itinerant *nembutsu* advocate: "All living things, from the mountains, rivers, trees and grass, to the winds that blow and the waves that sound, aren't not *nembutsu*."[22] And from Kūkai, the founder of the Shingon school: his "naturally" amplified imagination seems to lie at the center of Shingon esotericism. Yuasa Yasuo has examined this imagination in relation to Kūkai's mystical experiences:

> Unlike Saichō, who practiced scholarship and meditation in residential stability, Kūkai roamed through the wild, Japan's mountains and seas, in a fierce practice like that of the mountaineering ascetic. But there was no organization like the mountaineering asceticism [*shugendō*] that would arise later, and Kūkai must have frequently confronted Nature all alone. In the introduction to the *Sangō shīki*, where he describes his pursuits in Mount Ōtani in Awa province and the Cape Muroto in Tosa, we find the famous phrase, "Myōjō raieisu" [The morning star enters into oneself]. He seems to have been practicing the *Kokuzō gumonji no hō*, a form of meditation where one recites the eponymous scripture while praying to the morning star. The phrase "Myōjō raieisu" suggests a moment of contact with the mysteries of nature.[23]

It is almost trivially clear that Shingon Buddhism is welded to the mysteries of nature. Is it possible, however, that the mystical experiences of Hōnenbō Genkū—who belonged to the clearly exoteric Pure Land sect—were also tied to nature?

Unfortunately, there are no texts attributed to Hōnen that deal directly with nature. But we believe that he was no stranger to the experiences of the founder of the Shingon school, who gazed at the morning star as he meditated in caves or atop cliffs. Kurodani is situated halfway up the western slope of deep Hiei, and looking down one sees the city of Kyoto and, right across, Mount Atago and the Nishiyama (western mountains) range. In short, for a quarter-century Hōnen saw the sunset; almost every day he saw the Nishiyama range swallowing the burning ball, dying Kyoto a deep red. Let us look at the description of *nissōkan* in the *Kanmuryōjukyō* in this light: "You, and all others, should concentrate and focus your mind and heart on the Western land. You might ask, 'But how can we make the image?' Unless blind from birth, all people have seen the sunset. Strengthen your imagination, sit facing west, and gaze at the sun. Set your mind firmly, let it not wander, and see how the sun takes on the form of a drum, as it desires to set. Afterwards, evince the scene, opening and closing your eyes."[24] The source of light that allows vision but that blinds forever if seen directly is caught by the human gaze as it approaches the earth in the metaphorical form of an instrument. Thereafter the condition of vision is a tool to be summoned at will, regardless of vision. But Hōnen probably never forgot the anterior transcendence of infinite light. Did not the ritual of the drumlike sun setting without fail, regardless of the pictures of hell deployed in the city below, show Hōnen the overpowering landscape of the paradisal Pure Land in the immeasurably distant west? Did not the scarlet, burning orb become in his imagination—as in the picture of Yamagoeno Amida in Konkai Kōmyōji in Kyoto—the figure of the Buddha hovering high above the mountains?

There is yet another religious experience whereby Hōnen may have incorporated his natural environment—the dream known as "Niso taimen" (Two Masters Meet):

> I, Genkū, have practiced *nembutsu* for many years without neglecting to chant for a single day. One night, I had a dream in which there was a huge mountain, with long shoulders sloping north and south and a peak reaching extremely high. At its western foot, there was a

large river that curved around the mount, springing from the north and flowing south. Because there was a fog, it was hard to tell where the bank began and where the water ended. There was also vegetation so dense that its extent was unfathomable. As I flew up the mountain, gazing at a distant peak in the West, I saw a waft of purple cloud in the air. . . . A high priest appeared out of the cloud and stood before me. I immediately worshiped the figure in awe: above the waist, it was that of an ordinary monk, but below the waist, it was the golden one of the Buddha. I put my palms together, bowed, and asked, "Master, who are you?" The reply was, "I am Shantao of China." So I asked, "But time has passed, eras have changed. Why are you here now?" The reply: "You have preached the way of exclusive-*nembutsu* very well. That is rare and noble. I have come to encourage you." Then I asked, "Will all practitioners of exclusive-*nembutsu* attain salvation?" I woke up before he replied. Even in my awakened state, it seemed as if the holy appearance was still present. (*HSZ*, 862)

Salvation is not a question of dreaming. With some imagination on our part, the dreamscape is reminiscent of the plains of Kyoto. From the Higashiyama (eastern mountains) range, running north to south on the east side of Kyoto, one can see the Kamo River; splitting the city in two and, far beyond, the Nishiyama range. Hōnen could well have substituted Shantao, whom he always revered, for the shining disk in the unconscious of his dream. The clause "below the waist, it was the golden one of the Buddha" suggests the almost golden hue that the scarlet, setting sun takes on as it is about to conceal itself behind the gentle skyline. The sense of social crisis in Hōnen's times unquestionably amplified his imagination to an inordinate degree, but at the same time we cannot neglect that the raw material of Hōnen's everyday life played a crucial role in his imagination of the Pure Land.

NEMBUTSU AND CORPORALITY

But what of the other *nembutsu hijiri* who practiced on Hiei? Why did they not acquire the imagination that Hōnen did? It is because, trusting in contemplative-*nembutsu*, they practiced the *nembutsu* of remembrance, or the gentle sing-song *goe nembutsu*, but not vocal-*nembutsu*—the repeated, vigorous enunciation of one phrase over ten thousand times. We must remember the body.

As exemplified by the declaratives of Tibetan Buddhism and the mantras of esoteric (Shingon) Buddhism, the voice as such is an important factor in the gradual transformation of the meditating ascetic's consciousness. The Hindus who heatedly chant Viṣṇu's name are purifying their *bakhti* for god through enunciation, and the Gregorian chants of Roman Catholic tradition intensify the piety of the singing monks; they are not intended as human communication. In Japan too, *kotodama* worship, which holds that human utterances have the power to materialize thoughts, still has a residual presence in the felicitations that Shintō priests incantate. Scientists can probably prove that voices ripple through the body and influence brain waves; all we can do is to point out a mundane example of the relationship between the voice and spiritual states: *karaoke*. Much stress seems to be released as bodies shake to emit all-too-loud voices; the total level of stress in the milieu is carefully transferred and conserved.

There is a plane on which vocal-*nembutsu* functions as a voice irrelevant to human communication as such. We might lend an ear to what Slavoj Žižek says about "the hypnotic voice: when the same word is repeated to us indefinitely we become disorientated, the word loses the last traces of its meaning, all that is left is its inert presence exerting a kind of somniferous hypnotic power—this is the voice as 'object,' as the objectal leftover of the signifying operation."[25] The passage assumes that the hypnotic voice belongs to another person ("is repeated to us"). This does not have to be the case. In fact, we might say that the voice-as-object is most disorienting when it is one's own. Uninterrupted chanting is disowning one's "proper" voice as bearer of meaning. This is what differentiates *nembutsu* from, for example, the reading of sūtras, which is also pure form, which is also one's voice, whose monotony indeed exerts a "somniferous hypnotic power," but is literate, priestly expression. Insofar as the voice is the medium of communication, its surrender in vocal-*nembutsu* exerts more than just a somniferous hypnotic power. It exudes human mortality—not sleep, but death.

Hōnen was aware of the relationship between *koe* and *kokoro* (voice and mind/spirit). The body cannot be left behind: "Chant strong from the bottom of your heart, never doubting that one chant will grant you salvation according to Amida's True Vow. Although a single chant is sufficient if you utter it with conviction, you should continue chanting vigorously with the thought of responding to the Buddha's great favor. If you are faithful, then *nembutsu* will issue from your mouth effortlessly" (*HSZ*, 891). In all manners of religious pursuit, the preliminary, goal-oriented stage is difficult to endure, but as the practice begins to practice itself regardless of the subject's will, body and mind are released into ease—the "high" stage of practice where chemicals are released into the body and mind. Unlike Shinran, for whom a successful chant is a signifier linked to a signified (the interior faith which is what matters), Hōnen seems to prioritize the ceaseless repetition of the signifier itself (a repetition that is *facilitated* by faith). Hōnen must have relished the *nembutsu* that flowed automatically from his mouth. As for his disciple Shinran, although he reported oneiric visitations in his youth, he entertained very few mystical experiences in general; a possible explanation is that his position—one *nembutsu* is enough—missed the whole corporal point of vocal-*nembutsu*. On the contrary, Ippen, who applied himself to the frenetic dance-*nembutsu*, was not simply being creative in his numerous accounts of spiritual encounters, of meeting bodhisattvas Kan'non, Fugen (Samantabhadra), and Monju (Mañjuśrī) in dreams he had in Iyo Iwayaji, or of running into Kumano Gongen in the mountains. His imagination was supported by the corporality of dancing and mountaineering.

The corporal basis of uninterrupted-*nembutsu* endowed Hōnen with something more than visionary experiences. Hōnen, who sometimes conducted ceremonies of confirmation at the behest of aristocrats, healed through *nembutsu*. Yuasa Yasuo compares the power of *nembutsu* with that of *kikōhō* (*qi-gong*) in our own times:

> He had the power to heal, as his follower the regent Kujō Kanezane recorded in his diary. According to the research of *kikōhō* experts, it is through ascetic pursuits that many have gained the power to heal; I believe the reports are quite true in Hōnen's case too. In some accounts, disciples and followers report that when Hōnen meditated, light emanated from his body. In the *Kōsō wasan*, Shinran writes that "While Genkū [Hōnen] lived, he emitted a golden light, and Zenjō Hakuriku [Kujō Kanezane] saw it first-hand," or that "His disciples always saw the rays of light that Genkū radiated." Some will find this hard to believe, but I do not think Shinran was completely lying. I myself have never witnessed such incidents, but it is said that some of India's yogis are capable of similar feats. The point is that people never join a new religion because its doctrine and philosophy are interesting. They gather in pursuit of real effects.[26]

Hōnen won a wider support base than any *nembutsu* preacher before him partly because the salient corporal factor of exclusive-*nembutsu* gave him a kind of mystical aura. If we focus too much on exclusive-*nembutsu*'s epochal appeal as a thought system and neglect Hōnen's shamanistic charisma, we fail to understand it as a religious phenomenon.

4

Death and Imagination

Hōnen's singularity lay neither in simplifying the practice nor in popularizing the theory of Pure Land worship. Various *nembutsu hijiri* before him had practiced vocal-*nembutsu* in place of contemplative-*nembutsu*, and as for popularization, there was the precedent of Kūya (903–72), as well as the notable follow-up of Ippen (1239–89). If we joined Japanese Buddhologists in labeling Hōnen, without second thought, as the simplifier and popularizer of *nembutsu*, then we would run the risk of overlooking the most significant characteristic of Hōnen's labor: turning inside out the meaning of death, imaginatively. Previously, Buddhist transcendence had been limited mostly to abstract ideas such as the Buddhist law and the body of the law, in any case without concrete images; moreover, access to those ideas had been limited to monks with special ascetic experience and to eccentrically virtuous spirits, monsters of goodness. The contemplative-*nembutsu* that Hōnen opted not to preach indeed involved images, but their occurrences were strictly confidential, as it were. By discovering a transcendental meaning precisely in the inevitable and visible phenomenon of bodily death, Hōnen presented Amida's mercy and his vow to accept all without exception. Thus was born a paradoxical theory of salvation that ascribed a positive value to death, within and against an Age of Death.

Pure Land thought is often simply characterized as being otherworldly (the expression *onri edo, gongu jōdo* admittedly calls for such a summary), but Hōnen's case clearly differs. By taking death as his starting point, he not only conquered weariness for the world but affirmed it despite its saturation with suffering: death, which was for Hōnen the transcendent truth and Amida's mercy, ran through the relative opposition of life and death. The paradox reminds us of those survivors of nearly fatal accidents who begin to believe with their five senses that life after death is not to be feared but, rather, awaited as full of repose. Upon revival, they adopt an increasingly *affirmative* perspective toward the life that remains to be lived. Death held no threat for Hōnen because his experiences of *zanmai hottoku* had functioned like such wanderings on the horizon of life. "As long as I live, the virtue of *nembutsu* will accumulate, and when I die, I shall go to the Pure Land. Knowing that either way I have nothing to worry about, I worry about neither life nor death" (*HSZ*, 495). In other words, Hōnen's message is to live, vigorously, the life run through with absolute death; life is the tip of the iceberg—that is to say not simply opposed to death but in fact resting on its immense underwater mass. Perhaps it was because the security of death cheered him on that Hōnen lived to the ripe old age of eighty, a full life rare amongst his contemporaries, full of incidents, difficulties, resistances, persecution. We cannot rule out the possibility that the simplicity of exclusive-*nembutsu* actually did not attract Hōnen's contemporaries as much as the vitality he exuded, the stalwart life on display, grounded in an absolute lack of anxiety toward death.

The flip side of this peace of mind was the absolute disparity between the profane world he saw with his eyes and the blissful, sacred cosmos that deepened in him: pictures of hell occurred in reality and in representation, while paradise shimmered in his mind. If Hōnen harbored any anxiety, it was toward neither life nor death, neither the real world nor the visionary but, rather, their unbridgeable gap. Our hypothesis is that Hōnen's encounter with Shantao's injunction, the reputed "moment of conversion," was more accurately the symbolic moment of his realization that *nembutsu* could actively dissipate that nagging contradiction.

It was not until almost two decades after he descended from Mount Hiei that Hōnen dictated the *Senchakushū* to his disciples, in response to Kujō Kanezane's request. Hōnen probably needed those twenty years to treat the gaping wound between his spiritual world and the vicissitudes of reality, the latter having been presented to him more vividly than ever before by the spectacle called late Heian Kyoto. It was, of course, impossible for a single person to avert the material misfortunes that plagued Heian society due to the disintegration of the statute system. Hōnen instead tackled the no less difficult project of liberating the masses from the illusions of death assembled for powerful interests. As a kind of outline for this liberatory endeavor, the *Senchakushū* marked a modulation in Hōnen's religious conviction regarding salvation: the plane of its attainment shifted from the individual to the social. The book was a secret document for the eyes of close disciples only, and not a manifesto for public perusal. But the very fact that he wove a web of thoughts that threatened traditional religious values—thinking in that unavoidably public realm, language—already signaled Hōnen's willingness and readiness, we might say courage at long last, to transmute imaginary convictions into a system of teachings.

The *Senchakushū* has an essence. It is the phrase inscribed at the beginning in Hōnen's own hand: "To attain salvation, chant *nembutsu* first." We would be quite mistaken to interpret this as saying simply that *nembutsu* is a necessary condition for salvation. Under the critical circumstances that Hōnen shared with the common people, the concept of a passive *nembutsu* chanted in response to imminent death, in the form of desiring the Pure Land or of praying for the welcome of holy personages at the moment of demise, had little solace. Instead, to those standing on the brink of death and calling for help, Hōnen could offer an entirely new practice of *nembutsu* that would instantaneously overcome both life and death: *nembutsu* not as reaction but as action. The active understanding of *nembutsu* as that which runs through life and death is evident in the following exchange from "Nembutsu ōjōyōgishō": "Question: Is either daily *nembutsu* or final *nembutsu* superior to the other? Answer: They are equal. There is no difference in kind between the two. The daily *nembutsu*, if you die, can become the final *nembutsu*. The final *nembutsu*, if you survive, will be daily *nembutsu*" (*HSZ*, 686). The passage captures how the new *nembutsu* effaced the merely relative opposition between life and death. This understanding of *nembutsu* was not the same as the strategic mannerism practiced up until then.

Exclusive-*nembutsu* annulled spatiotemporal givens, not "in the name *of*" Amida but "*in* his name." The teaching was effective because Hōnen's contemporaries had an acute sense of the abyss between this world and the other and of the inconceivable, irrecoverable distance between the true law and its latter days. *Nembutsu* could no longer be practiced as a tactical maneuver with chances both of success and of failure, or, in other words, as a means of transport at the moment of transition. It was not a question of transition, for no bridge could connect such disparate realms; rather, the chant had to efface the disparity entirely, in one transcendent maneuver, so that one realm, the previously negative limit of death, could become that which ran through life and death as the ground of both.

THE HIEROPHANTIC VOICE

Be it the contemplative-*nembutsu* of aristocrats and Tendai monks or the vocal-*nembutsu* of the *hijiri* saints, *nembutsu* in the Heian period was generally a plea for salvation to the Buddha Amida. Hōnen's *nembutsu*, on the contrary, was practiced with the understanding that salvation was already realized precisely to the degree that death was inevitable. His was the *nembutsu* of expression. "When you are to get something from someone, which is better: having it already or not having it yet? I myself chant *nembutsu* in a mood of already having the thing" (*HSZ*, 495). The statement has as its background the jubilant world of shapes, colors, voices, and aromas that Hōnen's imagination brought to him every day. His growing valuation of the enunciatory vocal-*nembutsu* over and above the visual contemplative-*nembutsu* rested on an awareness of the corporal basis of the imagination. It was also, however, a desire to express the particularity as such of the Pure Land which he knew from his interior experience. "Do not worry how heated your passions are, do not bother how grave your sins are, but simply chant *namu Amida butsu:* think how certain salvation is, with your voice" (*HSZ*, 495). When Amida's mercy appears in a human body, it takes the form of a voice chanting *namu Amida butsu* and has no regard for the particulars of the body that chants.

In the *Senchakushū*, Hōnen asserts the unity of solicitude and voice, *nen* and *koe. Nembutsu* (the *nen* of *butsu*, or solicitude for the Buddha) becomes self-sufficient to the extent that Amida's mercy is expressed. "*Nen* and *koe* are one. We know this because the 'gebon geshō' section of the *Kanmuryōjukyō* says, 'If you make ten *nen* by chanting *namu Amida butsu*, without allowing your voice to falter, then, because you have chanted the Buddha's name, every sin in your eons-long past of transmigration will be eliminated, in each of the *nen*.' The meaning of this passage is clear: the *koe* is *nen*, and the *nen*, *koe*" (*Z*, 2:203). This reciprocal equation is the kernel of Hōnen's *nembutsu*. If we are right in taking *nen* to mean internal awareness, then *koe* is its expression or practice. But despite his belief that a single chant would ensure entry into the Pure Land, never in his whole life did Hōnen cease to practice its expression, for *nembutsu* was the supremely active deed whereby the infinity of death was cast toward and into the finitude of life. This expressive function brings exclusive-*nembutsu*, usually categorized as a *tariki* practice, close to the *jiriki*-centered practice of Shingon Buddhism. In the *Ben kenmitsu nikyōron*, for example, distinguishing esoteric from exoteric Buddhism, Kūkai says that even though the body of the law permeates the universe, the ordinary man cannot comprehend its teachings, which therefore must be recognized through the *sanmitsu* incantation of the body, the word, and the will. Thus Kūkai's argument is not fundamentally different from Hōnen's belief that Amida's mercy appears through vocal-*nembutsu*.

Mircea Eliade has given a name to objects through and in which the "sacred" presents itself: hierophanies. Common examples are statues, stones, trees, rivers, mountains, the starry heavens, myths, rituals, symbols, and concepts; in the case of a mountain or a tree, for instance, it may also be a "cosmic pillar," an intersection between a higher world of transcendent beings and a lower one of the dead. In *The Sacred and the Profane*, Eliade describes the hierophantic experience:

> [T]he experience of sacred space makes possible the "founding of the world": where the sacred manifests itself in space, *the real unveils itself;* the world comes into existence. But the irruption of the sacred does not only project a fixed point into the formless fluidity of profane space, a center into chaos; it also effects a break in plane, that is, it opens communication between the cosmic planes (between earth and heaven) and makes possible ontological passage from one mode of being to another. It is such a break in the heterogeneity of profane space that creates the center through which communication with the transmundane is established, that, consequently, founds the world, for the center renders *orientation* possible.[1]

In our context, the orientation is toward the west. But what center? The space of *nembutsu*, as we shall see shortly. Because hierophanies have the power to synthesize the sacred and the profane, the absolute and the relative, existence and nonexistence, the "discovery" of one smoothes out the wrinkles in a certain part of heterogeneous time and space. We find a hole there, it becomes the "center of the world," and the repetition of divine signs makes it a holy locale. Mecca for Islam and *ojiba* for the Tenri sect are two instances—we might add Wallace Stevens's anecdotal jar.

Nembutsu, then, is the hierophantic *voice*. For the utterance of *namu Amida butsu* effects a modulation from one existential mode (*edo*) to another (*jōdo*); in fact it functions as a cosmic pillar. Since, for Hōnen, chanting *nembutsu* was interacting with extraterrestriality (Amida's True Vow) and "founding a world," it gave him immense satisfaction. He deemphasized all other religious practices and rituals because the central, world-building vocal-*nembutsu* rendered them marginal. On this level, however, the world was not structured as a single center with a marginal circumference; rather, each chanting voice had the vibrant impact of a "center." Although Chion'in and Honganji came to be treated as holy locales after the Jōdo and Shin sects were organized, neither Hōnen nor Shinran, neither Kūya nor Ippen adhered to any given holy locale. For them, the chanting voice was the absolute hierophany. When Shinkū, one of Hōnen's disciples, laments that his master has not even tried to leave memorial constructions behind him, unlike other major ecclesiastics—what were to be Hōnen's monuments?—the master replies, "Monumental edifices occupy the space of their construction but obstruct the spread of the monumental law. My monuments must exist in every region. The practice of *nembutsu zanmai* is what this old fool has been preaching all his life. From the dilapidated abodes of the vulgar to the straw huts of fishermen, my monuments are wherever *nembutsu* is practiced" (*HSZ*, 722). The disciple's suggestion to leave material memento mori did not appeal to the master, for whom the only way to leave life-and-death was *nembutsu* and the only place that mattered, the vocal site of a *namu Amida butsu*.

Hierophanies can be separated into "universal" ones (the sun, etc.) and those confined to a culture or epoch. According to Eliade, the valuation and significance of both kinds are historically determined and fluctuating. *Nembutsu* as hierophany is no exception, with cultural limitations and a life span. The moment it is hypostasized as an eternal universal for sectarian interests, we are left with lifeless, dogmatic *nembutsu*.

NEMBUTSU AND THE PHILOSOPHY
OF NISHIDA KITARŌ

Having investigated *nembutsu* as hierophany, we are now inclined to apply to exclusive-*nembutsu* the concepts formulated by Nishida Kitarō—*basho* (place or topos), practical intuition, and contradictory identity. It is true that, during Japan's fascist enterprise, Nishida expressed support for militant statism much as Heidegger did for Nazism. In and out of Japan, the Eastern philosopher has been criticized for having stated, for example, that "the essence of the Japanese spirit is to become one in things. It is the imperial center as contradictory self-identity."[2] Here, however, we would like to focus on Nishida's understanding of *nembutsu* rather than on the extent of his complicity with imperialist expansionism.

As is well known, Nishida constructed his philosophy partly out of his own experiences in Zen Buddhism. It is less well known, however, that his mother was a devout *nembutsu* worshiper and that Nishida himself began, in old age, to entertain a more than flirtatious interest in Shinran. Whether or not maternal influence was finally taking effect, let us consider the following passage from "The Logic of the Place of Nothingness and Religious Worldview":

> For any religion, any true religion, when a person gains religious
> faith, or deliverance, there always appears a principle of the absurd,
> which expresses the absolutely contradictory identity of God and
> mankind. This principle is neither sensory nor rational. It must be
> the Word of God, the self-expression of the absolute. It is the creative
> Word itself. Thus in Christianity it is written: "In the beginning was
> the Word." Concerning Christ, it teaches: "The Word became flesh
> and dwelt amongst us." In Buddhism there is a structural similarity
> to this teaching in the Buddha's name as precisely the Buddha.[3]

We have already elaborated on the content of the last sentence of the passage. Nishida was writing immediately after the death of his eldest daughter; the seventy-five-year old himself would pass away only two months later. His sharp philosophical mind nonetheless did not miss the crucial point that the heart of *nembutsu* is "the creative Word itself." The vocal-*nembutsu* of Hōnen and Shinran was perhaps not so much a *tariki* attitude of utter dependence—please save us, take us to the Pure Land—but rather a subjective *nembutsu* in which the divine being limits and manifests himself as voice in our bodies.

Nishida believed that a human being (the chanter of *nembutsu* in this world) and the absolute (Amida in the other world) could meet only upon the death of the self. By death he meant not physical death but an absolute negation of the self's character—that is to say the *nembutsu* worshiper's relentless, soul-felt contrition for his or her irremediable sins:

The religious standpoint must negate character absolutely. This absolute negation does not mean mere death, which is death in relative opposition to life—death as the affair of merely human reality, which must be negated absolutely. We must die to human life and death; therein lies absolute life. Thus absolute death is absolute life, and absolute negation is absolute affirmation. But to attain such absolute negation we must transcend the spirit and culture, to deepen the awareness of self-contradiction and sin concealed at the bottom of free will.[4]

To gain "absolute life," or in Hōnen's phrase *shōji o hanareru*: this "awareness" was in Hōnen's thought the return to ignorance, without which contact could not be made with Amida's mercy, as embodied in his name.

The cap mentioned at the beginning of the following confession of incompetence belongs to the high priest whose rough training Hōnen purports to be incapable of emulating. "I am a man who does not even wear a cloth cap. It is the ignorant Hōnenbō of ten evils who is trying to attain salvation by *nembutsu*. There is not the slightest difference between the *nembutsu* that I chant and the *nembutsu* that the illiterate *onmyōshi* Awasuke chants" (*HSZ*, 458). This confessional Hōnen was already spiritually at ease, however, unlike the young Hōnen in Kurodani who could affirm nothing he saw or knew or felt—after all, Kurodani means "Black Valley"—the Hōnen who had not yet awakened to vocal-*nembutsu*. In fact, it may have been precisely such psychological pressure that effected saturation, at which point Hōnen could open his metaphorical eye. In Zen too, a self-negation thorough enough to induce *gidan*, a kind of melancholic state, must precede the spiritual turning point of *kensyō* (self-awakening). Regardless of the type of religious training, the spirit must sink low for the knowledge of *non savoir* to sink in; without the relative minima of the psyche, there is no relative or absolute maximum. To put it in Nishida's language, it is when the self encounters the contradiction of its existence and becomes truly nothing, truly dies, that the absolute is seen. And of course, the etymological meaning of "martyr" is witness.

Nishida describes this relationship between the self and the absolute as an "inverse proportion":

Death involves a relative being facing an absolute. For the self to face God is to die. When Isaiah saw God he cried out: "Woe to me! For I am undone; because I am a man of unclean lips; for my eyes have

seen the King, the Lord of hosts" [Isaiah 6:5]. What is relative cannot
be said to stand up against an absolute. Conversely, an absolute that
merely opposes the relative is not the true absolute; for in that case, it
would merely be relative, too. When a relative being faces the true
absolute it cannot exist. It must pass over into nothing. The living self
relates to the divine, encounters the divine, only through dying—
only in this paradoxical form.[5]

Death, in the philosopher's discourse, is a momentary encounter with
"the absolute" and not necessarily physical death. But surrounded
by people from all walks of life, our Pure Land thinker could not speak
of such an abstract death; he therefore preached more simply that it
is in the moment of physical death that a hundred out of a hundred
are saved, approaching the divine "only in this paradoxical form."
This last phrase recurs in Nishida's texts: "The world of the self, the
human world, is grounded in this paradox of the absolute. God's creation is God's absolute affirmation through his own absolute negation. Or, in Mahāyāna Buddhist terms, because there is Buddha there
are sentient beings, and because there are sentient beings there is
Buddha. The human self's relation to the absolute is not a matter of
imperfection, but of the self-negation of the absolute."[6] The asym-
metry is absolute.

The great slogan of Hōnen's *nembutsu*—sometimes called *gudon* or
ignorant-*nembutsu*—was "Back to *Gu!*" as touted for example in *Ichimai kishōmon. Gu*, or *oroka*, is usually translated as "ignorance." Although the translation is not mistaken, it does not fully convey the
pejorative tone that the character carries in Japanese—a tone perhaps
better captured by "stupidity." In terms of Foucault's stirring homage
to stupidity, Hōnen is the philosopher rather than the scholar:

> Intelligence does not respond to stupidity, since it is stupidity already
> vanquished, the categorical art of avoiding error. The scholar is intel-
> ligent. But it is thought that confronts stupidity, and it is the philoso-
> pher who observes it. Their private conversation is a lengthy one,
> as the philosopher's sight plunges into this candleless skull. It is his
> death mask, his temptation, perhaps his desire, his catatonic theater.
> At the limit, thought would be the intense contemplation from close
> up—to the point of losing oneself in it—of stupidity; and its other
> side is formed by lassitude, immobility, excessive fatigue, obstinate
> muteness, and inertia—or rather, they form its accompaniment, the
> daily and thankless exercise which prepares it and which it suddenly
> dissipates.[7]

We are reminded of the opening line of Tanizaki Jun'ichirō's "Tatoo-ist"—"Back in those times when people understood the virtue of *oroka* . . ."—a story in which the divine proves to be not God but the goddess Beauty. Although we must not mistake Pure Land faith for modernist aestheticism, Amida, as we have said, shines with beauty. In our opinion, it is to the credit of Pure Land faith that vocal-*nembutsu* resembles the dialogue between the philosopher and the "candleless skull," the "death mask" of stupidity. One wonders if Nishida's austere rhetoric of "paradoxical form" might not amount to the same since, according to him, self-abasement is the only route to God. The god of absolute stupidity is not a displeasing idea.

If we realize with Nishida that piety is a divine voice, then we have a clearer idea why Hōnen inscribed "First, chant *nembutsu*" at the beginning of the *Senchakushū*. This "epigraph" in his own hand, preceding the whole book, indicates the precedence and priority of chanting over any possible intellectual grounding. Salvation is not attained through *nembutsu* but, rather, already realized where *nembutsu* is practiced. In this sense, it is creative expression. Since the voice of Amida breaks forth from our bodies, chanting *nembutsu* is a creative act in *this* world. "Our corporal selves are creative elements in the historical world, and historical life manifests itself through our bodies. The historical world forms itself through our bodies, and our bodies function to rationalize the irrational."[8] This kind of Hegelianism is easy to, and often rightly under, attack, but in our case it is precisely the insistence on a process whereby transcendence unravels itself through empirical particularity that makes aspects of Nishida's thought a pertinent commentary on Hōnen.[9] In Pure Land terminology, the driving force of history would be Amida's True Vow and the doctrine of absolute dependence; the *place* where that life limits or defines itself in the historical world would be *nembutsu*. Within what Nishida calls the "corporal self," utter dependence on the one hand and the creation of the historical world on the other, the passive and the active voices, so to speak, are absolutely contradictory and identical.[10] "The true self," continues Nishida, "stands in an absolute relationship to the absolute. Where the self heedlessly embodies the transcendent, where the self becomes the transcendent's point of self-projection and forms the absolute historical worldview, there is our true praxis."[11] If we take "absolute" and "transcendent" to mean the absolute death that is also Amida's mercy, then the mercy takes place in real life through its "projection" into the vocalizing body.

It would be extremely facile to dismiss Pure Land thought as an otherworldly belief that dismisses this world, ours; in any event, such a sweeping characterization does not do justice to a thinker like Hō-nen, who held a paradoxical theory of salvation. For him as for Ni-shida, everyday life becomes truly creative only when the self is com-prehended as a *topos*, where absolute death defines itself, in each *namu Amida butsu*, in fact in each lived moment. That is why Hōnen, who lived in desperate times and overcame despair, found in *nembutsu* the medium for optimistic living. Here is our last citation from Nishida: "When we become creative as elements of the creative world, things are no longer merely instrumental but expressive. Things become ex-pressions of life. The world limits and defines itself—in other words, forms itself. We intuit practically and define ourselves dialectically." [12] Hōnen urged his disciples to practice uninterrupted-*nembutsu* as of-ten as possible not to bolster pessimistic fears that salvation may not be attained otherwise but because he knew it to be a creative act whereby everyday life becomes the site of practical intuition.

Doctrinal debates regarding single- and multiple-*nembutsu* raged in the Pure Land sect before and after Hōnen's death. As for Hōnen himself, he never doubted his own position: *chōjishū*, or sustaining a given session of chanting as long as possible. Thus his great differ-ence with Shinran, whose main principle was *shin*—trust, faith, or conviction. Hōnen denied the validity of *ichinengi*, the logically sen-sible position that, if there is faith in the True Vow, a single *nembutsu* should be enough. Why not? But Hōnen had a "practical intuition" of the functional merits of *nembutsu* itself.

Needless to say, Hōnen himself did not indulge in the kind of philo-sophical explication that is part of our delightful vocation. As a mem-ber of a still quite ancient society, he probably felt no need at all to con-duct any investigation into the mechanical anatomy of *nembutsu*. His only task was to sympathize, or "feel together," with a people living in a difficult era and to indicate, as directly and concretely as possible, the way to dissipate the fear of death. If Hōnen had merely followed in the wake of the long tradition of *nembutsu* worship, his thought would not have set off the social ripples that turned into the waves of a sect and encountered massive resistance. Hōnen used the tradi-tional vocabulary of Pure Land thought and coined hardly a single word, but, more than almost all other practitioners of *nembutsu*, he could persuade. He was articulate, although he intuited the central function of *nembutsu* from within religious experiences that transcended what we call reason. Once upon a time, the production of concepts was not about inventing neologisms but connecting, separating, and reformulating everyday language with the "is" and the "not" and the "and."

Words are wise. "On the Sacred path," Hōnen was fond of saying, "one consummates wisdom and departs from life and death. Then, on the Pure Land path, one returns to ignorance to be reborn in paradise" (*HSZ*, 696). The return is also to a verbal formula where the name is the thing.

WHY HE PERSISTED
IN THE OBSERVANCE OF PRECEPTS

Grasping the function of *nembutsu*, in which the infinity of death penetrates the finitude of life, brings us to another major contradiction: the question of precepts. Unlike Shinran, who chose to become a married meat eater, Hōnen observed the Tendai Enton precepts all his life. Hōnen's adamance regarding such matters is one reason moderns prefer Shinran.

Indeed, for many of the aristocrats who visited Hōnen, he was not the theorist of exclusive-*nembutsu* but a precept-observing, "clean" priest. As such, he was given the right to give commandments (*jukai*), which, if properly obeyed, would facilitate the rehabilitation of a sick relative, the maintenance of a post at the imperial court, and so on. The most famous of these aristocrats was the regent himself. In his diary *Gyokuyō*, Kujō Kanezane records Hōnen's frequent visits: "On 30 September, my wife fell gravely ill. I immediately invited Hōnen for a *jukai* service, and he helped my wife recover. He ought to be revered!"[13]

In the entry for 29 September of the second year of Kenkyū (1191), Kanezane hints how his peers have been criticizing him for inviting into the palace and for religious services a monk who after all did not come from the established temples. Kanezane adds that he shall not lend his ear to any of his critics since no monk observes precepts and embodies shamanistic powers like Hōnen does.[14] Yet conversion to exclusive-*nembutsu* was not high on Kanezane's agenda. Although he approached Hōnen, the regent's acts of worship circled around Fudōson, Aizen Myoō, Kisshōten, Kasuga Myōjin, and contemplative-*nembutsu*—in short, the regular Heian aristocrat's routine of religious observations.

Hōnen responded to the aristocrats' demand for confirmation, but he did not ask them to observe precepts at all costs. "Neither observing precepts nor worshiping ancestors is part of Amida's Vow, so practice them only as far as you can" (*HSZ*, 535). This attitude toward precepts reflected his basic attitude toward all practices not included in the True Vow: just do not go overboard. But if the "sales pitch" of exclusive-*nembutsu* was *igyō ōjō*, salvation through an easy practice and in disregard of all other practices, why did Hōnen himself observe precepts so stringently, and why did he give commandments to aristocrats? Although it is possible that Hōnen hoped to retain the attention the aristocrats paid him, along with the shamanistic reputation they attached to him, it is difficult to believe that Hōnen would jeopardize, out of such secular motives, the principle that he preached so passionately. Another possibility is that Hōnen's long training as a *shukke* on Hiei made the precepts an inalienable part of him, and that changing the pattern of his daily life would have felt *un*natural. Still, this practical possibility does not explain the risky upkeep of a blatant contradiction between theory and practice. We shall offer what we believe were the three motives—social, physical, and spiritual—that persuaded Hōnen to observe precepts when continuing to do so compromised the fundaments of exclusive-*nembutsu*.

Hōnen observed precepts, first of all, because the banner of exclusive-*nembutsu* had its support in something as subjective as his own personal imagination. Moreover, the religious ideology that he hoisted included radical factors that could be taken as challenging secular and religious law. In other words, as the leader of a religious movement, Hōnen had to conform to socially accepted standards of morality. He had to control himself, his ego and his imagination, in order not to invite ungainly criticism. In fact, his unchanging adherence to Enton precepts and to his official status as a Tendai monk resulted, for better or for worse, in the Old Buddhism's tendency to direct its criticism not at Hōnen but at the association of *nembutsu* exclusivists as a whole.

Second, Hōnen had to actively regulate his physical conditions so that the purity of his meditations would remain pure. In "Shōkō Shōnin densetsu no kotoba," he is quoted as saying that "If one's *shira* is impure, one cannot expect to have the *samādhi* experience of visualization" (*HSZ*, 459). *Shira* is of course *śīla*, the Sanskrit original for precepts. Hōnen had sensed an intricate relationship between body and mind through his *zanmai hottoku* experiences and had emphasized the corporal dimension of practice. He hoped to keep up the bodily tension that strict observance helped him maintain, a tension that supported the strenuous imagination that endowed him with a vivid imaginary world. Just as he intuited the unity of *nen* and *koe* in *nembutsu*, he could not ignore the unity of body and mind in precepts; continued observation, then, was not surprising.

Third, and again parallel to *nembutsu*, precepts might have been understood by Hōnen as the form that the expression of transcendence takes in the human body. Could it not have been the case that efforts to express Amida's mercy in everyday existence gave rise to the deed known as the observance of precepts in the first place? According to Hōnen's own teachings of exclusive-*nembutsu*, salvation is guaranteed even if precepts are broken, and his disciple Shinran, ruthlessly faithful to the implications of the master's teaching, indeed chose to have a wife and to devour meat. Shinran thus offered an evident proof of his faith in Amida's mercy and pioneered a new terrain for *nembutsu* worship. We might add, however, that his successors in modern Japan have offered empirical proof for a different proposition: breaking precepts can become a daily habit that returns, before one can realize, as life's intolerable punishment—as flames of desire that engulf everything and obscure Amida's power to save. Was it not perhaps because Hōnen sensed the blindness of life that he attempted to stab it with the transparent rod—the suprasecular practice of precepts? It is not difficult to imagine that after Hōnen descended from the mount and plunged into the human chaos of the capital, every new act in the tragicomedy only increased his belief in what Michel Foucault called the "Care of the Self."

In his career-long investigation of power and the body, Foucault's aim changed from dismantling the subject as such to negotiating one's place in society through appropriation, counterappropriation, and so on. For Hōnen, the two tendencies more or less coexisted. The self-identical subject was destabilized through the dependent chant of ignorance, but this never made Hōnen neglect self-creation through the body.

Let us consider the nature of rituals while keeping precepts and chanting in mind. According to Žižek: "When we subject ourselves to the machine of a religious ritual, we already believe without knowing it; our belief is already materialized in the external ritual; in other words, we already believe *unconsciously*, because it is from this external character of the symbolic machine that we can explain the status of the unconscious as radically external—that of a dead letter. Belief is an affair of obedience to the dead, uncomprehended letter."[15]

Let us consider precepts first. One might say that Hōnen did not eschew them because they were a set of taboos, or nonacts, rather than ritual. But we can put this differently. Taboos (in the form of precepts) are *negative* rituals because, by ruling out some acts, they negatively determine a kind of routine in everyday life (eating vegetables, etc.). As such, we must add a crucial fact that is missing in Žižek's description: a ritual is a ceremony led by a priestly leader. We must not underestimate the effect that such leadership in "external" ritual can have on "internal" belief. For Hōnen, the observation of precepts not only did not conflict with vocal-*nembutsu* but was similar to it because, although in different ways, they both negate ritual as the reiteration of a caste system. Regarding exclusive-*nembutsu*, the very fact that it matches Žižek's description almost too well should inform us that chanting is not merely a ritual but also a kind of *understanding* of ritual. As the verbal repetition of a name, chanting brings the mechanism to a self-elucidating and self-negating extreme; it functions as a meta-ritual even if it is not consciously understood as such by the practitioner. Chanting *namu Amida butsu* fosters belief precisely to the extent that it is a repetition enforced by oneself. "Venerate the unbounded light"—this command repeated formally, by oneself, beyond the guarantee of salvation after the first chant—this is a consummate recognition of the exteriority of belief, parallel to the recognition of dependence on Amida. It is no accident that this recognition of utter dependence (on Amida and on chanting) rendered the practitioners independent (of priests).

Hōnen did not simply break with the tradition of precepts. They functioned as a lens through which he could comprehend the way belief can rest on "the dead, uncomprehended letter," be it the precept "No" or the phrase *namu Amida butsu*. If there is a difference between the two, if Hōnen in fact recommended only the latter to his followers and denounced the former vehemently, it was because precepts were, quite simply, too *complicated*. They invite meaning and interpretation—the domain of a priestly caste. Hōnen's task as an interpreter was to put an end to "interpretation," and this end was to be exclusive-*nembutsu*. If precepts are negative rituals, then chanting negates ritual because it is, on the contrary, an *excessive* ritual.

But we may surmise from the accounts of Hōnen's death that, far from conflicting with his own religious life as a whole, the observation of precepts was, in private, one with *nembutsu:*

> Generally, the saint never relented in his practice of *nembutsu,* but he chanted with an especially loud voice from the twenty-third to the twenty-fifth days of the first month. The people around him were astonished because he kept up the vigorous chanting for half an hour, or, at times, for a full hour. . . . The holy man donned the *kesa* robe of Kujō that had come down to him from the great master Jikaku, and he chanted as he lay, his pillow to the north and his face turned toward the west. He attained *ōjō* in the afternoon of the twenty-fifth. Afterwards, there was no end to the flow of people who came to worship him at his side. (*HSZ,* 873)

Hōnen's final *nembutsu*—emitted from an unconscious that must die with the man—was that voice not a curious visitor from a realm in between this one and the other? The *kesa* robe, which the corpse-to-be had worn in preparation, symbolized the status of the observer of precepts, although the body had advocated a heretical principle. Precepts and *nembutsu* had united to form the skeletal structure of the corpse's religious livelihood.

RELIGIOUS EXPERIENCE AND EROTICISM

We must point out about *nembutsu* what might be a general characteristic of religious experience: shutting out the "white noise" of the mind through intense concentration can produce physiological ecstasy. This feeling was probably familiar to the man who chanted *nembutsu* "truly from the bottom of the heart" (*Saihō shinanshō*). Mircea Eliade, who concurs that shamans experience ecstasy when they enter into trances, divides shamanism along two opposing vectors: the spirit leaving the body ("cataleptic trance") and a spirit entering the body ("epileptic trance").[16] *Jōzenkan* accords with the former category, for the practitioner's body is not so much occupied by a foreign spirit as emptied of itself—the self sees paradise. *Nembutsu* fits the latter category better, for Amida's True Vow is an external transcendence that descends into the body.

The aged Hōnen customarily defied the cold to repeat the experience of *nembutsu zanmai* every New Year and by all accounts remained chaste, despite the presence of many female followers around him. This was because his religious experiences, backed by his imagination, already brought unsurpassable bliss to his flesh. It has been said that Anraku and Jūren, two of Hōnen's disciples, were sentenced to death in the Ken'ei persecution partly on grounds of public morals; their seductively beautiful chants of *rokuji raisan* had gathered many admirers from the other sex. We invite the reader to produce the contemporary analogy. A profound ecstasy can also be read in the records of the dance-*nembutsu* initiated by Kūya and continued by Ippen and his followers. It involved stomping, for a few days or even weeks, so vigorously as to crash through wooden floors. It is almost trivial to note that religious experience and eroticism find a common ground in ecstasy and that there exist sects in Hinduism, Tibetan Buddhism, and Shingon Buddhism that aim at spiritual awakening via sexual heightening. These blissful experiences are not the exclusive domain of religious practice, for any deed that creates harmony between body and mind, or makes us forget their "duality," can induce such a state. Even scholarship might not be an exception. Our point is that Hōnen's *nembutsu*, accompanied by deep *zanmai*, is almost by definition an experience of erotic ecstasy.

We owe the most explicit analogy between religious apotheosis (whereby the sacred is approached) and erotic transgression (whereby the contours of the ego disappear) to Georges Bataille. According to him, modern man and woman are caught in the factual framework of the restricted economy of productive labor. We can elevate life to the point of death only through eroticism:

> Life is a door into existence: life may be doomed but the continuity of existence is not. The nearness of this continuity and its heady quality are more powerful than the thought of death. To begin with, the first turbulent surge of erotic feeling overwhelms all else, so that gloomy considerations of the fate in store for our discontinuous selves are forgotten. And then, beyond the intoxication of youth, we achieve the power to look death in the face and to perceive in death the pathway into unknowable and incomprehensible continuity—that path is the secret of eroticism and eroticism alone can reveal it.[17]

Thus Bataille's argument for liberation into the great continuity proceeds along the same line as Hōnen's *shōji o hanareru*. Bataille also asserts that the love of one person for another is an opportunity for connecting to the universe. At the extreme of *nembutsu* as a "cosmic pillar," then, one can expect to find eroticism. The issue that Bataille explored as a literary thinker was a variation on Freud's psychoanalytic meditation upon Eros and Thanatos, the desire for life and death, respectively, which Freud already considered to be closely associated with each other. The psychological urge to equate Amida's mercy with physical death was not a surprising outcome of Hōnen's ecstatic mysticism.

Freud's hypothesis that Eros, which when repressed becomes the cause of difficult neurotic situations, can instead be sublimated as creative expression and generate culture and art, inaugurated, as we all know, a fertile discourse on civilization that has continued beyond his death. We can trace this mode of thought back to the classical theory of Eros (love), which Plato makes Socrates utter in the *Symposium:*

> When a man, starting from this sensible world and making his way upward by a right use of his feeling of love for boys, begins to catch sight of that beauty, he is very near his goal. This is the right way of approaching or being initiated into the mysteries of love, to begin with examples of beauty in this world, and using them as steps to ascend continually with that absolute beauty as one's aim, from one instance of physical beauty to two and from two to all, then from moral beauty to the beauty of knowledge, until from knowledge of various kinds one arrives at the supreme knowledge whose sole object is that absolute beauty, and knows at last what absolute beauty is.[18]

Eros, the god of love in Greek myth, is defined by Plato as a daimon who loves the beautiful, the good, the wise, and the immortal; as it walks the path of love, it awakens to the beauty of the body, of the soul, of thought, and then of god, until it is finally liberated from the body and desires death. Thus did Greek philosophy connect Eros to death. Hōnen's association of Amida's transcendental love (mercy) with death was not particularly peculiar.

Just as Freud recognizes Thanatos's aggressive impulse to destroy, just as Bataille links eroticism to the violent destruction of social regulations and of other human beings, we too have to note the fact that the eroticism at the heart of *nembutsu* was not unrelated to the negative power of transgression. Hōnen's hostility toward the Old Buddhist order was not simply a dogmatic stance but an effect of the eroticism that he experienced in *zanmai hottoku*. The violent behavior of *nembutsu* exclusivists, and later of Ikkō sectarians, was not entirely due to political and economic circumstances. There was also the destructive potential inherent in *nembutsu*.

5

The Ethic of Inversion

Soon after finding its way to sixth-century Japan, Buddhism became a battleground for the Sogas and the Mononobes, two powerful clans for whom the arena was not staked out for highfalutin theoretical debate—this they agreed upon. It was, rather, a decidedly administrative choice between the "foreign god" Buddha and the eight million deities indigenous to Japan: which of them could secure, with greater certainty, real-life benefits such as political stability, agricultural plenitude, and the containment of epidemics? With a host of nobly unabashed secular motives, the victors of the day accepted Buddhism as the new sorcery. Its thought content was not comprehended until after the Nara period, and even then only by a handful of scholarmonks. For the rest of the populace, the thought content was almost exclusively a certain law of causes and effects: retributive justice. We shall briefly survey the power this law was exercising in Japan before Hōnen tried to annul it.

That the popular reception of Buddhism assumed the form of retributive justice is evident in an early Heian work: the *Nihon-koku genpō zen-aku ryōiki*, by Kyōkai of Yakushiji. "What guideline is there in repenting evil and practicing good," says the introduction, "if not in the law of retribution?" (*NKT*, 70:55). The author's purpose was to disseminate Buddhism through unambiguous tales of rewards and punishments, for good and bad deeds respectively. Because Kyōkai was a private monk with a family, or a *shidosō* not formally accredited by the templar establishment, he strove to preach the Buddhist principle of causality through attention-grabbing episodes, not excluding rumors from the marketplace.

We shall quote *Nihon ryōiki*'s twenty-first anecdote in its entirety:

Once upon a time, in the land of Kōchi, there was a vender of gourds by the name of Isowake who always overburdened his horse. Whenever it balked, Isowake yelled and beat it to spur it on. Exhausted

by the heavy burden, the horse shed tears from both eyes. It was Isowake's practice to kill the horse after having sold all his gourds. Many
horses did he kill thus. When he later looked into a cauldron of soup,
his eyes dropped in and boiled. Retribution is always near, believe
the causal law. A beast is the form your parents took in the past. The
six ways and the four lives are the house in which you were born.
Do not lack pity. (*NKT*, 70:121)

This is a typical plot of *kanzen chōaku* (literally, recommending the
good and chastening the bad). Precisely the banality of the setting
must have given the many persecutors of domestic animals something
to ponder.

Another interesting episode is the thirty-fifth, for which we shall
simply provide a summary. The Hi-no-kimi, or lord of fire, a provincial aristocrat of the Bizen province, falls to hell; he sees its cauldron
and therein a black object bobbing up and down. It happens to be a
human being called Mononobe no Komaro; he is atoning for having
exploited peasants for many years as a tax collector; he would like Hi-
no-kimi, if the lord finds his way back up again, to copy Lotus Sūtras
to purge Komaro of his sins. Hi-no-kimi indeed does survive the infernal experience and submits a report to the Imperial Bureau at Da-
zai. The report takes twenty years to reach the Emperor, who is told
by a priest, however, that a human century lasts only a night and day
in hell. The Emperor arranges for the copying of sūtras and the
appropriate memorial services, and Komaro's spirit is finally saved
(*NKT*, 70:421–24).

Although, in the early Heian, the fear of hell had not yet acquired
the urgency that it later did, such a tale reveals to what extent the
masses tried to understand Buddhism as a metrics of justice: close to
half of the episodes in the *Nihon ryōiki* are variations on the theme.
That all deeds would be appropriately rewarded or punished, regardless of one's caste, probably consoled those who felt socially oppressed; that the direct agents of their oppression (tax collectors) were
suffering in hell must have been almost soothing. Narrative remind-
ers of retributive justice continued to proliferate in the late Heian with
the great *Konjaku monogatari*. But, crucially, the causal principle did
not provide a feasible link to salvation. In fact, because the good the
priests preached involved constructing temples and statues, copying
and reading sūtras, sponsoring services, giving alms, releasing creatures to the wilderness, and other deeds that were beyond the reach

of people whose daily lives were already a struggle, the teaching of *kanzen chōaku* only exacerbated the masses' alienation from Buddhism. Thus, in the *Ryōjin hishō*, for example, we find songs that convey the honest opinion of people who had to slaughter to live: "In passing through this ephemeral world, in earning our livelihood from the seas and the mountains, we earn the disdain of ten thousand buddhas: what are we to do with ourselves?"[1] If we mean by "ethics" the questioning of "moral" codes shared unreflexively by a community, then the popular authors of the lyrics were far more ethical than priests moral and immoral.

Laypeople were fleeing from the Buddhist death machine, its vindictive spirits, hell, and apocalyptic despair. They groped for the rope that was thrown them; it was dyed with the Buddhist element of retributive justice; they let go. Perhaps it was in accordance with an ecclesiastic sense of duty that the high priests of Nara and Kyoto recommended goodness and chastened evil, but the *rokuharamitsu* ways that they advanced—charity, observing precepts, perseverance, dedication, meditation, and wisdom—were far too removed from everyday life to be actualized. The impossible demand only increased the masses' despair and also gave rise to a feeling of moral oppression. It is unlikely that the peasants swallowed whole the good deeds and virtues recommended by the religious organizations that were also powerful landowners of expanding *shōen* estates. We have no way to ascertain exactly what percentage of peasants sensed that the doctrine of virtue was intended to bind them to the temples, to impress the ecclesiastics' importance, and to secure for the religious venture, through *kanjin hijiri*, a steady financial resource.

The peasants could not escape the established temples' regime of maintenance because plots could be taken away and insecticidal incantations be denied. In addition, antagonizing the monks and the temples meant bringing down curses that could steer the course of one's afterlife toward the undesirable destination. The impossibility of the moral demands were not simply an issue for laypeople. There also existed monks who could not bring themselves to obey the commandments impeccably and who therefore had to fabricate a text like *Mappō tōmyōki* to justify their own "decadent" lapse from required standards. The conscientious amongst them could not have remained indifferent toward the reified ethic's severe contradictions with circumstantial actuality as well as human possibility.

THE PARADOXICAL THEORY OF SALVATION

It is in the nature of a system to counter its own growing inflexibility by differentiating itself. A religious system that loses doctrinal and institutional elasticity, and that oppresses a majority of its followers morally, sooner or later produces a potentially subversive element in order for the whole to survive. The Protestant Reformation in Renaissance Europe is a case in point. Liberating people from their deep-rooted dependence on an oppressive belief structure requires a negation of the traditional value system. In thirteenth-century Japan, it was Hōnen's exclusive-*nembutsu* that initiated the rejection of a religious ethic that many ecclesiastics and laypeople alike deemed stagnant. By defining vocal-*nembutsu* as an absolute good qualitatively superior to all prevalent practices, Hōnen annulled an older set theory of salvation or, rather, turned it inside out so it no longer bounded out, but was instead inextricably bound to, the production of a comprehensive view of humanity.

In the *Senchakushū*, Hōnen calls *nembutsu* the "absolutely best method":

> Q: If *nembutsu* is, as you say, the highest practice, then why do you
> preach it to the lowly and not to those of higher status?
>
> A: As I have said before, *nembutsu* can be practiced by people of all
> *kuhon* [nine levels]. By this we are referring to the passage in the
> *Ōjōyōshū* that reads, "People are to be divided into *kuhon* accord-
> ing to their qualities." The lowest are those who have commit-
> ted one of the five terrible sins. These sins are beyond the reach of
> all other practices. Only the power of *nembutsu* can annul them.
> That is why I preach the absolutely best method to the absolutely
> worst people. (Z, 2:256)

Hōnen recommends *nembutsu* as a supreme method, as one meant especially for those who have committed the five "cardinal" crimes—murdering your father, your mother, or an *arhat*, harming the Buddha's body, and destroying a sect's unity. The stance would eventually lead to the theory of *akunin shōki*: we owe Amida's Vow to the existence of villains. The theory is customarily associated with Shinran and his famous statement in *Tan'nishō*—"Since even the good can attain salvation, there is no question that the bad will"—but Hōnen already makes an identical assertion in "Sanshin ryōken oyobi gohōji": "About the idea that 'Since even the good can attain salvation, there is no question that the bad will,' I say this: Amida did not make his vow for good people, who have the means to depart from life and death. He made it because he pitied the worst sinners who would have no means otherwise" (*HSZ*, 454).

Such a reversal of values could potentially shake the fundamentals of social order. People who felt themselves to be completely exterior to the cone of salvation must have been astounded by Hōnen when he dismissed, confidently, the popular belief that the outcome of death was meticulously conditioned by worldly acts. He instead told the people about entry into the Pure Land via *nembutsu* and despite sinful crimes. The word "people" suggests a group of innocents persecuted by power, but this group unquestionably included a lot of cunning spirits who took advantage of social chaos for less than moral purposes. It is probable that every disaster produced new thieves and adulterers, and it was they who were most intensely moved by Hōnen's paradoxical theory of salvation. Hagiographies of Hōnen narrate his encounters with robbers and prostitutes who repent and reform upon meeting the saintly man. The accounts may be parables, but they must be understood as symbolic, verbal enactments of the life-affirming, all-encompassing attitude of exclusive-*nembutsu* at its best. To say the least, we can surmise that the immoral were not averse to Hōnen.

The point of Hōnen's idea of *igyō ōjō* was not so much the methodological ease of vocalization but the annihilation of the moralist conditionals for salvation—the innumerable, variegated set of causes and effects laid out as the system of retributive justice. Hōnen tried to annul these causes and effects not by denying the idea of causality but by overshadowing the causes and effects with the Cause and the Effect of vocal repetition. According to David Hume, only repetition establishes the link between cause and effect. When we "prove" that event A causes event B, we are only saying that event A has always been followed by event B *in our experience so far*. The repeated sequentiality of the two events makes the mind expect event A *always* to be followed by event B, in the past, present, and future, but this is just a mental habit and not something as metaphysical as "causality." The idea of causality is simply an "effect" of repetition (in our experience so far).[2]

We can make two points in this regard. Obviously, we cannot apply the Humean argument directly to theories of salvation, since salvation (event B, the effect) is never observed. But this is precisely our first point. The fact that event B is *never* observed can be as secure a ground for "causality" as the fact that, up until now, event B has *always* followed event A. (The law of causality would be most threatened by the "sometimes.") As long as the effect, salvation, is never observed, this "never" can actively posit an entirely other space where the effect *always* takes place. With the law of retribution, on the other hand, effects must be posited and described as empirical occurrences in order to scare the public; sometimes, the effect that should follow a certain cause will not be observed. Unlike paradisal salvation, the causes and effects of retributive justice have to function in this unstable domain of the "sometimes." Our second point concerns Hōnen's insistence that the cause of salvation, the chant of *namu Amida butsu,* should be repeated over and over. We said earlier that we should locate the radical nature of exclusive-*nembutsu* partly in the fact that it is a kind of metaritual, by virtue of its excessive character. Here too, exclusive-*nembutsu* overwhelms the causes and effects of retributive justice by enacting the very mechanism of causality itself, repetition. Precisely because the effect is not observed, the cause has to be repeated tirelessly.

For Hōnen, the sublimation of the existing moral structure was not possible without liberation from causal minutiae: "Salvation by *nembutsu* does not exclude the worst criminals. The welcome responds to ten chants, or possibly just one. The other sects of the Holy Path promise salvation only to good people who have practiced much. But in these our latter days, there are bad people only. Instead of trying to follow difficult teachings, you should follow the easy practice of chanting Amida's name, and thus exit the house of life and death" (*HSZ*, 681).

While prior Buddhists had examined life as such, and had indicated moral codes that were to be revered to elevate *life,* Hōnen on the contrary gazed at the workings of life from *death,* which negated all moral codes not immanent in human mortality. In other words, Hōnen did not survey life on earth from high above, from the elevated point of view of the enlightened man; rather, he lay supine on the floor of death to observe life from underneath. If he had thrown the net of salvation from above, he could not have captured the fish swaying like reeds at the bottom of the river. By making death the point of origin of faith, Hōnen cast the net of salvation from the riverbed toward the surface. According to his teachings, then, those who would have been necessarily caught in the net eluded the net, and on the contrary, those whom nets had never quite reached were the first to get wrapped up in the joyous twine. But if exclusive-*nembutsu* and its paradoxical theory of salvation were to gain influence as a movement, it had to become entangled in an older network of religious values and secular *idées reçues*.

CHANTS AND BATTLE CRIES

For those who were in a position to defend the older religious ethic, Hōnen was a tricky menace: he was a "clean" monk with a high reputation for observing precepts, who nevertheless announced vocal-*nembutsu*, heretically, as an absolute good capable of eliminating all evils. In expounding this ethic of inversion, however, Hōnen assumed the line of sight of the desperately insecure—on whom he had fixed his eyes—and lamented his own worthlessness as a *bonbu* (an ordinary/mediocre man):

> There are many Buddhisms. Yet a cursory overview reveals to us that none of them goes beyond the tripartite teaching of Precepts, Meditation, and Wisdom. All we have are the precepts, meditation, and wisdom of Hīnayāna Buddhism, the precepts, meditation, and wisdom of Mahāyāna Buddhism, the precepts, meditation, and wisdom of exoteric Buddhism, the precepts, meditation, and wisdom of esoteric Buddhism. As for myself, I do not observe a single precept; I have never succeeded at meditation; and I have not gained the just wisdom that staves off ungainly thought. (*HSZ*, 459)

We could accuse Hōnen of a kind of reverse hypocrisy (the good dissimulating the bad) since, in actuality, he observed precepts with an extraordinary, lifelong self-discipline, not to mention the visionary experiences he enjoyed on multiple occasions. Far from being properly autobiographical, then, Hōnen's confession was rather an attempt to construct an "Everyman's biography."[3] His motive was not a desire to be condescending but a need to establish commonalities— that is to say, if indeed fictional, then fictionally convincing points of sameness—so that his horizons may coincide with those of his contemporaries.

Hōnen lamented his own insufficiency often enough that we might impute a certain conviction to the sum of his statements: "human beings are born evil." Yet he refused to recognize the existence of any evil that surpassed the good of *nembutsu*. "Even if you have made evil all your life, each and every one of your sins will be naturally effaced as long as you chant persistently and wholeheartedly.

Your salvation is certain. So why not stop worrying, why not put your mind to rest?" (*Z*, 2:163). Since all evils are wiped clean by *nembutsu*, why worry about this world? This form of indifference, however, was the diametric opposite of the more familiar religious inclination to negate the real world. For Hōnen's ethic of inversion also functioned as a logic of the most inclusive affirmation of reality. "Chanters should chant as they are—the good person as the good, the bad person as the bad" (*HSZ*, 450). There were those who had striven all life to accumulate goodness through almsgiving and the observation of precepts; there were those who were incapable of such deeds, for various reasons; there were those who did not even try or who made valiant efforts toward entirely contrary goals. They could all remain as they were.

This new ethical system that made no amends for common sense liberated the members of an increasingly powerful class from their guilty conscience. These were the warriors caught in a dilemma between the Buddhist law of nonviolence and the temporal law of their field of labor—slay or else. Hōnen himself came from the rising warrior class, and his exclusive-*nembutsu* provided an ethical system for a professional group with a unique set of demands and interests that had not previously existed, at least not in the same organized manner. Perhaps it was Pure Land thought and other currents of the New Kamakura Buddhism that allowed those demands and interests to coagulate into a set and a class. "Since Amida's True Vow was taken specifically for sinners, any sinner who chants Amida's name is saved *as a sinner:* this is the mystery of the True Vow. He who was born in a house of bows and arrows should not doubt—not even in his dreams—that the chanting of *nembutsu* will summon the welcome. Salvation according to the True Vow is certain even if he expires on the battlefield" (*HSZ*, 717). The precept against murder, in short, may be virtually ignored; no other words could have been so simply relieving for those whose métier was murder. In the *Genpei seisuiki,* Hōnen appears to dispense spiritual relief to a certain Amakasu Tarō Tadatsuna as the warrior embarks upon his way to carnage: "The high priest taught Amakasu that, if he chants ten times, his salvation is indubitable whether he dies by the sword or by the arrow. Amakasu set off for Sakamoto happily" (*HSZ*, 1105). Taira-no-Shigehira in *The Tale of Heike,* Minamoto Tameyoshi in the *Hōgen monogatari,* and Kumagai Naozane in the *Azuma Kagami* all repent in the presence of Hōnen. In each case, he tells the warrior that the virtue of *nembutsu* annuls the sin of willful violence. Not every religious personality encounters various warriors in various works; this repetition in fiction was not entirely fictional, for warriors indeed flocked to Hōnen.

Even if you have committed as grave a sin as murder, you will be entirely forgiven as long as you conform to that highest good, *nembutsu*. The assertion was a ray of light in the spiritual dark—to use the Japanese proverb *jigoku ni hotoke,* or the buddha in hell—for those who could be thus liberated from guilt. On the one hand, although exclusive-*nembutsu* ran against the grain of the accepted standards of good and evil and elicited much criticism, it was not unsuccessful in liberating a people from a moral oppression interiorized as the law of retributive justice. On the other hand, this assent to murder—not particular to Pure Land worship but, in fact, a general characteristic of Japanese Buddhism—has had enduring sociopolitical reverberations whose analysis we defer to the end of this book.

FORGIVENESS RUNS AMOK

The ethic of inversion, which exclusive-*nembutsu* embodied, was apparently so contrary to common sense that even those who heard it from Hōnen himself had to doubt their own ears. We can fathom the extent to which Hōnen's discourse was deemed astonishing and suspicious if we unroll the *Ippyaku shijū gokajō mondō* (One Hundred Forty-five Questions and Answers) exchanged between the high priest and the unbelieving wives of court officials:

Q: They say a baby is impure for the first hundred days and should not be brought to a shrine for worship. Is that so?

A: Newborn babes are not impure. If you think of them as impure, then they are. But that applies to many things other than babies.

Q: If one has eaten scallions, onions, spring onions, or meat, is it okay to chant before the smell has disappeared?

A: Nothing obstructs *nembutsu*.

Q: My seven-year-old has died. But you have said that purification is not necessary?

A: Buddhism does not know of purification. All that is secular.

Q: Is it true that it's sinful to die before one's parents do?

A: In our impure land, we cannot do much about that anyway.

Q: Should one ask a priest for the reading of sūtras?

A: If you can read, then go ahead yourself.

Q: Is it sinful to drink saké?

A: It's better not to, but it's a custom.

Q: Can one attain salvation simply through daily *nembutsu*—that is to say, without the presence of a respected monk at the moment of death?

A: As long as you have chanted, you will be saved—even if there is no attendant monk, and even if your death is not as calm as you thought it would be.

Q: Should the dead be shaven bald?

A: Not necessarily.

Q: Is it okay to read sūtras when I am having a period?

A: I don't see why not.

Q: Is it possible to attain salvation without becoming ordained?

A: Many people have attained salvation practicing solely at home.

Q: If a woman and a man have just been one, should they take a bath before reading sūtras?

A: As in the other cases, properly speaking, you ought to take a bath. In the case of chanting, however, you need not worry. But for sūtras, it's better to take a bath first, even if that means every day.

Even the seasoned Hōnen scholar cannot help being entertained once again by the boldness with which the master demolishes various superstitions and folk beliefs. After a few exchanges, Hōnen's response was not hard to guess. Nevertheless, he shocked the wives into multiplying their particularistic questions, and together they produced a precious document for future cultural historians if for nobody else.

The following more or less pragmatic assertion was a hint that the dawn of the spirituality of a new era was imminent: "There is a limit to human destiny. When you fall sick, it makes no difference whether or not you pray to the deities. If praying could cure sickness and defer death, then no one would ever fall sick and die" (*HSZ*, 604). These words could not have fallen softly on the ears of those who were diligently following esoteric Buddhist guidelines in order to obtain supernatural powers. It was perhaps simply because Hōnen was thick-skinned that he could make such claims in an era when people of all castes were trapped in an intricate web of superstitions, first and foremost the *onmyōdō*. At the same time, we sense a kind of rationalist spirit, heterogeneous to the eloquence of Heian literature, in the simple beauty of Hōnen's replies—the spirit, perhaps, of a rising class of military professionals.

But it was almost inevitable that a teaching radical enough to liberate people from an oppressive morality would begin to walk on its own, to tread its own path heedless of the creator's will, to cause monstrous social problems. When the umbilical cords that tied vindictive spirits to the imagination of the people were cut loose, the spirits served the powers to be. The revolt of Hōnen's teachings against him, however, perturbed the configurations of power. For better or for worse, exclusive-*nembutsu* was the imagination of freedom through the choice of dependence on Amida. Religion, which so often enforces the reproduction of order across generations, also includes in its very core a violent element that can explode the frameworks of power. In the case of Pure Land thought, the explosive growth branched off from the theory of *akunin shōki* to become the infamously immoral concept of *zōaku muge,* or the lack of any obstacle to doing evil— "licensed evil."[4] In "Ichinengi chōji kishōmon," Hōnen laments the fact that such a trend was observable amidst his own disciples:

> In search of ephemeral delights, they have ceased to fear the prospect of eternal life on the other side of the river of Sanzu [hell]. When they preach at all, they preach that believers in Amida's Vow need not eschew the five terrible sins, that they should wholeheartedly commit them; that believers should wear the clothes of laypeople instead of donning the *kesa* robe; that believers need not avoid fornication, nor the devouring of meat—that they should eat deer and fowl as much as they wish. (*HSZ*, 804)

The text is believed to have been written in the sixth month of 1209 at Settsu Katsuoji, two years after Hōnen returned from his exile in Shikoku. We can thus surmise that Amida's Vow to accept all without exception was already reinterpreted by many as a kind of indulgence, as a moral free-pass for abandon. The imperial court had to exile Hōnen, in the first place, to make a prohibitory example out of him. Antisocial behavior among his followers must have intensified during his exile. By the first decade of the thirteenth century, the ethic of inversion was running far ahead and irrevocably out of reach of the vigorous but old man.

THE POINT OF *ZAIJARIN*

No one was more enraged by Hōnen's assault on traditional religious values than Myōe Kōben (1173–1232).

Although Hōnen had dictated the *Senchakushū* in 1198 in compliance with Kujō Kanezane's request, copies of the text did not circulate until the year of the death of the author, 1212. In November of that same year, however, only two months after Hōnen's work appeared, Myōe finished writing the third volume of *Zaijarin*. The next year, he added an extra volume, the *Zaijarin shōgonki*. The rapidity of the output revealed Myōe's strong objection to the content of the *Senchakushū* and an equally urgent desire to staunch the bleeding influence the work might have on the general public.

Hōnen and Myōe's doctrinal differences have been indicated, repeatedly, only at the price of neglecting several crucial points the two men had in common. To begin with, their biographical origins were astonishingly similar. Myōe, the son of a local warrior named Yuasa Muneshige, was born in 1173 in Kishū, between Taira-no-Shigekuni of the Arita village. When Myōe was eight, his mother died; the same year, his father would not return from a battle. Myōe's mother had decided before her son was even born that he should enter a monastery. A year after his parents died, the young Myōe, or Yakushimaru, indeed ascended to the Jingoji in Takao. Hōnen too had been the son of a warrior who died violently, and he too had become a monk early in his youth. And just as Hōnen is said to have read ravenously in the *issaikyō* (the complete collection of Buddhist scriptures) in the Hōon Hall during his hermit days in Kurodani until Shantao's *Kuan ching shu* at last nudged him spiritually, so too did Myōe discover a copy of the *Yuikyōgyō* (The Last Teaching Sūtra) in a hall of scriptures, in his nineteenth year, and gained from it the awareness that he was a "lost child of Shākyamuni Buddha."

Both refused to rely on the teachings of their respective masters and instead cultivated religious terrains on and of their own. It is true that Hōnen experienced *zanmai hottoku* while he was under the tutelage of Eikū, but, as we saw earlier, master and disciple were implacable regarding the relative merits of the contemplative and vocal forms of *nembutsu*. Meanwhile, Myōe's master Mongaku was a famous eccentric who also appears in *The Tale of Heike* and the *Genpei seisuiki*. He was exiled to Sado, and then to Tsushima, there to perish. Myōe had removed himself to Kishū to spend most of his days alone and away from his master, even while the latter still lived.

Despite the salient biographical parallels, the ridges on which they stood were unbridgeable. That Hōnen not only refused to distinguish between laypeople and ecclesiastics but, in fact, ridiculed the latter more than once touched on Myōe's nerves. In "Gyakushū seppō," Hōnen writes that *nembutsu ōjō* is superior to all other salvatory routes for six reasons, of which the second reads: "The light of Amida Buddha illuminates practitioners of *nembutsu* and only them. Because of the vow that Amida made when he was still the bodhisattva Hōzō, the light that emanates from his beautifully adorned face illuminates all *nembutsu* practitioners without exception, saving them without fail. He does not save other kinds of practitioners" (Z, 2:48). According to this claim, also made in the *Senchakushū*, Amida's light shines on the amateur vocalists but not on the priests making solemn bids through other practices. Hōnen's view was visualized by his disciples, who drew a *sesshu-fusha mandara* in which Amida's light shines upon a wide variety of people that conspicuously excludes traditional monks. The simple, almost simplistic inversion of religious and social common sense could not have sat well with Myōe, the idealist whose foremost passion in life was to resuscitate the dying precepts and to revive spiritual vigor in Buddhist organizations. But Hōnen goes even further in the *Senchakushū* when he is explicating Shantao's allegory of the two rivers and the white path, where a path flanked by water, fire, and other perils leads from this world to the other. There Amida beckons with his hand, but, "A tenth or a fifth on the way down the path, bandits call to the walker to head back. This is an analogy: those who uphold conflicting understandings and practices preach their wrong views and confuse each other, fomenting evil and returning to sinful ways" (Z, 2:248). According to Hōnen, the bandits are those who preach anything other than *nembutsu*.

Myōe used to respect Hōnen. The latter was well read and virtuous, precept observing and revered by people from all walks of life. When Myōe discovered that Hōnen was comparing the priests of the Holy Path to bandits, his rage knew no bounds. His intense emotion is expressed with eerie concision at the beginning of the *Zaijarin*:

> Recently, a certain high priest has authored a book called *Senchakushū*. It distorts the scriptures and commentaries, has betrayed and misled many people. It purports to focus on the practice of salvation but hinders it. I, Kōben, have respected the holy man profoundly and for many years. The various evil views that reached my ears, I simply dismissed, thinking them to be the inanities of unordained people who appropriated and abused the high priest's fame. Thus I never

criticized the high priest—not once. When others spoke ill of him,
I tried not to believe them. I have just read the *Senchakushū*. I am
immersed in the deepest sorrow and disappointment. (*NST*, 15:44)

The doctrine of exclusive-*nembutsu* was probably newfangled enough
for Kyoto's laypeople to circulate it by word of mouth. At first, it
seems, Myōe relegated the talk to the domain of rumor. How surprised he must have been when he realized that in the *Senchakushū*
Hōnen was indeed expounding an ethic of inversion that did not attribute the least significance to precepts. One did not have to recognize in Indian Buddhism the highest values, as Myōe did, to hear Hōnen's topsy-turvy teachings as the unmistakable voice of evil. Many
serious practitioners of Buddhism must have felt the same way.

In addition, Hōnen and Myōe disagreed about something more
fundamental than religious mores. Their hermeneutic divergence
concerned a central issue of Buddhist thought: the will to enlightenment. In the *Senchakushū*, Hōnen insists that both Shākyamuni and
Amida chose *nembutsu* only, or in other words, rejected all other
paths including the will to enlightenment.[5] Myōe launched a virulent
counterpolemic against Hōnen's system because it failed to advocate
a struggle for enlightenment from our side, mediocre as we are. "You
are like a beast. You are a gravely sinful man. If you jettison the will
to enlightenment, then Shākyamuni's whole life, the precious teaching of the Holy Path, would all have been for naught" (*NST*, 15:86).
For Myōe, the will to enlightenment was the *primum mobile* of life, the
first and last word of the Buddhist way.

Hōnen, who had a formidable imagination, was at the same time
an astute realist: he saw the diminutive stature of human beings in
the torrent of history. In fact, looking around him, the various theaters
of society presented modalities of what could actually have been a
twilight of the law. Nothing lent itself to idealization, and much of
the ecclesiastic world was also growing tired and ashamed of calling
for a return to Shākyamuni's times. For Hōnen, there was little incen-
tive, less hope, and no sense in demarcating good and evil, do's and
don'ts, in some misguided effort to construct ideal religious lives. Although Hōnen concentrated on the meaning of death instead, the differences between him and Myōe were perhaps less temperamental
than generational, even historical. While Hōnen faced a reality that
defied moralization, Myōe was born half a century later and came of

age in the early Kamakura, when the chaos ignited by the disintegration of the statute system was beginning to subside. Although the early years of Hōnen and Myōe were congruent in many ways, their lives took shape in contexts that were quite distinct.

By the time Myōe entered his productive years, the sociopolitical situation had restabilized to the point that he could trumpet the fundamental principles of the religious way of life. The *Toga-no-o Myōe shōnin yuikun* begins with the following two points:

> [1] We ought to hold fast to this seven-syllable phrase: "That which is appropriate" (*arubeki yō wa*). There is that which is appropriate for the monk and that which is appropriate for the layman, that which is appropriate for the emperor and that which is appropriate for his subjects. Every evil arises from disregarding what is appropriate for each of us.
> [2] I am not one who looks forward to being saved in the afterlife, I simply want to do what is appropriate for me in this life.[6]

As condensed in his maxim *arubeki yō wa,* Myōe's ethical standpoint was the maintenance of lives as they actually ought to be. Nothing was clearer to Myōe than that the Buddhist way is keeping commandments in mind, arranging life virtuously, and receiving Buddha's wisdom. It was also clear to him that Hōnen's stubborn emphasis on the other world was nothing but evil. In the background of Myōe's idealism lay an exigent, incessant admiration for the life of Shākyamuni Buddha, who achieved the most perfect state as a human being. Myōe dreamed of treading the earth on which the Buddha had lived as such a perfect human being, and he thrice planned to travel to India. For this enthusiast, the Buddhist way meant approaching the Buddha as best one could—*imitatio buddhi,* so to speak. No compromise was allowed on spurious grounds such as that precepts could not be sustained in the latter days of the law. Laypeople ought to revere and support monks, who engaged in scholarship and meditation with a will to enlightenment.

Hōnen has left us a passage that argues the exact opposite of Myōe's "that which is appropriate":

> You should live in this world in such a way that chanting may come to you easily. You ought to abandon anything that might hinder your practice of chanting. If you can't as a bachelor, then marry. If you can't in transit, then stay at home. If you can't while earning your own liv-

ing, then rely on others. If you can't while relying on others, then earn
your own living. If you can't without company, then chant in company. If you can't in company, then chant in seclusion. (*HSZ*, 462)

If the will to enlightenment was unnecessary, as it was for Hōnen,
then why not simply leave life to nature? Hōnen thought the only
path to salvation was turning, returning to absolute death in the form
of Buddha's mercy as expressed in his name, while Myōe found the
way out of eternal transmigration in the imitation, in everyday life,
of the Buddha's character. For Hōnen, the infinite transcendence lay
in temporally finite reach, namely in death. For Myōe, the finite figure
of transcendence, Buddha as man, lay infinitely far away, albeit in the
perspective of life and will; the impossible project of becoming identical would necessarily fail, but it was more a question of degree. The
practice of the one is, in itself, a contact with salvation, while that of
the other is a line that negates such contact but also includes a point
that will be translated into the same. Imitation is analog and *nembutsu*
is digital, so to speak.

But finally, we must reiterate that the doctrinal opposition between
Hōnen and Myōe existed on a plane that they shared: both ascribed
immense value to the interior world of the imagination and used it as
a means to open up fresh spaces of religious truth. Specifically, we
mean Hōnen's *zanmai hottoku* through *nembutsu* and Myōe's analyses
of his own dreams: we have discussed the former's *jōzenkan;* as for the
latter, he practiced his active imagination in the form of sequential
dreams that unfolded over many consecutive nights. Conversely, Hōnen took his dream of *niso taimen* (encounter with Shantao) quite seriously, while Myōe practiced something called *kōmyō shingon* that was
quite similar to vocal-*nembutsu*. The latter also experienced a *bukkō
zanmai* in which he saw a shining white disk. Although their teachings appear irreconcilably different, this must not make us neglect
the common grounds on which they disagreed. Both of them stringently observed precepts and ceaselessly meditated: they valued the
corporality of practice as well as the fertility of the imagination.

THE PHENOMENOLOGY OF *JIRIKI* AND *TARIKI*

In Derridean deconstruction, the painstaking displacement of bi-
narisms and logocentric assumptions also occurs at the very scene

of deconstruction. Insofar as deconstruction takes place in the world, time, and language, the menacing possibility is always present. Yet Derrida has constantly evaded the danger. As practiced by him, the rigor of deconstruction is moving—not only in the affectative sense—for it always questions the ground on which it stands and moves perpetually.

But what if Jacques Derrida is an adventurer on an Antarctic expedition? Always pointing to the south of "here," sliding sidereally, he has reached the South Pole—and why not, since you can't go farther south from there? He has stood the flag of thought at the limit. That such tireless, uncompromising vigilance was humanly possible! Derrida's books are reels from this expedition: we are proud, we applaud, we are mesmerized by the beauty of the landscape. But the question arises: *Do you want to live there?*

Some of us doubtless do. All of us who traffic in thought know that the first step we take commits us to the austral journey. And if we do not reach the pole—if we sojourn a bit too long in some warm land we find along the way—then it is only because we have fallen short, because we lack the requisite will and light, as well as that enduring spot of interior darkness. Then comes the man of religion. He tells us, "Do not take the first step! If you have, then stop now. For it is an endless path that leads to ice. Believe, instead, in the faraway west."

The doctrinal differences between enlightenment and paradise, between *jiriki* (through one's own efforts) and *tariki* (dependence on faith) have been belabored over several centuries. Through transcendental phenomenology, however, we would like to question the terms of this reigning distinction. To grasp consciousness as an intentional function, Edmund Husserl sets up the two interrelated categories of *noesis* (cognition, understanding, judgment, imagination, and other functions of consciousness) and *noema* (objects of consciousness). All existences in the world have "meanings" that are given by the intentionality of *noesis* and *noema*, both of which belong to consciousness. The transcendental ego at the functional center of intention is therefore positioned in a subjective world full of "meanings" that the ego itself has assigned. Because the world that the transcendental ego experiences is also there for others, there begins the multilateral construction of a common subjectivity that we habitually refer to as the "objective world." Phenomenology is not about bracketing out this objectivity forever; it involves finally removing the brackets and returning to the bracketed thing, with a better understanding why it appears evident.

In phenomenological terms, Hōnen and Myōe's *noeses* intended different *noemata* and resulted in two contradictory subjective worlds. Whereas Hōnen's imagination turned toward Amida in paradise and gave death the meaning of infinite happiness and light, Myōe's imagination turned toward the body of Shākyamuni Buddha and gave life the purpose of representing Buddha's land. In this sense, the *Zaijarin* was not a work "by" Myōe but, rather, the impact of a head-on collision between two similar *noeses* that intended divergent *noemata*. In a sense, it is meaningless to delve in the distinction between *jiriki* and *tariki*. The worldviews will vary depending on whether it is the Buddha within or Amida in a radically other realm that is intended. But most important, both enlightenment and paradise are products of a rarely intense interaction between *noesis* and *noema*. It is this *intensity* that matters. A third instance will indicate that whichever path may be chosen, the "transcendental ego" ultimately alights upon the same spot. We are referring to Dōgen's famous statement in the *Shōbōgenzō*: "To learn the Buddha Way is to learn one's own self. To learn one's self is to forget one's self. To forget one's self is to be confirmed by all dharmas. To be confirmed by all dharmas is to cast off one's own body and mind and the bodies and minds of others as well."[7] *Shinjin datsuraku* (body and mind falling away) refers to the removal of the barrier between the self and the world of objects, the inside and the outside, in the course of the Zen practice of sitting.

It is true that Hōnen himself drew a thick double line between "the Amida in one's heart" encountered in *jiriki* meditation and the Amida of Pure Land thought who reigns in a paradisal west, metes out his bottomless mercy, and saves all. Unable to believe anything other than what he constructed subjectively from Shantao's experiences (Hōnen's Shantao *henne*, or obsession), his imagination intended Amida in the faraway west. He gave an absolute meaning to what he took to be an external object, as is clear in the following exchange from the *Ippyaku shijūgokajō mondō*:

Q: Is the Shingon worship of Amida a correct practice?
A: The figures [of the Shingon and Pure Land versions of Amida] are similar, but they differ in content [*kokoro*]. The Amida of the Shingon sect is the Amida in one's heart and nowhere else. The

Amida of our teaching is the buddha whom Hōzō became.
Because he is in the faraway west, he is of immense capacity
[*kokoro*]. (*HSZ*, 668)

"The Shingon worship" refers to the esotericists' adoption of Amida as an idol of worship that disturbs the distinction between *jiriki* and *tariki*. Pure Land thought influenced late Heian Tantric Buddhism significantly.[8]

Although Hōnen formulated an absolute binarism between the Buddha and human beings, the distance between the two was often warped: "When people worship the Buddha, the Buddha sees this. When people chant the name of the Buddha, the Buddha hears this. When people think of the Buddha, the Buddha thinks of the people. Thus the three deeds of Amida Buddha and the three deeds of practitioners become one, and Buddha and people become as parent and child" (*HSZ*, 559).

One might be tempted to ask if this was not the *nyoraizō* (*tathāgata-garbha*) theory that Tendai Buddhism underscored. Although Hōnen is actually talking about an Amida who responds to a good-for-nothing's *nembutsu*—not a word is said about an interior "buddhisticity" to be developed through practice—it is nevertheless inappropriate for a practitioner of *nembutsu* to say that the Buddha and the ordinary man can become one. Hōnen extended Shantao's concept of *shin'en* (affinity) to a point where life and death, this world and the other, the ordinary man and the Buddha, could be united in *nembutsu*.

In the following sentence, then, it becomes unclear who is the *jiriki* practitioner and who the *tariki*, although the tenor of the reference to *nembutsu* removes all possible doubts about who the author might be: "Those who are remote from *nembutsu* lose countless treasures. Those who engage in it attain limitless *satori*" (*HSZ*, 638). Although intentional expressions such as "attaining *satori*" are usually foreign to the theorists and practitioners of *nembutsu*, such a phrase is not at all surprising coming from a man who intuited his truths through an imagined world supported by incessant chanting. Was Hōnen wandering in our temporal world, or was he roaming in a pure and paradisal land? If we find this dispute difficult to settle, it was not the problem of Hōnenbō Genkū: he picked up innumerable treasures in this world as his body became one with that of the Buddha.

6

The Degeneration of Death

Now at the beginning of the end, we shall survey, retrospectively and from the point of view of death, the basic character of the religious tradition that preceded the rupture called exclusive-*nembutsu*.

Unlike, for example, Christianity's grassroots crawl through the Roman Empire, Buddhism was introduced into Japan in the interests and under the auspices of the islands' rulers. Scriptural exegeses had a marked tendency to favor the ruling class politically and socially, and Buddhism took on a secular, temporal, this-worldly character from its very first years. The main output of Prince Shōtoku (574–622)—who in the Asuka period became, at least according to legend, the first serious Japanese student of Buddhism—was called *The Seventeen-Article Constitution*, essentially an administrative manual for imperial bureaucrats. Shōtoku is the signatory of numerous other works such as the *Sankyō gisho*, but in the final analysis he studied Buddhist thought as a guideline for duties that a person had to fulfill in order to live justly as a social being.

In *Ways of Thinking of Eastern Peoples*, Nakamura Hajime observes:

> Like a torrent of water rushing forth from a broken dam, Buddhism spread all over Japan within a very short time. However, it was impossible for Buddhism to transform the this-worldly inclination of the Japanese general public completely. On the contrary, it was the Japanese who, having imported continental Buddhism, transformed it into a religion centered upon this world. With the advent and spread of Buddhism, the Japanese came to think seriously of life after death. But even then Buddhism was accepted as something thisworldly.[1]

This secular tendency intensified when the Nara regime officially sanctioned Buddhism, which soon became a public organ for the spiritual defense of the state. As the temple establishment grew into a leviathan shoulder-to-shoulder with the imperial bureaucracy, the monks churned out scholarly products in competitive bids for seats at the head. Because humble phrases like "In the Memory of Seven Generations of Fathers and Mothers" (*shichisei fubo no tameni*) were inscribed in statues of the Buddha, it has been pointed out that ancestral worship was very popular in the Nara period. The people's eyes, however, were focused on their own world. The memorial services were meant to dissuade the dead from bringing misfortune to the living, to persuade them to be guarantors of peaceful lives; it was not that death itself was positively valued.

In the Heian period, Kūkai founded the esoteric Shingon sect with a steadfast exclusion of any philosophy of death. He instead applied himself persistently to the completion of a philosophy of life, condensed finally in his theory of *sokushin jōbutsu*, or living Buddhahood: Tantric practices like manual signs, chants of dhāraṇī, and concentration on *maṇḍalas* could unite Mahāvairocana (Dainichi) Buddha, the body of the law, and human flesh. Saichō, the other towering figure of Heian Buddhism, preached that it was possible for anyone to achieve *satori* in life and to become a "national treasure" for secular society—given the appropriate practices and studies. It was on Saichō's "universalist" (*ichijō*) stance, based on the Lotus Sūtra, that the Tendai sect was founded. It gradually welded itself to state authority and turned into a formidable political force.

But a cultural trend against state orientation intensified after the final years of the ninth century, when Japan stopped sending governmental delegations to China. Buddhists correspondingly awakened to a mode of worship that prioritized individual salvation over the defense of the nation. But the very *hijiri* (itinerant monks) of the middle Heian who fortified this trend were eventually sucked into and organized by the powerful temples; thereafter, the wandering *hijiri* did not forget to remind people of the connection between almsgiving and salvation. Afterlife became a pecuniary issue, a kind of life insurance to be collected by the dead themselves. The *hijiri* recommended *nembutsu*, but as a rule, only to the "inferior."

In short, ancient Japanese Buddhism was first and foremost a "religion of life" backed by a secular cultural bias. The question of this Buddhism was, "What can a person living in this world do in this world to escape the quagmire of passion and obtain repose in this world?" Vulgar primitivists would idealize this affirmation of life as a paradisal "pre-." If the solace of life after death was preached at all, it was as the by-product of a religiously correct life. For that reason, when the mechanism of death crouched forth on its three limbs of the bedeviling, the below, and the belated, it found a people unaccustomed to negative images of death, a people who scuttled about with no terrain whereby to take a collective stand.

THE TURNING POINT AND HŌNEN'S STANCE

A cruel sun mercilessly scorched an innumerable multitude, many of them barely alive and all of them strictly divided into castes, in the land where Buddhism was born. It is perhaps not surprising then that Indian Buddhism found the highest significance in a logic of negation, in extinguishing the flames of time; it is not surprising either that in the relatively Mediterranean climate, the nurturing nature of Japan, there could be no worldview that viewed this world as trivial, no worldview that was truly the view of another world.

But if there *have* been epochs in Japan that we might provisionally term "life negating," then one of them would be the years of the Heian and Kamakura during which Hōnen lived. Oppressed by a caste system, beset by serial disasters, exploited materially and spiritually by a gargantuan religious authority, the majority of Japanese faced a reality that exterminated the returning buds of secular optimism. As Ienaga Saburō maintains, it was not until the Kamakura period that the logic of negation, which had been so prevalent in Buddhism since its beginnings in India, finally grew to be appreciated in Japan for better or for worse.

> Kamakura Buddhism had no starting point other than the direct, unflinching confrontation of life's negative dimension. The founders of the new faiths grasped life in its gravely negative aspects and the essential figure of humanity in its sins. By theorizing this discovery through teachings, by heightening it also into experiential forms of worship, through their personal lives as well as through the experiences of their times, the founders erected astounding bodies of thought.[2]

But even for Ienaga, the protagonist of Kamakura Buddhism and its project of enabling absolute affirmation through absolute negation is Shinran and not Hōnen.

Our thesis has been otherwise: the first one to engage a logic of negation that indeed perfectly matched a negative reality whose emblem was death; the first one to wrestle with this logic, to transmute it into a logic of affirmation by emphasizing the active function of *nembutsu* the first was Hōnenbō Genkū. He was a major turning point in Japan's religious history, not only as the fulcrum by means of which a religion of death, rooted in the other world, took ascendance over a religion of life rooted in this one. Hōnen also contributed to the transition from "religion for the state" to "religion for the person." In these two interrelated, inversely symmetrical movements away from the objective realm, then, Hōnen is the point at which a One (Amida) includes the all but also at which a different One, the state, is excluded by the particular.

Unlike monotheism, where a transcendent God reigns as a single absolute, and where consequently there is no room for selection—the No of Jonah or the Why of Job notwithstanding—exclusive-*nembutsu* recognizes the existence of multiple deities. However, it also crucially calls for a choice: specifically, of the Amida Buddha, as a path suitable for the helpless people living in the latter days of the law. The choice of *nembutsu:* as we have seen, this exclusive option is also a response, a responsibility, to the True Vow as an event. Ironically, many of those who criticized exclusive-*nembutsu* were deeply influenced by Hōnen and followed his method of choosing a single practice out of thousands and making it accessible. For example, shortly after he wrote the *Zaijarin,* Myōe invented a new practice that he called *sanji sanbō-rai:* three times a day, one must worship a *honzon*, a verbal triptych where words for buddhahood flank a word representing a *buppōsō* (the Buddha, Dharma, Priesthood). This method, which Myōe recommended to many, was clearly the simplified form of a Tantric Buddhist counterpart.

Dōgen, another Kamakura Buddhist who disdained the practice of *nembutsu,* expressed his low regard in the *Shōbōgenzō:* "To think that merely moving your tongue or raising your voice has the merit of buddha-work is a truly futile notion. . . . To read the words without an awareness of the way of practice is just like reading a medical prescription while neglecting to concoct the compound—altogether worthless. Lifting your voice in endless recitation resembles the croaking, from morning to nightfall, of frogs in the spring fields."[3]

Dōgen was thirty-two when he wrote this; in other words, he was already the Dōgen who had the unction to deny all practices other than sitting. By his forty-fifth year, however, his attitude changed, and he counted the reading of sūtras and the chanting of *nembutsu* among the possible methods for attaining buddhahood ("Hotsu mujōshin"). Yet Hōnen's most important influence on Dōgen was not this shift in opinion but, rather, the Zen master's choice of sitting as the highest practice of Buddhism, as well as his understanding that sitting is, finally, not so much a means to *satori* but a manifestation of the Buddhist law itself. He thus repeats, in form, the content of Hōnen's thought. There is no proof that Dōgen was influenced by what we might call Hōnen's "optionism," but one fact allows us to advance the hypothesis that Dōgen was at least intensely aware of it: he opened Eiheiji, the Zen monastery, precisely on the Japan Sea coast where *nembutsu* worship was extremely popular, very possibly out of a desire to lure the misguided chanters back, via sitting, to the real Buddhist way.

Another critic of Hōnen was Nichiren, who showers the founder of exclusive-*nembutsu* with sarcasm. The passage from the *Shugo kokka-ron* is only one of many:

> Some time ago, a misguided high priest wrote a volume called
> *Senchakushū*, which distorted all the teachings of Buddhism for the
> sake of latter-day fools. Relying on the authority of the three masters
> T'anluan, Taoch'o, and Shantao, he divided Shākyamuni's teachings
> into the Holy Path and the Pure Land Path, called true scriptures
> false, ignored the just paths of Tendai and Shingon, and preached
> instead a narrow, crooked way based entirely on the three Pure Land
> scriptures. Not even to the content of these was he loyal. With his
> erroneous views, the slanderer of truth blocked off the way to wis-
> dom and brought the hell of shrieks much closer to us. (*NSI*, 2:89)

Although he points his ever-accusatory finger at Hōnen and his followers, Nichiren might not have come to assert his own theory of *shō-dai jōbutsu* (attaining Buddhahood through the recitation of *daimoku*) without the precedence of exclusive-*nembutsu*. It was thus not only his finger that pointed toward "optionism." Although Nichiren paid exclusive attention to the temporal world for most of his life, he took to the Pure Land and other postdeath issues in his final years.

We have already insisted that Hōnen's most significant exploit was not popularization. His foregrounding of absolute equality before death, nonetheless, opened the gates of salvation to the masses, and contributed greatly to the popularization of Buddhism. Those who followed Hōnen by founding sects indeed formulated, and stood for, teachings that differed from exclusive-*nembutsu*, but it was through the medium of "optionism" that they could popularize religious experience. The new Buddhist leaders may inscribe their names in history without Hōnen's prior cultivation of a new terrain of religious experience—that is to say, the exclusive choice of one practice for the purpose of overcoming the opposition between life and death and other oppositions. Hōnen exerted an immense impact on medieval Japanese Buddhism not by being received but by being firmly rejected—a familiar mode, after all, of historical irony.

THE MAN OF IMAGINATION
AND THE MAN OF LOGIC

Hōnen and Shinran: their relationship has often been assumed to be that of the master who transmitted vocal-*nembutsu* and the disciple who inherited it. This view would accord well with Shinran's profession of faith in *Tan'nishō*: "I have no idea whether *nembutsu* will lead me to paradise or consign me to hell. But even if saint Hōnen is fooling me, even if I fall to hell, I shall never regret my decision."[4] Because Shinran has become so famous, there is a dominant impression that this disciple who admired his master so deeply must have also been a special intimate, but Hōnen's "fellow traveler" of half a century was a different disciple, Shinkū. In the *Shiju in'nen-shū*, written forty-five years after the master's death, his five most important disciples are said to have been Kōsai, Seikō, Ryūkan, Shōkū, and Chōsai.

The general misunderstanding about the Hōnen-Shinran relationship is given a paradigmatic articulation in the *Hōnen to Shinran no shinkō* by Kurata Hyakuzō, a literary disciple of Nishida and no fool.

> But if Shinran had not appeared after Hōnen to radicalize thoroughly the essence of the faith, it would have developed along Hōnen's lukewarm [*futettei*] ways, in a direction that would have emphasized *jiriki*, diligence, the observation of precepts, and miracles. The essence of the faith would have been clouded over, its popular appeal would have been lost, and it would have regressed back to elitism and idealism. . . . Shinran was respectful toward his master, but on the point of faith he rejected Hōnen's inconclusiveness and developed the religion in the way it clearly should have developed. It was in this fullest sense that Shinran succeeded Hōnen. It was with Shinran that Pure Land faith and practice were consummated.[5]

Characterizing Hōnen's faith as "lukewarm" simply because it contains elements like *jiriki* and so forth is the sign of a lukewarm examination of Hōnen's faith. Kurata, however, is not alone in comparing Hōnen with Shinran according to an oversweet dialectic of fruition and completion. For us, the dialectic has been a more sour one of negation and excess that little green buds of resistance assume here and there. Instead of succumbing to a developmental schema where Hōnen is not only chronologically, but logically, a mere "stage" on the way to Shinran, we would like to probe three of their central theoretical differences.

The first is the content of the despair that motivated them religiously, that is to say, along religious paths and with a "religious" fervor. We have already pointed out that the content of Hōnen's despair was death on the social and individual planes. In the case of Shinran, it was *mumyō* or the nonlight—the source of all sin and evil that reigned in what we might call the recesses of his "Dostoyevskian" soul: "It is truly sorrowful that, as an ignorant monk, I am drowning in the ocean of lust and wandering in the mountain of greed. I have not struggled to join the company of the enlightened. Nor have I approached the true domain of wisdom. Let me begin with this sense of shame" (*SZ*, 1:200). Shinran had a rare ability and compulsion to engage the demonic nature grovelling at the bottom of his existence—to unearth the monster, to bring it to his consciousness. Of course, Hōnen too was a master of almost self-punishing introspection, and that is why he insisted on the importance of being earnestly stupid; however, when he took notice of the demon within, as it were, he abandoned his ego entirely, imagined the Pure landscape instead, and strove to give images a kind of virtual reality until, at last, a body of thought began to take shape. It was indeed a body, a surface: the phrase *namu Amida butsu* chanted with ritual vitality until it becomes a chain of signifiers—not so much without a referent, for Amida was out there—but without the signified, the static image of conviction. In Shinran's case, on the contrary, he persisted in his razor-sharp introspection. The blade was not meant to shave along the surface but to cut. *His* unflinching gaze was directed not at death but at his own sinful existence, which encapsulated a nonlight that made him, in his own words, *jigoku hitsujō* or doomed to hell.

It was here that Shinran's energy was spent, in repeated movements of thought that groped for a way to switch that nonlight within into limitless light ("Amida"). His *Gutoku hitan jikkai* begins with a hymn:

> Convert I have to Pure Land faith
> without an ounce of honesty
> I love to lie and love the false
> I haven't the least sincerity
>
> Whenever there are others about
> I try to look like I'm trying
> But I'm a greedy hypocrite
> Quick to lose my temper
>
> There's not much I can do
> My heart's a snake a scorpion
> The little good I sometimes do
> Turns venomous in me. (*SZ*, 4:566)

Unlike Hōnen, who exuded a charisma that was not only not effaced but, in fact, produced to a large extent by the multiple contradictions that he learned to endure seemingly without anguish, the "underground man" of Kamakura Japan had something violent in him—perhaps an oversized superego—that refused to accept the tiniest morsel of falsity in himself, probably including the violent something as well. Such differences were no doubt partly due to temperament, but difference in historical background also contributed to the divergence between their varieties of despair.

Sueki Fumihiko divides the Kamakura era (1192–1333) into three periods.[6] Period one stretches from the final years of the twelfth century, when the Shogunate was founded, to the Jōkyū Rebellion (1221). As the consolidation of warrior rule proceeded, Chōgen, Eisai, Jōkei, Shunjō, Jien, and of course Hōnen, laid the foundations of Kamakura Buddhism. The second period coincides with the epoch of peaceful regency, when, in relative social stability, Myōe, Ryōben, Dōgen, and Shinran could deepen their religious systems. The third period began sometime in the middle of the thirteenth century. While warrior rule destabilized, the Mongol invasion heightened national consciousness, and the Buddhist arena welcomed Eison, Ninshō, Gyōnen, Ippen, and Nichiren. Whereas Hōnen had seen a reality buried to its neck in death, Shinran lived in an epoch that was stable enough for him to conduct a ruthless investigation into subjectivity. The guilt experienced in everyday life by practically all of his contemporaries (if not ours too) became the turning point for his spiritual "resurrection." The resurrection was accompanied by a theory of salvation based on absolute dependence. A sequel to the critical religion known as exclusive-*nembutsu*, Shinran's theory was the necessary apparition of a religion of human dignity.

The second major doctrinal difference between Hōnen and Shinran concerned salvation. Hōnen's faith manifestly equated physical death with ultimate salvation, but for Shinran it was not death but faith that had to be absolutized. Thus he denied the final welcome, or *rinjū raigō*: "Salvation at the moment of death applies only to those who pursue practices other than *nembutsu*—that is, to those who have not established true faith" (*SZ*, 4:319). If Shinran is asserting that only the lack of true faith makes one think that salvation is deferred to the moment of death—as he indeed seems to in the above opening passage of *Mattōshō*—then, strictly speaking, it is a kind of blasphemy against his master Hōnen, who never budged in his affirmative stance on *rinjū raigō*. Perhaps the two thinkers shared very little apart from their common faith in the True Vow, and we have placed them too closely side by side for too long. For Shinran, salvation meant the death of a self that depended on *jiriki* and the birth of a self that depended on the True Vow; it had absolutely nothing to do with physical death. In the *Kyōgyōshinshō, Wasan* (hymns), and *Shōsoku* (correspondence), he reiterates that a single chant, if made in absolutely dependent faith, suffices to bring about the ten grand benefits in this life and to place the chanter in a position on a par with Miroku (Maitreya). Hōnen struggled to separate the real images of death from its illusionary imagination and actualized absolutely egalitarian salvation by attributing a transcendental status to physical death. Shinran instead worked through the nonlight of the self and located salvation in the moment faith is attained, through self-negation without reserve.

Because Shinran had wiped out all factors remotely resembling *jiriki* from *nembutsu* worship, he came to hold that faith itself was no human achievement but rather a unilateral gift from Amida Buddha. "For the eternally drowned common and ignorant men and the transmigrating multitudes, the Highest, Excellent Fruition is not difficult to attain. But the True Serene Faith is very difficult to gain. Why is it so? Because it is attained through the endowment of the Tathāgata's Power and through the Power of Universal Wisdom of the Great Compassionate One."[7]

The *Kyōgyōshinshō* was supposed to be a reasoned defense (against Jōkei and Myōe's criticism) of the Pure Land belief that Shinran's master had preached. But it appears that, despite his preliminary intentions, as Shinran wrote, his thoughts—perhaps his words, language itself—dug a different terrain; there welled up a doctrinal system of *nembutsu* worship that was fresh. Shinran realized that, taken to its logical conclusion, dependence on the True Vow implied the exteriority of *kyō, gyō, shin,* and *shō* (teaching, practice, faith, and evidence); none of the four were ruptures in the human world but events from the outside, from Buddha's side. Hōnen's exclusive-*nembutsu* still maintained intentional elements, and belief in Amida's True Vow was a choice, as was the option of vocal-*nembutsu*. His disciple, however, rejected this optional mode—to an extent that not even the master's critics did—while still agreeing on the importance of the optative mood regarding the True Vow.

The third and final major difference between the two *nembutsu* worshipers was their interpretation of *nembutsu* itself. Enlightenment thought (not Voltaire, of course, but *satori*) had a sizable effect on Shinran, and he advocated a faith-centered *ichinengi* (the doctrine that a single chant is sufficient for salvation). This position, also held by other disciples of Hōnen (Gyōkū, Kōsai), brought *tariki* worship to an extreme: not only is salvation guaranteed by a single chant, but *we cannot prevent salvation*—that is to say, no deed on our part can cancel Amida's acceptance of all without exception. This belief differs significantly from *tanengi*, the position that one must chant as many times as possible, advanced by Hōnen in "What He Said about *Ichinengi*": "Amida Buddha's Vow was made for the salvation of the worst sinners and the least learned; therefore, the point is to practice uninterruptedly, sincerely, and as long as one lives. It is not right to obstruct multiple chanting by advocating the nonpractice of a single chant" (*HSZ*, 807). Hōnen insisted that one should chant thousands of times every day until the moment of death, in heartfelt response to Amida's True Vow. In addition, based on Shantao's teaching, he offered four fundamental rules of chanting, to be obeyed as carefully as possible: *chōjishū* (for long intervals), *kugyōshū* (reverently), *mukenshū* (uninterruptedly), *muyoshū* (to the exclusion of other practices) (*Z*, 2:253–54).

Hōnen took *nembutsu* worship without corporality to be insufficient probably because applying his mind and body to chanting endowed him with a fertile imagination. "If you chant *nembutsu* carelessly just because one chant, or ten chants, guaranteed your salvation, then your belief is hindering your practice. But if you chant incessantly because you think one chant, or ten chants, might not be enough, then your practice is hindering your belief. Hence, you must believe that one chant is enough but practice all your life" (*HSZ*, 464). What Hōnen is advancing is not a "happy medium" of belief and practice but their *lived contradiction*. The recommendation befits a man who built his religious worldview on both theory (belief) and practice. Instead of deemphasizing either dimension, Hōnen calls positively for a split between the two. Hōnen's answer to the impossible question of the relationship between "theory and practice"—namely, his injunction to choose neither theory nor practice, to choose instead the "and" in between that borders on the "but"—should be named "wisdom" as opposed to "intelligence." Meanwhile, the basis of Shinran's worship was acute, philosophical introspection. For the pellucid thinker who chopped up his own self-contradictions with the blade of logic, it was exigent to understand *nembutsu* not in its practical function but as a symbolic moment of the establishment of faith. To put it differently, for Hōnen, *nembutsu* is the place where human intention and divine mercy, coming from different directions, meet. For Shinran, for whom faith too is Amida's gift, there is no point of entry or of intervention, no point in intention, on the human side, for *nembutsu* as absolute dependence is Amida's unilateral call.

VISIBLE AND INVISIBLE AMIDA

We have differentiated the two religious leaders on the three planes of religious motivation, views on salvation, and views on chanting. It is on these planes that we must indicate any line of continuity. In short, Shinran's greatest contribution was the logical systematization of Hōnen's experiences—not an overcoming but a translation or a reconfiguration into a different mode of persuasion. In hindsight, Hōnen's historical destiny was to challenge the extant religious tradition by clearing, with his rare imaginative faculty, a personal field of religious experience. He was not a man of logic, as we can infer from Myōe's comment in the *Zaijarin*: "The master is indeed profoundly wise, but he is not a good writer. He has not written anything on his own" (*NST*, 15:45). Although Hōnen did expound his beliefs orally to scholar-monks of the older Buddhist order (the Ōhara Debate, the Tōdaiji Lecture), he did not produce a substantial corpus. It was twenty-three years after Hōnen descended from Mount Hiei that the *Senchakushū* was finally written—and this not by Hōnen but by his disciples, who recorded the master's words. The text itself is a kind of long essay, a collection of Hōnen's religious convictions spewed out with some reason but no rhyme; it is not a treatise, nor probably was it intended to be. But its style did not hinder exclusive-*nembutsu* from taking on a revolutionary nature, both socially and theoretically. If "concept" implies a certain noncontradictory unity, a certain identity across time, then there is hardly a single concept that Hōnen articulated anew. He was a man of imagination and not of logic. Most of his words were ambiguous and conflicting because they faithfully expressed a subjective world where repetitions alter. In this sense, it was not Shinran who stood close to Hōnen but his uncompromising critic, Myōe.

Shinran was an uncompromising reasoner. His purpose was to give systematic form, logical definition, and universal applicability to the exclusive-*nembutsu* that Hōnen had constructed regarding the Pure Land. This reconfiguration, which had a particularity and a body heat that could almost be felt, also had to be applied to Hōnen's Amida. Hōnen's Amida was Eros—Eros as the desire for meaning, beyond Thanatos. But Shinran had to disfigure, or more precisely refigure, the colorful Amida Buddha that Hōnen had witnessed. According to Shinran, "Amida's vow was to turn us into supreme buddhas. Supreme buddhas have no form, and that is why they are natural. The indication of form would not be consonant with supreme nirvāṇa. I have heard that Amida Buddha appeared precisely to teach us this absence of form" (*SZ*, 4:331). Hōnen's image of the embodied Amida was not expected to be the signified of the chant *namu Amida butsu*. In Hōnen's *nembutsu*, what mattered was the repetition of the signifier, and the signified image could alter from person to person. On the contrary, the Amida that won Shinran's conviction hid his figure and could therefore enter into the *kokoro* (mind/heart) as such.

The signified of *ichinengi* had to be *shin*, the conviction sent by Amida himself. In one, singular chant, the phrase *namu Amida butsu* had to signify a moment of absolute dependence. Through the concept of *nishu ekō*, or the double movement of *ōsō* and *gensō*, Shinran abstracted and formalized Hōnen's personal myth. *Ōsō:* it is not through one's good deeds that salvation is attained but through an attitude of dependence, sent from the Amida himself. *Gensō:* the saved ones are sent back to this world as bodhisattvas, again by Amida, to assist the living. The latter leads to the idea of *jinen hōni:* "The word *jinen* [nature/natural] is made up of two characters. The first, *ji*, means 'on its own.' In other words, the intention of practitioners does not matter. The second, *nen*, means 'becoming thus.' Again, it is not the doing of the practitioner. And *hōni* means that salvation happens only because it is Amida's Vow" (*SZ*, 4:332). The absolute will of Amida is expressed, much in a Spinozist manner, in the "natural" behavior of people.

The equation of life-and-death with enlightenment, of passions with buddhahood, expressed in effortless, ordinary behavior, resembles the mechanism of *nembutsu* in Hōnen. But Shinran shifted the emphasis of religious awareness away from the world of the individual. According to him, the self that chants in absolute dependence works positively and to the benefit of other selves. You are not alone in facing death, and your salvation is not a selfish matter. Shinran thereby planted the seed that would make his Shin sect the largest *nembutsu* organization in Japan.

LUTHER, CALVIN, AND RESISTANCE

Hara Katsurō's *Tōzai no shūkyō kaikaku* (Religious Reformation East and West [1991]) has revitalized a justifiably persistent comparative urge. But the resurgent analysis of similitudes is still centered on an all-too-familiar frame of reference. In short, Shinran-and-Luther was precisely the matrix for classic scholars of religion such as Karl Barth, F. Heiler, and, of course, Max Weber. It is beyond doubt that Shinran and Luther (1483–1546) have points in common. But if we are interested in the process whereby radical doubt toward a religious tradition initiates a large new stream of thought, then is not the more appropriate pair Luther and Hōnen? Why have Western scholars tended to compare the inaugurator of the Protestant break with Shinran? Is it because the comparison is meant to draw out doctrinal similarity rather than historical positionality? Or is it simply because Hōnen has been unfamiliar territory except for specialists of Japanese Buddhism? If we desire a counterpart to Shinran in the history of Christianity, we should in fact turn to Calvin (1509–63). But Martin Luther first.

He was born to a miner in a small German town. As a university student, he nearly lost his life when he was struck by a lightning bolt. This almost too symbolic event triggered an abrupt decision on Martin's part to become an Augustinian monk, against his parents' objection. When he took up an opportunity to visit Rome, he witnessed the decadent state of the Vatican and was overcome with despair. Martin's disappointment with Catholicism reminds us of the young Hōnen, who, disillusioned by the degeneration of Mount Hiei, fled to Kurodani and the solitude it promised. But what most troubled the Augustinian monk was not institutional corruption but the figure of the fearsome God who punished sinful human beings. We hear his agonized voice in a treatise against Erasmus: "It gives the greatest possible offense to common sense or natural reason that God by his own sheer will should abandon, harden, and damn men as if he enjoyed the sins and the vast, eternal torments, of his wretched creatures. . . . And who would not be offended? I myself was offended more than once, and brought to the very depth and abyss of despair, so that I wished I had never been created a man."[8] The feeling of alienation from God was probably a result of his Occamite training: forgiveness is not delivered automatically by God; his salvation is won only through adherence to an ascetic, virtuous lifestyle. Such an uninviting invitation to do good was precisely what had generated anxiety in Japanese Buddhists before Hōnen.

Just as Hōnen encountered Shantao's text while gobbling up the *issaikyō* in a hall of scrolls, Luther was reading the Bible in a tower of his Augustinian monastery when he came across the famous passage in the Epistle to the Romans—chapter 1, verse 17—that radically altered his faith. This legendary moment of conversion, the well-known "tower experience," can be found in the introduction to his Latin works:

> At last, by the mercy of God, meditating day and night, I gave heed to the context of the words, namely, "In it the righteousness of God is revealed, as it is written, 'He who through faith is righteous shall live.'" There I began to understand that the righteousness of God is that by which the righteous lives by a gift of God, namely by faith. And this is the meaning: the righteousness of God is revealed by the gospel, namely, the passive righteousness with which merciful God justifies us by faith, as it is written, "He who through faith is righteous shall live." Here I felt that I was altogether born again and had entered paradise itself through open gates. There a totally other face of the entire Scripture showed itself to me. Thereupon I ran through

the Scripture from memory. I also found in other terms an analogy, as, the work of God, that is, what God does in us, the power of God, with which he makes us strong, the wisdom of God, with which he makes us wise, the strength of God, the salvation of God, the glory of God.[9]

Thus Luther realized that the good news preached in the New Testament was the figure of a God who forgives human beings mercifully—a God who has the sole power to save humanity, through his son the Lord Christ, without any contribution on the part of the church. Hōnen likewise denied the temples' role, given Amida's True Vow to accept all without exception. The similarity follows directly from the affinity between the True Vow and the Good News: "When you feel depressed, harassed by your sins, attend the sacraments and mass, train and strengthen your faith [*den glauen ubist*]. . . . You will be convinced that Christ and the saints wish to come to you, in you, to share everything, to live, work, suffer, and die with you, in all their virtue, suffering, and grace."[10] *Den glauen ubist* was a concept shared by Hōnen, who held faith and practice to be inseparable, but not by Shinran, who absolutized dependence. Luther probably came to feel the presence of Christ very palpably, and we are not surprised that he felt compelled to criticize a church whose practice was to sell indulgences. The flames of religious reformation were ignited in 1517 when he publicized his ninety-five theses against the Church's right to mediate between God and humanity.

Playing the role that Jōkei did for Hōnen, Silvester Prierias, the chief of the Vatican palace at that time, issued in 1519 a pamphlet boldly denouncing the treacherous heretic—*Epitome of a Reply to Martin Luther*.[11] Although Luther was excommunicated in 1521, he refused to retract his words. Instead, he added many more in the form of his famous vernacular translation, which he completed in the castle of Wartburg under the aegis of the Saxon prince Friedrich. Again, this reminds us of Hōnen, who opposed the templar authority that sent out itinerant monks all over Japan to advertise the good deed of almsgiving. Hōnen had also persisted in preaching his ideas within the stronghold of his own movement, despite the counterattack of eight powerful temples (the *Kōfukuji sōjō*). Moreover, just as exclusive-*nembutsu*, which began as an intensely personal need to overcome death, left the creator's hands to develop into insurrections at the hands of future followers, Luther's good news began as a personal matter of faith but became, in hindsight, one of the causes of the mas-

sive peasant uprisings against feudal landlords who imposed un-
payable taxes on the serfs.

These historical phenomena seem to indicate a rule: the more revolutionary the religious innovation, the more unlikely it is to remain
on a purely religious plane; sociopolitical interpretations follow, and
give rise to more or less interventionist movements. We might further argue in hindsight and strictly in the case of exclusive-*nembutsu*
that it may have been partly its radically atemporal, ahistorical, apolitical form that gave it revolutionary force—first through the warrior class and later through peasants rebelling against feudal oppression. It was through the in itself apolitical practice of chanting a
phrase over and over that proved—in its idiotic annihilation of time,
in its stupid refusal to reflect in itself the historical context in concrete
detail—impervious to co-optative mechanisms to which a more nuanced system might easily have succumbed. The inane simplicity of
chanting (a facility foreign to the Lutheran practice of *reading* on one's
own, where literacy was a privilege shared tellingly by a rising bourgeoisie) indeed perturbed a material and cultural hierarchy, but if
Hōnen's sole intention were political, he might never have chosen to
advocate such a single-mindedly atemporal practice empty headed
opposed to "timing."

It was precisely because Hōnen intended to open up a space exterior to the order of things, to guarantee a form of spiritual solace
independent of it, that the space left such an indelible trace on the
very order it was meant to transcend. In his final years, however, Hōnen criticized his own followers in the *Shichikajō seikai* (*The Seven-
Article Oath*). Similarly, Luther felt accountable for the increasingly
violent peasant uprisings and rushed to defend feudal oppression in
a denunciatory work *Against the Robbing and Murdering Hordes of
Peasants*.[12] If anything is more complex and paradoxical than the
thought of great religious leaders, it is their political effect. It is partly
in this sense that Hōnen and Luther form a pair, while Shinran's
counterpart in the Protestant Reformation ought to be Calvin. Shinran and Calvin radicalized the sociopolitical oppositionality of the
new religious currents. Following Luther in attributing the highest
authority on earth to the Bible, Calvin led Geneva in what became the
Protestants' central counter-countermovement against the Catholic
church. Shinran's followers were more insouciant of social mores
than Hōnen's.

Calvin's well-known doctrine of predestination, where divine will is independent of human desires and deeds, resembles Shinran's theory that those who find themselves capable of believing in the True Vow are already the chosen crowd who will enter the Pure Land, achieve *satori*, and become bodhisattvas. The undisguised fatalism of the Calvinist paradox—"submission to God is true liberty"—exerted an influence that was also paradoxical. In brief, the middle classes, liberated from the authority of the church, turned themselves into the willing means of God and toiled in his glory with an ascetic work ethic, in this world, that was anything but fatalistic. The destination was predetermined, but one's course in this life, which supposedly reflected the *fait accompli*, depended paradoxically (speaking from a non-Calvinist viewpoint) on the Calvinists' own "hard work."[13] It is well known that Calvinism won the overwhelming support of the rising bourgeoisie in Switzerland, Holland, France, Scotland, England, and North America and that Max Weber saw the curious ideology of "inner-worldly asceticism" as the sociological basis of capitalism.[14] This aspect of Calvinism is extremely similar to the way Shinran's doctrine of absolute dependence won immense support from Japanese peasants and merchants, who fetishized virtues such as thrift and diligence to feel secure about their afterlives; their need for spiritual assurance, despite there being only one possible outcome, contributed significantly to the ideological foundation of Tokugawa society.

THE ART OF DEATH

With Hōnen as the pivotal point, Japanese Buddhism, which had been a religion of life, turned into a religion of death. Although Hōnen was never a direct influence, similar radical changes took place in the various arts. In painting, the *yamatoe* that used gold and silver abundantly were replaced by *sumie*, which located beauty in desolation and the monochromatic style as if to symbolize the Zen spirit of quelling one's attachment to life. Architecture likewise made a transition from opulent chambers and Amida halls to the simple, functional abodes of warriors and Zen halls. For Sen no Rikyū (1521–91), who eventually angered his newly rich patron Toyotomi Hideyoshi (1536–98) and was forced to disembowel himself, the unadorned tea room was the ephemeral space of transition between this world and the other. In literature, the resplendent writings of Heian court women, which deftly described the folds of human affect, gave way to essays by hermits steeped in Buddhist sentiments of transience and to accounts of war that saw warriors to their deaths in battle. The ethos of the new literature was the emptiness of life in our "drifting world," seen from the inevitability of death.

This is not the place to explore the mysteries of historical causality, but it is beyond doubt that the thirteenth century did mark a fundamental change in the composition of Japanese art. Yet, there is really only one candidate for *the* art of death: the one that father and son, Kan'ami (1333–84) and Zeami (1363–1443) of the Muromachi period, established: Noh theater. Supernatural phenomena are also employed in Western drama—we think of Ibsen's ghosts—but not in the systematic, generically obsessive manner that would call for the title of the art of death. (The notable exception is the Hollywood cinema of horror, which is unfortunately obsessed with presenting those horrors "realistically," with special effects.) In Noh, not only spirits and embodiments of gods but ogres, long-nosed goblins, foxes, and monsters taking forms such as the spider are acted as concrete existents playing central roles. The works that are referred to as the masterpieces of Noh theater are precisely the ones in which spirits return from the land of the dead to enact dramatic conflicts on earth—we are speaking of Mugen Noh, dream Noh.

There is a reason for this. In the *Fūshikaden*, Zeami himself ascribes *hana*, the highest value, to works that feature spirits of the living and the dead and other suspicious entities belonging to the category *monogurui* (the mad, deranged):

> Acting a mad person is most dramatic and intriguing. There are various characters in this genre, so that if one excels in acting a role such as this one can act a whole range of similar characters. Many devices are required for this kind of impersonation. For example, if a character is distraught because they are possessed by a ghost, or the spirit of a dead or a living person, one can easily get suggestions for one's performance by imitating the being possessing them. It is not easy to impersonate a mad person who is distraught, suffering from a quite different kind of misfortune, such as being separated from parents, being deserted by a husband or lover, being left by a wife, or searching for a lost child. Even if an actor is skilled, his acting will not appeal to an audience if he performs without taking into consideration the different causes of madness. If the cause of the madness is the result of being overcome with emotion, one should act so that one looks

pensive, and appears to be deep in thought, and then one should try
to present *hana* at the scene where the character goes mad. If one presents the scene of madness, identifying oneself emotionally with the
character, one's performance will become impressive and moving.[15]

There are many Noh plays, with various plots, but Zeami insists that
he who has mastered the dance of *monogurui* can act in any kind of
Noh. Be it vindictive spirits from the other world or vengeful, obsessive people in ours, it is the condensation of human affect that constitutes *monogurui*—madness as the bridge between this world and
the other, entrancement as the "flower" of Noh. Zeami's insight is as
sharp as death.

Corporality plays an irreducible role in the Noh enactment of death
and madness. Yuasa Yasuo offers a valid analysis in his *The Body: Toward an Eastern Mind–Body Theory*:

> Zeami compares training to Zen cultivation. In Zen cultivation,
> whether one is engaged in seated meditation or in everyday chores,
> one is instructed to assume a certain "form" (*katachi*) or posture for
> meditation, eating, worship, or working in compliance with the mo-
> nastic regulations. At any rate, Zen corrects the mode of one's mind
> by putting one's body into the correct postures. Zeami seems to un-
> derstand artistic training in a similar manner. Training, it seems, is a
> discipline for shaping one's body into a form. Art is embodied through
> cumulative training; one comes to learn an art through one's body.[16]

This view recognizes the role of the body in deepening one's "consciousness"—in the case of Noh, to the place where sanity and madness, life and death, share a common border. The Noh actor cannot
portray the chaotic emotional realm that festers in the "depths" of
the human psyche, cannot dig into his *kokoro*, without arranging the
external "forms" of the body as in Zen. We believe that Hōnen, who
preached salvation through a nonspecialist practice, had similar reasons for offering to his disciples the four rules of chanting—for a
long time, reverently, uninterruptedly, and without mixing in other
practices. Whether it is theater or religion, thought cannot be subjec-
tivized without piercing the body.

More directly, corporality in Noh involves the manner of enunciation. In an essay on "Ōchō no koe to Kamakura no koe [The Voice of
the Monarchic Age and the Voice of Kamakura]," Kamei Katsuichirō
characterizes Noh enunciation—which seems "to squeeze life out"

of the stomach—as a "life-sound." He also touches upon the voice of the *shite:*

> I have used the term "life-sound" concerning the unique method of enunciation, but in the case of the *shite,* another important element is added. We mean the mask. The "life-sound" goes through another fabrication. In other words, because the mask blocks the voice, it takes on a muffled quality. The central character of the song can be a man or a woman, but the voice is not gendered. In addition to this muffling, words take on the air of incantations, resulting in a voice neither male nor female but neuter. What we hear as a result is a meaningless voice that we can only call a "ghost-sound." [17]

What Kamei calls the "ghost-sound" is the voice emitted in the conflict between human beings and vindictive spirits, life and death, Eros and Thanatos.

Noh is the symbolic expression of the phantasmal that arises from the melee between Apollonian beauty and Dionysian chaos, as it were; its mode of expression is not only the actors' movement but also the voices, the masks, on and off "stage." Noh has been appreciated outside of Japan to the extent that it brilliantly acts out, under a phantasmal light, a drama that can be, if not universally recognized, then universally misrecognized as shared human truth. Such misrecognitions testify to the force of a genre, its power to carve out a depository for cathexes. The Japanese "religion of death" has never succeeded in creating an art of death that surpasses the Noh theater, the partnership of genius father and genius son.

THE MERCHANTS OF DEATH

We have discussed at length how Japanese Buddhism after the Kamakura period, beginning with exclusive-*nembutsu,* set up the transcendental meaning of death as a stepping board for a leap toward life, in a paradoxical movement from death to life. As long as death is seen from the viewpoint of life, memorial services such as ancestral worship are deemed important, but when life is seen from the viewpoint of death, such religious rituals begin to appear secondary. As captured in Shinran's assertion that he has not chanted a single *nembutsu* for his parents' sake (the *Tan'nishō*), the leaders of Kamakura Buddhism, with the exceptions of Eisai and Ippen, were not generally interested in the appeasement of the dead. In *The Rhetoric of Immediacy*, Bernard Faure describes Chan/Zen's transcendental attitude toward death:

> Death was furthermore relativized by the notion of the constant arising and cessation of psycho-physical aggregates and the belief that the true break in the stream of consciousness was the result of awakening. Reinforcing the no-self theory of early Buddhism, the Mahāyāna doctrine, as exemplified by the Heart Sūtra, further blunted the scandal of death by denying its ontological reality: in emptiness (śūnyatā) there is neither birth nor death, neither coming nor going. Accordingly, temporality and finitude were ultimately negated as karmic delusions. Mahāyāna Buddhists could have made theirs the Roman motto: "Non fuit, fuit, non sum, non curo" (I was not, I was, I am not, I do not care).[18]

In theory, Mahāyāna Buddhism rejected funerary rituals, having relativized both death and the afterlife. But time passed. The currents of Japanese Buddhism, including Shinran's Shin sect, veered toward paths that were not the ones indicated by their idiosyncratic founders, if indeed the various paths indicated were self-identical, noncontradictory "ones" in the first place. It is already a piece of common sense that as soon as a religious (or any other) movement is organized, the indications of the founder can no longer be heeded by the institutional machine. Faure aptly analyzes the ritual domestication of death in the Chan/Zen tradition:

> The dominant impression left by Chan/Zen documents is that of an increasing ritualization and collectivization of death. As a form of mediation, ritual simultaneously hides and reveals death: it marks its apotheosis, but it also diffuses or defers its suddenness by turning the corpse or its substitutes into signifiers. In the Chan/Zen case, these signifiers point toward a form of ancestral, corporate transcendence of awakening. We also witness what we could call an undramatization of death (as a traumatic event) through its "dramatization" (as ritual performance). This ritualization affects all the "stages" (in both senses) of the death process.[19]

In Japanese Buddhism, the process attained its high plateau during the Tokugawa period: the sects submitted themselves to the Shogunate's control; the temples became outposts of the state in a parish system; the relationship between people and religion was maintained only in terms of memorial services for ancestors.

Buddhist sects assigned discriminatory *kaimyō* (posthumous names)—*kanji* characters for slaughter, beast, leather, and so on—to the *burakumin,* or clans segregated because of their forms of livelihood. The vicious Heian practice of extending the caste system to life after death was thus resurrected in a sharper form of exclusion, in complete disregard for the principle of absolute equality upon death. Pure Land thought, which sets up a distinction between the "pure" and the "impure" worlds, is not free of blame regarding this form of injustice. The practice of discriminatory *kaimyō* continues today in the posthumous gradating of the quality of names according to the degree of "piety" shown through almsgiving.

It is precisely in such economic terms that modern Japan casts death. Priests have commercialized death, and the Japanese now speak understandably of *sōshiki bukkyō,* or funereal Buddhism. Death is now run as a profitable business venture by temples, stonecutters, and funeral-organization agencies, a triumvirate that well-nigh surpasses the auto industry. Customs of human death, plots for tombs and fees for confirmation, are the largest source of income for temples. By "merchants of death" we usually mean those entrepreneurs who profit immensely by fomenting warfare and selling weapons; in Japan, the term seems to apply to a different profession.

THE IDEOLOGY OF DEATH

It might be too simplistic to lament the fall of Buddhism if we regard the exaggerated funerals and the overall ritualization of death as a modern, synthetic reincarnation of the spiritual worship practiced during Japan's animistic past. But we can hardly deny that contemporary Japanese Buddhism lacks the acuity of religious thought and practice that is won only through a direct confrontation with death. The taboo on direct confrontation has ironically meant the sensational proliferation and mass consumption of images of death—in other words, an increased obsession with death, a total engagement with it in all possible ways except as a personal matter. This is not a uniquely Japanese phenomenon; the point of DeLillo's acclaimed novel *White Noise* is that the usual clichés about the media (that it sells things through sex if not sex itself) miss the fact that the media are obsessed with death—in order to help us forget, paradoxically, the fact that death is a necessary outcome of one's own life. Perhaps the

Heideggerian counterrhetoric of being-toward-death, which we too have been mouthing, also sounds tired, clichéd. No wonder that has had to be the case. Although the degeneration of death is far from a uniquely Japanese phenomenon, one might like to hope from Japan— as one of the few nations with a Buddhist background *and* an exceptionally advanced technological infrastructure—a medical ethic, for example, based on a view of life that transcends individual physical death by engaging it. However, in organ transplants, euthanasia, and other subfields of medicine, Japan is tirelessly dependent on U.S. leadership. If the only effect of the degeneration of death were the production of petty merchants of death, then it would simply increase the headcount of gluttonous priests in hell. In fact, if we take Hōnen for his word, anyone who has chanted *nembutsu* even once is now in the Pure Land, and a serious recession must be tormenting all the stages of hell. If the priests do not become selfless enough to commit themselves to hell, there would be chronic unemployment for the demons down there.

But leaving all jest aside, we must note that Japan has manipulated death in a manner that cannot be dismissed as petty. The most fearsome degeneration of death is its aestheticization—especially on the massive scale of nationalist propaganda.[20] It would be easy for us to criticize the complicity of intellectuals (active participation in the case of not a few), but we ought first to be shocked by the fact that neither their often admirable character nor their liberal humanist education hindered them from bellowing out support, murmuring assent, or maintaining silence. The seemingly sudden consolidation of fascist power in Japan was due to multiple factors that we leave to historians. It is not because we think Buddhism was the only or even the major cause but because it is our focus that we shall analyze the role it played in Japan's plunge into totalitarianism. As we said earlier, exclusive-*nembutsu* must be seen in this dark light.

In the simplest terms, Buddhism began as an intensely personal religion centered on self-improvement through introspection; its ideal is to link oneself to the eternal life, with an awareness that all living things partake in this life; its moral spine is a taboo on killing not only human beings but any animate form. This faith underwent a radical change in Japan—namely, the emphasis on individual dignity fizzled away—largely because religious authority as such was placed under the supervision of state authority, at least in form and often in fact, throughout Japan's history. The early years of the reign of the Showa emperor Hirohito were only an extreme case of this tendency. Hardly a single Buddhist rose up to cry out against war, and no Buddhist draftee risked his life by declaring himself, in our language, a conscientious objector.

In some cases, the assent was not tacit and passive but noisily active—the case of various Buddhist leaders, for instance. The following passage is an excerpt from a 1938 article by Katō Seishin, ex-president of Taisho University and ex-leader of the Shingon sect's Buzan subsect:

> Originally, the teaching of Mahāyāna Buddhism revolves around mercy. Since its intent is to help living things, it affirms whatever is consonant with the intent. And without this *kokoro*, Prince Shōtoku would not have defeated the Mononobes; the spirit of Mahāyāna Buddhism is not so stiff as to call war as such a breaking of precepts. Of course, if Japan were fighting an unjust war, it would be inappropriate to follow along, but it is a holy war for the sake of Eastern peace; Shākyamuni Buddha himself waged a war of justice in his past life, and we do not need to discuss this matter further. If Japan were to be led in accordance with a precept so stiff as to ban killing altogether, it would collapse. Thus, what some Chinese take to be Buddhism is Mahāyāna Buddhism in name but Hīnayāna Buddhism in content. It is fundamentally mistaken to use it to criticize the rational [*rironteki*] Mahāyāna Buddhism.[21]

We would like to say that such a distortion of Mahāyāna Buddhism would be unthinkable today, but Aum Shinrikyō's recent repetition of the very same theoretical maneuver forbids us.[22] The excerpt exhibits all the symptoms of rationalization, and under different circumstances the final appeal to the rational might be enjoyed as the punchline of an exemplary parodic text. Similar communiqués justifying warfare were repeatedly issued by priests and Buddhologists as well as by other followers of the faith. In those times, fanning the "patriotic spirit" was one of the social duties of ecclesiastics.

It was the ideology of death that enabled the connection between Buddhism and war. The idea that eternal life is gained through the supersession of physical death did not displease the military command; the fascists solicited the cooperation of Buddhist leaders, who taught the people that it is a good thing to serve the emperor and the nation to the point of death. A character called Kuno Kyūran tries to fulfill the collaborative task in the following excerpt from "The Essence of Bushidō [the Warrior Spirit]," published in an illustrious Buddhist journal shortly after the bombing of Pearl Harbor:

> "I have discovered that *bushidō* is about dying." Yamamoto Tsune-tomo's *Hagakure* begins with the above incisive formulation. Simple and clear, it captures the essence of the warrior spirit. . . . In the current war, the Japanese forces' sublime spirit of martyrdom, of offering a death to His country, shows that the warrior spirit has become the flesh and blood of our race, has built our throbbing history for 2,602 years. The warrior spirit that was latent, the natural characteristic of the Japanese race, has shone forth proudly to the whole world, in this war.[23]

This is the ideology of death that loomed behind the *kamikaze* corps, the human torpedo *kaiten,* the youth whose lives were abruptly terminated in attempts to terminate other equally promising ones. "The Life to Be Offered to the Nation," "The Immortality of the Soul beyond Death," these were the slogans hammered into the populace. But often, not much hammering was necessary, the hammering was happy. The ideology of death had a propensity to latch onto physical violence in premodern times as well. We know how Hōnen helped the *bushi* themselves (the historical referents of the warrior spirit) discover moral ground for slaughter in the exclusive-*nembutsu* policy of *zōaku muge.* But it was only with the early Showa that the ideology of death contributed to the organized brainwashing of virtually the whole people. These more insidious merchants of death did not single-handedly cause militarism—but neither did they retract their ideology of death in the face of a historically anomalous situation. They instead formulated a general theory.

The ideology of death embodies both Eros and Thanatos; Eros itself already involves both creation and destruction; it is precisely through Eros that Thanatos can and does express itself. The same goes for the imagination. Let us recall that a world called the Greater Asian Co-Prosperity Sphere (Daitōa Kyōeiken) was carefully prepared and grafted onto the people's minds—it was a thoroughly imaginary world. Death and the imagination, the twin themes of our book, always contain these dangerous vectors. However, our guiding conviction has been that it is not a question of abandoning them—for that is impossible—but of entering the arena of their antagonisms, of partaking in the eternal life of stopgap measures, makeshift arrange-

ments, and temporary adjustments, if we wish to avoid political catastrophes whereby erroneous state and unrepentant religion proceed hand in hand. We cannot control Thanatos without Eros. We
cannot avoid fanaticism without using our imagination.

HISTORY AND THE IMAGINATION

Hōnen's theory of option and dependence has functioned as a myth,
not withstanding its vicissitudes. It is with good reason that fascist
collaborators "discovered" a national spirit of loyalty. We concur that,
although not as some unchangeable essence, there *is* a Japanese tendency "to serve one master," including but not limited to the strictly
political sense of the phrase. It was Watsuji Tetsurō who pointed out
the common ground between Pure Land worship and the warrior
ethic of not serving more than one master;[24] indeed, we are not so
sure that feudalism could have become so well established in Japan
without the assistance of the homologous religious virtue. The feudal mindset was shared by peasants too, toward their landlords, and
it seems in many ways to have persisted beyond the dissolution of
the corresponding economic structure.

In modern Japan, it sometimes seems as if the "*nembutsu*" has
crumbled away from "exclusive-*nembutsu*" without taking the "ex-
clusive-" with it. We assert with confidence that you can live in Japan
for a long time without running into a single person chanting reverently, let alone uninterruptedly. You are likely, however, to find traces
of the "exclusive-." This modern, more than residual "optionism"
cannot simply be traced back to Hōnen, of course; all sects belonging
to the genealogy of Kamakura Buddhism have contributed to the
ideological sedimentation of choosing-and-depending. We must also
take into account the possibility that such a tendency existed before
Kamakura Buddhism to welcome it in the first place. However, we
believe that in large part it was Hōnen who introduced, with a radical negativity that constituted a kind of discursive rupture, a religious theory and practice of exclusive choice. If the doctrine had been
introduced as a political or moral principle, it might not have had
such an immense impact on culture; perhaps it was because the medium was religion, a new religion centered upon a numinosity transcending, by definition, the domain of the intellect, that it ramified so
many facets of Japanese society.

The only possible way to go beyond Hōnen's myth of option and dependence lies precisely in the faculty that he used: the imagination. Just as Hōnen wielded his imagination as a hammer against the mechanism of death that constituted his times, what is necessary now is a moment of imaginative transcendence that will negate the mechanism of the option unto death. This necessity might not be limited to modern Japan. Myth has to be the skin that the snake sheds never for the last time. The imagination, the serpentine body, is not a fantastic abstraction, nor about fantastic abstraction; it begins with the hypnosis of reality. The active imagination does not move without the friction of the material ground. But we are not awaiting the rise of another man of imagination to whom we would listen as if listening to our own destiny but rather men and women, children of imagination who will find—in whatever field they find themselves—a plane of immanence.

We end here, now that we are no longer in a position to laud Hōnen, the man of imagination. Our defiance lies outside the book.

Appendix

Due to the scarcity of documents written by Hōnen himself, one must consult other primary sources in order to investigate his religious thought. The various materials that are considered authentic can be organized into four groups:

Group I: Texts proven to be handwritten by Hōnen

1. *Ichimai kishō-mon* (owned by Konkai Kōmyō-ji of Kyoto)
2. A letter to Kumagai-no Nyūdō (owned by Shakadō Seiryō-ji of Kyoto)
3. Three partial letters to Shōgyō-bō that were discovered in the Amida statue of Kōzen-ji of Nara
4. One line in the manuscript of the Amida-kyō (owned by Isshin-ji of Osaka)
5. The title and the opening phrase of *Senchaku-shū* (owned by Rōzan-ji of Kyoto)
6. Hōnen's signature on *Shichikajō seikai* (owned by Nison-in of Kyoto)

As can be seen, except for items 1 and 2, these materials are of little use in examining Hōnen's ideas.[1]

Group II: Texts that include Hōnen's works or words

1. *Saihō shinan-shō*, whose authorship and dating are obscure. It exists in the form of a manuscript in Shinran's hand dating from 1226 to 1258.
2. *Kurodani shōnin gotōroku*, edited by Dōkō in 1274 and 1275. It consists of three parts:
   Kango tōroku, 10 vols.
   Wago tōroku, 5 vols.
   Shūi go-tōroku, 3 vols.

These texts—the main source on Hōnen's thought—can be further subdivided into eight categories.[2] It should be noted, however, that since most of the materials listed below did not remain with Hōnen's own manuscripts, they cannot be attributed to him definitively. (I will list representative items for each category.)

A: Treatises and commentaries on Pure Land scriptures (kyōsho),
    17 items:

1. *Senchaku-shū*
2. *Ojōyōshū senyō*
3. *Muryōju-kyō shaku*
4. *Gyakushū-seppō*
5. *Hōnen shōnin go-seppō no koto*
6. *Jōdo-shū ryaku yōmon*

B: Teaching to his followers in general (hōgo), *32 items:*

1. *Ichimai kishō-mon*
2. *Nembutsu taii*
3. *Ichigo-monogatari*
4. *Zenshō-bō densetsu no kotoba*
5. *Tuneni ooserarekeru mikotoba*

C: Correspondence with particular disciples and lay followers (shōsoku),
    26 items:

1. A reply to Hōjō Masako
2. A reply to Kanezane's wife, Kitano Mandokoro
3. A reply to Princess Shokushi
4. A reply to Kumagai Naozane

D: Dialogues with priests and lay followers (mondō), *50 items:*

1. *Ippyaku Shijū-go kajō mondō*
2. *Tōdaiji ju-mondō*
3. *Nembutsu ōjō-gi*
4. *Jūni mondō*

E: Words that people transmitted as Hōnen's (dengo), *23 items:*

1. His words to Shōkō-bō
2. His words heard by Shinran

F: Disciplinary edicts that Hōnen imposed on his disciples (seikai),
    8 items:

1. *Shichi-kajō seikai*
2. *Ichinen-gi chōji kishōmon*
3. *Sanmon ni okuru kishōmon*

G: Miscellaneous:

1. *Sanmai hottoku-ki*
2. *Go-rinjū-nikki*
3. *Hōnen shōnin go-musō-ki*

H: Forged (Den Hōnen-sho), 86 items:

1. *Nyonin ōjō-shū*
2. *Rinjū-gyōgi*
3. *Ōhara dangi kikigaki*

Group III: Contemporaneous texts (primary texts by
contemporaries that refer to Hōnen)

1. Jōkei, *Kōfukuji sōjō*
2. Myōe, *Zai-jarin*
3. Myōe, *Zai-jarin shōgon-ki*
4. Jien, *Gukan-shō*
5. Unknown, *Enryaku-ji daishūge*
6. Shinran, *Kyōgyōshinshō*
7. Shinran, *Tan'ni-shō*
8. Nichiren, *Risshō ankoku-ron*
9. Nichiren, *Shugo kokka-ron*
10. Nichiren, *Nembutsu muken jigoku-shō*
11. Nichiren, *Shinkokuō gosho*
12. Jōshō, *Dan senchaku*
13. Kujō Kanezane, *Gyokuyō*
14. Fujiwara Teika, *Meigetsu-ki*
15. Sanjō Nagakane, *Sanchō-ki*
16. Unknown, *Heike monogatari*
17. Yoshida Kenkō, *Tsurezure-gusa*
18. Mujū, *Shaseki-shū*
19. Unknown, *Azuma kagami*
20. Fujiwara Arifusa, *Nomori kagami*

Group IV: Biographies of Hōnen

These organize themselves into two groups. The first emphasizes that the
exclusive-*nembutsu* collective is compatible with the Tendai school and that
Hōnen's teaching continues the Tendai tradition. They practically ignore
Hōnen's major work, *Senchaku-shū*, and the saint's indebtedness to the teaching of Shandao (613–81). Instead, they stress that Hōnen practiced *nembutsu*
in conjunction with many other kinds of traditional practices, including
hokke-sanmai (the visualization of sacred images through chanting the Lotus
Sūtra) and the esoteric worship of Amida.[3]

Some of these tendencies are familiar characteristics of hagiography, but
others constitute a strategic maneuver. In other words, even after the organi-
zationally volatile initial years when declaring independence from the Tendai school was too risky, many of Hōnen's disciples had to try to placate con-
servatives in order to end the unflagging persecution of exclusive-*nembutsu*.
The major biographies in this first group are as follows:

1. *Genkū shōnin shi-nikki*, 1 vol. Shinkū? (ed.), ca. 1218.
2. *Hōnen shōnin-den*, only 2 vols. remaining. Myōzen? (ed.), ca. 1241.
3. *Honchō soshi denki ekotoba*, called Denbō-e, 4 vols. Tankū (ed.), 1237.
4. *Hōnen shōnin-e*, 4 vols. Gugan (ed.).

According to the second group of biographies, Hōnen the religious hero founded the Jōdo school: a staunch advocate of *senju-nembutsu* independent from the Tendai school, he practiced only *nembutsu* and nothing else. These biographies acknowledge Shandao's legacy and present extensive explanations of what Hōnen teaches in the *Senchaku-shū*. The representative biographies in this group are as follows:

1. *Daigo-bon Hōnen shōnin denki*, 1 vol. Genchi (ed.), ca. 1214.
2. *Chion-kō shiki*, 1 vol. Ryūkan (ed.), ca. 1218.
3. *Kurodani Genkū shōnin-den*, called *Jiūroku mon-ki*, 1 vol. Shōkaku? (ed.), ca. 1227.
4. *Hōnen shōnin-den ekotoba*, 9 vols. Editor unknown, ca. 1301.
5. *Shūi kotoku-den ekotoba*, 9 vols. Kakunyo (ed.), 1301.
6. *Hōnen shōnin denki*, called *Kyūkan-den*, 9 vols. Shunshō (ed.), 1311.
7. *Hōnen shōnin gyōjō gazu*, called *Shijū hakkan-den*, 48 vols. Shunshō (ed.), ca. 1311.[4]

Neither group of existing biographies nor their combination can give us a historically accurate image of Hōnen. For the most part, these hagiographies of a savior who transcended the secular world do not seem to care for the man who had to contend with his own problems while searching for religious truth.

The scholar's lament is amplified by the fact that many of the biographies represent the viewpoints of particular factions within the Jōdo school. Half a century after Hōnen's death, the Jōdo school contained five currents: the Ichinen-gi of Kōsai, Chinzei-gi of Shōkō, Tanen-gi of Ryūkan, Seizan-gi of Shōkū and Shogyō hongan-gi of Chōsai. Each claimed orthodoxy by asserting that its leader was the only authentic successor of Hōnen. For this purpose, a faction had to produce biographies that exaggerated its leader's relationship to the late saint.

For example, the *Shijū hakkan-den*, which is the most commonly read biography and the only one to have been translated into English (by H. H. Coates and R. Ishizuka in 1949), was produced by the Chinzei-gi group in the early fourteenth century, the end of the Kamakura period. Originally, under the leadership of Shōkō (1162–1238), the faction was based in Kyūshū and later in Kamakura. It found a foothold in the Chion-in temple in Kyoto, which eventually became its headquarters and from where favorable relationships could be established with the court and Kyoto's aristocrats. The *Shijū hakkan-den* is evidently heavy with the political purpose of the Chinzei-gi group. Similar biases riddle the *Genkū shi-nikki* of Shinkū and the Daigo-bon of Genchi, just as the *Shūi kotoku-den* edited by Kakunyo overestimates Shinran's place in Hōnen's circle.[5]

Biographies aside, sources on Hōnen's life include two collections of his own work, the *Kurodani shōnin go-tōroku* and the *Saihō shinan-shō* (group II), which contain articles, informal talks, and correspondence. These documents must be used with no less caution, however, since they were compiled by "insiders" of the Pure Land sect. The fact that Hōnen wrote very little in his own hand forces us to draw a composite figure of him by connecting the dots scattered among his biographies, his collected works, enemy polemic, and scraps of literature.

Notes

INTRODUCTION

1. Nichiren's condemnations of other leaders of Kamakura Buddhism were, if not personal, theological. Jacqueline Stone ("Rebuking the Enemies of the Lotus: Nichirenist Exclusivism in Historical Perspective," part 1, *Japanese Journal of Religious Studies* 21, no. 2 [1994]: 233) writes, "Nichiren was unique, not in making exclusivist claims per se, but in integrating confrontation with other Buddhist teachings into the formal structure of his thought, especially through his advocacy of *shakubuku*."

2. Cf. Helen McCullough, trans., *The Tale of the Heike* (Stanford: Stanford University Press, 1988), 334–35; Harper H. Coates and Ryūgaku Ishizuka, *Hōnen the Buddhist Saint: His Life and Teaching* (Kyoto: Society for the Publication of Sacred Books of the World, 1949), 488; and *NKT*, 30:121.

3. Hōnen's stance was, however, noticeably inconsistent. In 1186, he defended the *senju-nembutsu* in the Ōhara debate with the high priests of other schools by claiming that the vocal-*nembutsu* was inferior but more suitable to the apocalyptic age. See George Tanabe, *The Dreamkeeper: Fantasy and Knowledge in Early Kamakura Buddhism* (Cambridge, Mass.: Council on East Asian Studies, Harvard University, 1992), 88, and Enchō Tamura, *Hōnen* (Tokyo: Yoshikawa Kōbun-kan, 1988), 76–83.

4. The significance of Hōnen's teaching also lay in eliminating negativistic views of the afterlife from Pure Land belief. In the *Yōgi mondō*, he insists that the idea of the "evil realm" (*makai*), which people feared, was entirely false. See Z, 3:207–8.

5. Gustavo Gutiérrez, *A Theology of Liberation: History, Politics, and Liberation*, trans. and ed. Sister Caridad Inda and John Eagleson (New York: Oribis Books, 1973), 275–76.

6. Liberation theology unearthed spiritual force in the interests of revolution, and it influenced not only democratic movements in the Philippines and Korea but also battles against racial discrimination and gender subordination in the United States.

7. The temples gained their political power through their ever-growing landownerships from the tenth century to the thirteenth. George Sansom (*A History of Japan to 1334* [London: Cresset Press, 1958], 110) writes, "The truth is that the real source of power in Japanese life was the land."

8. Kuroda Toshio, "Shōen shakai to bukkyō" [The Estate Society and Buddhism], in *Kuroda Toshio Zenshū*, vol. 2 (Kyoto: Hozōkan, 1994), 22.

9. This campaign was notable because it reflected the apex of the medieval Buddhist clergy's military power. See Neil McMullin, *Buddhism and the State in Sixteenth-Century Japan* (Princeton: Princeton University Press, 1984), 100–145.

10. Yamaori Tetsuo, "Ikki izenno koto" [Things Prior to the Rebellions], in *Chūsei shakai to Ikkō ikki* [Medieval Society and the Shin-Buddhist Rebellions] (Tokyo: Yoshikawa Kōbunkan, 1985), 3–14.

11. We do not, however, deny that the *ikkō ikki* also emerged from motives other than the purely religious one of dying for *nembutsu* worship. The Ikkō sect, which defeated the feudal lord Togashi and ruled the Kaga region for a century after (1488–1580), encompassed warriors who were dissatisfied with their lords, and followers of the Hakusan Shrine who simply wanted to expand their estate. The siege of Ishiyama also mobilized warlords who sympathized with Ashikaga Yoshiaki, the last Muromachi shogun, whom Oda Nobunaga had displaced.

12. Robert E. Morrell, *Early Kamakura Buddhism* (Berkeley: Asian Humanities Press, 1987), 82.

13. Martin Collcutt (Review of *Buddhism and the State in Sixteenth-Century Japan* by Neil McMullin, *Journal of Japanese Studies* 12 [1986]: 406) suggests that "*ōbō-buppō*" (mutual dependence rhetoric) was a one-sided rhetoric on the part of the church and not the state. His claim may be justified in the late medieval period, but in the early thirteenth century the parity between them was still intact because they needed to defend their common political and economic interests.

14. Karl Marx, "Critique of Hegel's Doctrine of the State," in *Early Writings*, trans. Rodney Livingstone and Gregor Benton (New York: Penguin Books, 1974), 112.

15. Ibid., 107.

16. See Taira Masayuki, *Nihon chūsei no shakai to bukkyō* (Tokyo: Haniwa Shobō, 1992), 293.

17. For example, Taira Masayuki (ibid., 394–98) claims that Hōnen did not contribute substantially to eradicating sexism from the Buddhist tradition.

18. For an English translation of the entire text, see Morrell, *Early Kamakura Buddhism*, 75–88.

19. Karl Marx, "On the Jewish Question," in *Early Writings*, trans. Livingstone and Benton, 221.

20. Ibid., 218.

21. Pure Land belief provided the anvil on which low-level samurai and village peasants could forge religio-political leagues against oppressive feudal lords. See James C. Dobbins, *Jōdo Shinshū: Shin Buddhism in Medieval Japan* (Bloomington: Indiana University Press, 1989), 140.

22. Ryūkoku Translation Center, trans., *The Kyō Gyō Shin Shō* [Teaching, Practice, Faith, and Enlightenment] (Kyoto: Ryūkoku University, 1966), 206.

23. George Tanabe (*Dreamkeeper*, 86) points out the questionable authenticity of the *Shichikajō seikai*. This issue requires further examination.

24. Morrell, *Early Kamakura Buddhism*, 88.

25. Tanabe, *Dreamkeeper,* 84.

26. Katō Shūichi, "Jūsan-seiki no Shisō" [Thought in the Thirteenth Century], in *Katō Shūichi Chosakushū,* vol. 3 (Tokyo: Heibonsha, 1978), 99.

27. Marx, "On the Jewish Question," 235.

CHAPTER 1: CONSTRUCTED DEATH

1. See G. Cameron Hurst III, *INSEI: Abdicated Sovereigns in the Politics of Late Heian Japan, 1086–1185* (New York: Columbia University Press, 1976), 171–77 and 189–90.

2. Helen McCullough, trans., *The Tale of the Heike* (Stanford: Stanford University Press, 1988), 195.

3. *Gyokuyō,* ed. Ichijima Kenkichi, vol. 2 (Tokyo: Kokusho Kankōkai, 1907), 627.

4. Tsuji Zen'nosuke, *Bukkyōshi: Jōsei-hen* [The History of Buddhism: Ancient] (Tokyo: Iwanami Shoten, 1944), 695.

5. Karl Marx, "Economic and Philosophical Manuscripts," in *Early Writings,* trans. Rodney Livingstone and Gregor Benton (New York: Penguin Books, 1974), 324.

6. Ibid., 326–27.

7. On this point, see Georg Lukács, "Preface," *History and Class Consciousness: Studies in Marxist Dialectics,* trans. Rodney Livingstone (Cambridge, Mass.: MIT Press, 1972).

8. "Hauntology" is the suggestive pun on "ontology" developed in Jacques Derrida, *Specters of Marx,* trans. Peggy Kamuf (New York: Routledge, 1995). In our opinion, Foucault preserved the *epochè* (the phenomenological reduction) as a method while giving it the Nietzschean inflection of *savoir-pouvoir.* In other words, discourse analysis puts the referential truth value of a discourse in brackets in order to ask who or what gains socially through the production of that discourse.

9. Shigematsu Nobuhiro, *Genji Monogatari no Bukkyō Shisō* [Buddhism in the Tale of Genji] (Kyoto: Heirakuji Shoten, 1967), 97.

10. Edward G. Seidensticker, trans., *The Tale of Genji* (New York: Alfred Knopf, 1992), 599.

11. Yamaori Tetsuo, *Jigoku to Jōdo* [Hell and the Pure Land] (Tokyo: Shunjūsha, 1993), 134.

12. Ivan Morris, trans., *The Pillow Book of Sei Shōnagon* (New York: Columbia University Press, 1991), 87.

13. *Saigyō Hōshi Zenkashū,* ed. Itō Yoshio (Tokyo: Daiichi Shobō, 1987), 256.

14. Marx, "Economic and Philosophical Manuscripts," 331.

15. Kuroda Toshio, *Kuroda Toshio Chosakushū,* vol. 2 (Kyoto: Hōzōkan, 1994), 23.

16. Antonin Artaud, "Le théâtre et la peste," in *Le théâtre et son double* (Paris: Gallimard, 1964).

17. Fujiwara Sukefusa, *Shunki* [Spring Record], in *Shiryō Taisei* [The Collection of Historical Documents], vol. 7 (Kyoto: Rinsen Shoten, 1974), 13.

18. *Gyokuyō,* 2:455.

19. Saichō, *Dengyō Daishi Zenshū* [The Collected Works of Master Dengyō], vol. 1 (Kyoto: Sekai Seiten Kankō Kyōkai, 1989), 418.

20. Robert E. Morrell, *Early Kamakura Buddhism* (Berkeley: Asian Humanities Press, 1987), 53.

21. For a discussion of the Old/New dichotomy in the Japanese scholarship, see Sueki Fumihiko, *Nihon bukkyō shisōshi ronkō* [The Discourse on the Intellectual History of Japanese Buddhism] (Tokyo: Daizō Shuppan, 1993), 275–83.

22. George Sansom, *A History of Japan to 1334* (London: Cresset Press, 1958), 269–75.

23. Neil McMullin, "Historical and Historiographical Issues in the Study of Pre-Modern Japanese Religion," *Japanese Journal of Religious Studies* 16, no. 1 (1989): 17–18.

24. It did not simply mean a peculiar logic of aggression but often the obstinate and violent behavior of temple monks. See Allan G. Grapard, *The Protocol of the Gods* (Berkeley: University of California Press, 1992), 137.

25. *Nihon bungaku taikei* [Collection of Japanese Literature], vol. 15 (Tokyo: Kokumin Tosho, 1925), 325.

26. Tsuji, *Bukkyōshi: Jōsei-hen,* 884.

27. See Kuroda, *Kuroda Toshio Chosakushū,* 2:185–96.

28. Giovanni Boccaccio, *The Decameron,* trans. Mark Musa and Peter Bondanella (New York: Norton, 1982), 6.

29. Cf. William H. McNeill, *Plagues and Peoples* (Garden City, N.Y.: Anchor Press, 1976), 147–49.

30. Cf. Pierre Chaunu, *La mort à Paris* (Paris: Fayard, 1978), 28–59.

31. *The Poems of François Villon,* trans. Galway Kinnell (Boston: Houghton Mifflin, 1977), 53.

32. Cf. Philippe Ariès, *Western Attitudes toward Death: From the Middle Ages to the Present* (London: Johns Hopkins University Press, 1974), 33–39.

CHAPTER 2: THIS SIDE OF DESPAIR

1. Søren Kierkegaard, *The Sickness unto Death,* trans. Howard V. Hong (Princeton: Princeton University Press, 1980), 17–18.

2. There are fifteen biographies of him, not including those from the Muromachi period and after; the count puts him at the top of Japanese men and women of religion. All the biographies arose from within the Pure Land sect and were edited carefully for sectarian ends. But while texts such as *Genkū shōnin shinikki, Hōnen shōninden,* and *Chionkō shiki* were written by Hōnen's disciples only a few years after his death, a whole century had elapsed by the time *Hōnen shōnin gyōjyō ezu* was compiled. The differences in editorial strategies and methods of coloration create for us not only confusion but perspective—regarding their interrelationship as well as the relationship of each text to its own context. For detailed studies of Hōnen's biographies, see Mita Zenshin, *Seiritsushiteki Hōnen shōnin shoden no kenkyū* [The Study of the Development of Hōnen's Historical Biographies] (Kyoto: Kōnenji, 1966).

3. *Chūgai Nippō* [Chūgai Daily Times (Kyoto)], February 1, 1994, 10.

4. Genshin is in fact the reputed model of "the monk of Yokawa" in the Uji chapter of the *Tale of Genji*, but to what extent no one knows. See Shigematsu Nobuhiro, *Genji Monogatari no Bukkyō Shisō* [Buddhist Thought in the Tale of Genji] (Kyoto: Heirakuji Shoten, 1967), 8–26.

5. Genshin was the man of images, while Hōnen was the man of imagination, as we shall see. According to Foucault (*Dream and Existence*, trans. Forrest Williams [Atlantic Highlands, N.J.: Humanities Press, 1993], 71), "the image enables me to elude the real task of imagination. . . . That is why reflection kills the image, as perception does, whereas the one and the other reinforce and nourish imagination. . . . The image as fixation upon a quasi-presence is but the vertigo of imagination as it turns back toward the primordial meaning of presence. The image constitutes a ruse of consciousness in order to cease imagining, the moment of discouragement in the hard labor of imagining." As for the Heian aristocrats and death, perhaps fretting before its negative images was in fact easier than the "hard labor of imagining."

6. Genshin, *Eshin Sōzu Zenshū* [Collected Works of Abbot Eshin (Genshin)], vol. 1 (Kyoto: Hieizan Tosho Kankōjo, 1927), 683.

7. Ibid., 682.

8. "Strive to enter in by the narrow door: for many, I say unto you, shall seek to enter in, and shall not be able" (Luke 13:24).

9. See George Tanabe, *The Dreamkeeper: Fantasy and Knowledge in Early Kamakura Buddhism* (Cambridge, Mass.: Council on East Asian Studies, Harvard University, 1992), 137–41.

10. Hōryū, *Eshin Sōzu Eshiden* [Pictorial Biography of Abbot Eshin], vol. 2 (Tokyo: Ryūbunkan, 1989), 40.

11. "Introduction to *Purgatorio*," *The Divine Comedy*, trans. James Finn Cotter (New York: Amity House), 230.

12. Hayami Tasuku, *Jōdo Shinkō-ron* [Discourse on the Pure Land Belief] (Kyoto: Yūzankaku Shuppan, 1973), 164.

13. Karl Marx, "Letters from the *Franco-German Yearbooks*," in *Early Writings*, trans. Rodney Livingstone and Gregor Benton (New York: Penguin Books, 1974), 201.

14. Ibid., 208. In the next chapter, we will reconsider this point in closer detail.

15. William James, *The Varieties of Religious Experience* (New York: Macmillan, 1976), 78–142.

16. *Nomori Kagami*, in *Shinkō Gunsho ruijū* [Newly Edited Collection of Miscellaneous Materials], vol. 21 (Tokyo: Naigai Shoseki, 1930), 268.

17. "Zanmai Hottoku-ki" contains a foreword that indicates that the text was originally written by Hōnen himself and preserved by Seikanbō, one of his disciples. However, the original text was never recovered. See Mita, *Seiritsushiteki Hōnen shōnin shoden no kenkyū*, 42–43.

18. Foucault, *Dream and Existence*, trans. Williams, 59.

19. Given the fact that imagining the Pure Land means imagining death, Foucault's suggestion (ibid., 55) that "in every case death is the absolute meaning of the dream" resonates too. He is resuscitating the tradition of

dreams as prophecy (future) in order to combat Sigmund Freud's quasi-scientific relegation of dreams to individual traumata (past). However, the later Freud who sees the death instinct (a desire to return to undifferentiated being) at work in the "compulsion to repeat" should interest us, for Hōnen's imagination of death indeed involved a kind of repetition-compulsion: chanting *nembutsu* over and over. Cf. Sigmund Freud, *Beyond the Pleasure Principle*, trans. and ed. James Strachey (New York: Norton, 1961).

CHAPTER 3: IMAGINATION AND EXPERIENCE

1. Ōe Kenzaburō, "Geppō" [Monthly Newsletter], Sept. 1970, *NST,* vol. 6.

2. Michel Foucault, *Dream and Existence,* trans. Forrest Williams (Atlantic Highlands, N.J.: Humanities Press, 1993), 75.

3. Jacques Derrida, *Speech and Phenomena and Other Essays on Husserl's Theory of Signs,* trans. David B. Allison (Evanston: Northwestern University Press, 1973), 81.

4. Carl Jung, *Psychology and Alchemy,* trans. R. F. C. Hull (Princeton: Princeton University Press, 1968), 96.

5. "If it is true that the imagination circulates through a universe of images, it does not move to the extent that it promotes or reunites images, but to the extent that it destroys and consumes them. The imagination is in essence iconoclastic" (Foucault, *Dream and Existence,* trans. Williams, 72).

6. Carl G. Jung, *Psychology and Religion: West and East,* trans. R. F. C. Hull (Princeton: Princeton University Press, 1973), 559–60.

7. Jung's emphasis on the panhuman universality of the collective unconscious tempts the conscientious scholar, customarily and successfully, to abandon Jungian concepts altogether. We should remind ourselves, however, that there is a system of images, *in addition to* and *within* but never in exclusion of the material coordinates of existence, that can indeed be described as a collective unconscious—neither completely personal nor supremely universal but, rather, existing on the level of a family, an organization, a region, a nation, a cultural sphere, and so on. Instead of deriding Jung's concept of the collective unconscious, we should be prepared to reread his texts in the interest of constructively complicating theories of ideology.

8. As an aside, in Buddhist *yuishiki* (conscious-only) thought, there are concepts called *manashiki* (*manovijñāna*) and *arayashiki* (*ālayavijñāna*) that correspond to the personal and the collective unconscious respectively; *karma* is said to be rooted in the latter, which stores all memories, irrespective of time and space.

9. Carl G. Jung, *The Spirit in Man, Art, and Literature,* trans. R. F. C. Hull (Princeton: Princeton University Press, 1972), 82.

10. Yoshida Kenkō, *Essays in Idleness,* trans. Donald Keene (New York: Columbia University Press, 1967), 36.

11. If belief indeed has such a swaying performative function, the implication might be a radical relativism at odds with a positive ontology of paradise. Yet Hōnen was by no means a relativist; rather, he was thinking in a

realm where only intuition seems to lead us to a priori truths. In a sense, Hōnen was a positivist of the Pure Land, but not in the current epistemological sense of "positivism," the view that there is an objective reality unmediated by point of view. Hōnen was a positivist because he allowed the Pure Land to be posited as an inalienable idea in the psychological cosmos of individual human beings.

12. Dennis Hirota, *Plain Words on the Pure Land Way* (Kyoto: Ryūkoku University, 1989), 71.

13. Nakanishi Susumu, *Shinwaryoku* [The Power of Myth] (Tokyo: Ōfūsha, 1991), 18.

14. Slavoj Žižek, *The Sublime Object of Ideology* (London: Verso, 1989), might still be the most useful for the student of religion because it lays out the groundwork for the analysis of belief structures. It is not only possible but necessary to apply a "Western" concept like "signifier" to Japanese religious studies. Consider, for instance, the fact that deities were mass-produced through puns (the play of signifiers) in Edo: the ancient poet Hitomaro became the god of fire prevention simply because *hi tomaru* means "the fire ceases"; examples abound ad nauseum.

15. Ibid., 99.

16. We owe the term to Jacques Derrida. Cf. "The Double Session" in *Dissemination*, trans. Barbara Johnson (Chicago: University of Chicago Press, 1981).

17. "Reply to the Wife of Tarō Sanehide of Taiko," *HSZ*, 509.

18. Takagi Yukio, *Saichi Dōgyō* (Kyoto: Nagata Bunshōdō, 1991), 223.

19. See Daisetz Suzuki, *Japanese Spirituality* (New York: Greenwood Press, 1988), 167–213.

20. Gaston Bachelard, *Air and Dreams*, trans. E. R. Farrell and C. F. Farrell (Dallas: Dallas Institute of Humanities and Culture, 1983), 72.

21. Matsubara Taidō, *Dōgen* (Tokyo: Shūeisha, 1987), 176.

22. Kamata Shigeo, *Ippen* (Tokyo: Shūeisha, 1987), 40.

23. Yuasa Yasuo, *Nihon kodai no seishin sekai* [The Spiritual World of Ancient Japan] (Tokyo: Meicho Kankōkai, 1990), 279.

24. *Jōdo Bukkyō no shisō* [Pure Land Buddhist Thought], vol. 2, ed. Sueki Fumihiko (Tokyo: Kōdansha, 1992), 77.

25. Žižek, *Sublime Object of Ideology*, 104.

26. Yuasa Yasuo, *Shintai no Uchūsei* [The Cosmic Nature of Corporality] (Tokyo: Iwanami Shoten, 1994), 128.

CHAPTER 4: DEATH AND IMAGINATION

1. Mircea Eliade, *The Sacred and the Profane*, trans. Willard R. Trask (New York: Harcourt Brace Jovanovich, 1959), 63.

2. Nishida Kitarō, "Nihon bunka no mondai" [The Question of Japanese Culture], in *Nishida Kitarō Zenshū* [The Collected Works of Nishida Kitarō], 19 vols. (Tokyo: Iwanami Shoten, 1953–), 6:104. Such nationalistic tendencies were shared, in fact, by a vast majority of Japanese intellectuals, pre-

cisely in the form of a rhetoric of irony ("contradictory self-identity"). The collaborative stance and the rhetoric of irony were debatably of more than incidental affinity.

3. Nishida Kitarō, *Last Writings,* trans. David A. Dilworth (Honolulu: University of Hawaii Press, 1966), 106.

4. Takayama Tetsuo, *Nishida Tetsugaku* [The Philosophy of Nishida] (Tokyo: Iwanami Bunko, 1975), 292.

5. Nishida, *Last Writings,* 68.

6. Ibid., 78.

7. Michel Foucault, "Theatrum philosophicum," in *Language, Counter-memory, Practice,* ed. Donald F. Bouchard (Ithaca: Cornell University Press, 1977), 190. Foucault is in fact paraphrasing Gilles Deleuze—with a healthy dose of active imagination.

8. Nishida Kitarō, "Ronri to seimei" [Logic and Life], in *Nishida Kitarō Zenshū,* 8:324.

9. Nishida's sometimes precarious synthesis between modern European philosophy and medieval Japanese Buddhism is of immeasurable value insofar as the two domains might have more mechanisms of thought in common than we might like to admit. Such uncanny similarities menace our contemporary faith in absolute cultural difference.

10. Here we should recall another critical successor of Heidegger, namely Jacques Derrida. According to him, in the French language, "the ending *-ance* is undecided between active and passive. And we shall see why what is designated by 'differance' is neither simply active nor simply passive, that it announces or rather recalls something like the middle voice.... But philosophy has perhaps commenced by distributing the middle voice, expressing a certain intransitiveness, into the active and the passive voice, and has itself been constituted in this repression" ("Differance," in *Speech and Phenomena and Other Essays on Husserl's Theory of Signs,* trans. David B. Allison [Evanston: Northwestern University Press, 1977]), 137.

11. Nishida Kitarō, "Poeshisu to purakushisu" [Poesis and Praxis], in *Nishida Kitarō Zenshū,* 10:147.

12. Nishida, "Ronri to seimei," 8:364.

13. *Gyokuyō,* ed. Ichijima Kenkichi, vol. 3 (Tokyo: Kokusho Kankōkai, 1907), 944.

14. Ibid., 731.

15. Slavoj Žižek, *The Sublime Object of Ideology* (London: Verso, 1989), 43.

16. Mircea Eliade, *Shamanism: Archaic Techniques of Ecstasy* (Princeton: Princeton University Press, 1974), 24.

17. Georges Bataille, *Erotism: Death and Sensuality,* trans. Mary Dalwood (San Francisco: City Lights Books, 1986), 23–24. We must heed, however, the fact that Bataille himself complicates the schema: "In its vicissitudes eroticism appears to move away from its essence, which connects it with the nostalgia of lost continuity. Human life cannot follow the movement which draws it towards death without a shudder and without trying to cheat" (146).

18. Plato, *The Symposium*, trans. Walter Hamilton (New York: Penguin Books, 1980), 94.

CHAPTER 5: THE ETHIC OF INVERSION

1. *NKT*, 70:421–24.

2. Cf. David Hume, *A Treatise of Human Nature*, ed. L. A. Selby-Bigge, rev. P. H. Nidditch (Oxford: Oxford University Press, 1978), 165 and *passim*. "The several instances of resembling conjunctions lead us into the notion of power and necessity. These instances are in themselves totally distinct from each other, and have no union but in the mind, which observes them, and collect their ideas. Necessity, then, is the effect of this observation, and is nothing but an internal impression of the mind, or a determination to carry our thoughts from one object to another."

3. We are alluding to Gertrude Stein's eponymous work as well as to the Everyman plays of medieval England.

4. See James C. Dobbins, *Jōdō Shinshū: Shin Buddhism in Medieval Japan* (Bloomington: Indiana University Press, 1989), 47–78.

5. *Senchakushū*, chaps. 3, 4, 5, 6, and 12.

6. Robert E. Morrell, *Early Kamakura Buddhism* (Berkeley: Asian Humanities Press, 1987), 53.

7. Dōgen, "Shōbōgenzō Genjōkōan" [A Treasury of the Right Dharma Eye: Kōan in Reality], *Eastern Buddhist* 5, no. 2 (Oct. 1972): 134–35.

8. See Hayami Tasuku, *Heian Kizoku Shakai to Bukkyō* [Heian Aristocratic Society and Buddhism] (Tokyo: Yoshikawa Kōbunkan, 1975), 153.

CHAPTER 6: THE DEGENERATION OF DEATH

1. Nakamura Hajime, *Ways of Thinking of Eastern Peoples* (Honolulu: University of Hawaii Press, 1985), 362. Nakamura's work is more a compendium of various modes of thought in the East than a definition of Eastern thought as such.

2. Ienaga Saburō, *Nihon shisōshi ni okeru hitei no ronri no hattatsu* [The Development of the Logic of Negation in the Intellectual History of Japan] (Tokyo: Shinsensha, 1973), 90.

3. Dōgen, "Shōbōgenzō Genjōkōan" [A Treasury of the Right Dharma Eye: Kōan in Reality], *Eastern Buddhist* 5, no. 2 (Oct. 1972): 139; translation modified.

4. Shinran, *Tan'nishō* [Notes Lamenting Deviations] (Tokyo: Iwanami Shoten, 1969), 38.

5. *Kurata Hyakuzō Senshū*, vol. 7 (Tokyo: Daitō Shuppansha, 1948), 143.

6. Sueki Fumihiko, *Nihon bukkyōshi* [The History of Japanese Buddhism] (Tokyo: Shinchōsha, 1992), 140–64.

7. Ryūkoku University Translation Center, trans., *The Kyō Gyō Shin Shō* (Kyoto: Ryūkoku University, 1966), 89.

8. Walther von Loewenich, *Martin Luther: The Man and His Work*, trans. L. W. Denef (Minneapolis: Augsburg Publishing House, 1982), 78.

9. Ibid., 84.

10. Martin Luther, *D. Martin Luthers Werke: Kritische Gesamtausgabe,* vol. 2 (Weimar: Bohlau, 1883), 750.

11. Martin Luther, *Works of Martin Luther,* vol. 2 (Philadelphia: Muhlenberg Press, 1943), 58.

12. *Works of Martin Luther,* 2:248–54.

13. Žižek, among others, analyzes this paradox. Cf. Slavoj Žižek, *The Sublime Object of Ideology* (New York: Verso, 1989), 230.

14. Cf. Max Weber, *The Sociology of Religion* (Boston: Beacon Press, 1964), 166–83.

15. Masaru Sekine, *Ze-Ami and His Theories of Noh Drama* (Buckinghamshire: Colin Smythe, 1985), 90–91.

16. Yuasa Yasuo, *The Body: Toward an Eastern Mind–Body Theory,* trans. S. Nagatomo et al. (Albany: State University of New York Press, 1987), 105.

17. In Kanze Hideo, *Noh* (Tokyo: Sakuhinsha, 1990), 57.

18. Bernard Faure, *The Rhetoric of Immediacy: A Cultural Critique of Chan/Zen Buddhism* (Princeton: Princeton University Press, 1991), 180.

19. Ibid., 184.

20. Again, we must add that philosophical rhetoric of the Heideggerian brand did contribute to the totalitarian turn in the form of the Kyoto school.

21. Katō Seishin, "Daijō Bukkyō no Sensōkan" [The Mahāyāna Buddhist View on War], *Daihōrin* (Aug. 1938): 50.

22. D. W. Brackett, *Holy Terror: Armageddon in Tokyo* (New York: Weatherhill, 1996), 59–78.

23. Kuno Kyūran, "Bushidō no Shinzui" [The Essence of the Warrior's Spirit] *Daihōrin* (July 1942): 163.

24. *Watsuji Tetsurō Zenshū,* vol. 12 (Tokyo: Iwanami Shoten, 1962), 307–23.

APPENDIX: BIBLIOGRAPHICAL SOURCES

1. Tōdō Kyōshun and Itō Yuishin, "Hōnen shōnin shippitsu ruijū kaisetsu" [Commentary on Hōnen's Hand-written Materials], in *Hōnen shōnin kenkyū* [A Study of Master Hōnen], ed. Bukkyō daigaku Hōnen shōnin kenkyū-kai (Tokyo: Ryūbun-kan, 1975), 539–60.

2. I am following Ishii Kyōdō's *Shōwa shinshū Hōnen shōnin zenshū* [The Collected Works of Master Hōnen] (Kyoto: Heirakuji Shoten, 1955).

3. Tamura Enchō, *Hōnen shōnin-den no kenkyū* [A Study of Biographies of Master Hōnen] (Kyoto: Hōzō-kan, 1972), 57. The biographies, moreover, tell of mystic phenomena occasioned by the "embodiment of Seishi bosatsu (Mahāsthamaprapta)." Here are some examples: when Hōnen was born, two white flags descended from heaven as an omen; whenever Hōnen opened Buddhist texts at night, the light radiating from his head illuminated his room; when he was reading the *Avataṃsaka Sūtra,* a snake crawled onto his desk to listen to his teachings. One of the senior disciples who witnessed this

last incident had a dream in which the snake confessed that it was actually a blue dragon, Hōnen's guardian spirit. Also see Mita Zenshin, *Seiritsushiteki Hōnen shōnin-den no Kenkyū* [The Study of the Development of Hōnen's Historical Biographies] (Kyoto: Kōnen-ji, 1966), 117–22.

   4. This categorization is based on Tamura Enchō's *Hōnen to sono jidai* [Hōnen and His Times] (Kyoto: Hōzō-kan, 1982), 55–67.

   5. Tamura, *Hōnen shōnin-den no kenkyū,* 9–11.

Glossary

Aizen Myōō 愛染明王 (Skt. Rāga Vidyārāja, the God of Love)
Akashi Gen'nai Musha Sadaaki 明石源内武者定明
Akikonomu 秋好
akunin shōki 悪人正機 (the idea that the evil person is the primary object of Amida's vow to save sentient beings)
akusō 悪僧 (malicious monks)
Amakasu Tarō Tadatsuna 甘糟太郎忠綱
Angen 安元
Anraku 安楽
Aoi-no-ue 葵上
arubeki yōwa あるべきやうは (that which is appropriate)
asa daimoku, yū nembutsu 朝題目、夕念仏 (*daimoku* chants in the morning, *nembutsu* chants in the evening)
Asahara Saichi 浅原才一
Asuka 飛鳥
Atago 愛宕
Aum Shinrikyō オウム真理教
Awa 阿波
Azuma kagami 吾妻鏡
basho 場所 (topos, place)
Ben kenmitsu nikyōron 弁顕密二教論
bessho 別所 (a secluded place)
bessōkan 別相観
Betsuji nembutsu 別時念仏 (intensive *nembutsu* practice)
Bettō Chōen 別当長円
biwa 琵琶 (a Japanese mandolin)
bonbu 凡夫 (an ordinary man)
bukkō zanmai 仏光三昧 (concentration on the radiance of the Buddha)
buppō 仏法 (Dharma)
burakumin 部落民 (outcasts)
bushi 武士
Butsumyō 仏名
Buzan 豊山
byakugōsō 白毫相 (the white curl between the Buddha's eyebrows)
Chion'in 知恩院
Chionkō shiki 智恩講私記

177

Chōgen 重源
chōjishū 長時修 (sustained *nembutsu* practice)
Chōrakuji 長楽寺
Chōsai 長西
chūin 中陰 (purgatory)
chūu 中有 (the synonym of chūin)
Dainichi 大日 (Skt. Mahāvairocana)
daishakunetsu jigoku 大灼熱地獄 (the great inferno)
Daitōa Kyōeiken 大東亜共栄圏 (the Greater East Asian Co-Prosperity Sphere)
Daochuo 道綽
Dazaifu 太宰府
Dōgen 道元
Eiga monogatari 栄華物語
Eikū 叡空
Eisai 栄西
Eishō 永承
Eison 叡尊
en 縁 (karmic relation)
Enchin 円珍
Ennin 円仁
Enryakuji 延暦寺
Fa-chao 法照
Fudōson 不動尊
Fugen 普賢
Fujiwara Michinaga 藤原道長
Fujiwara Sukefusa 藤原資房
fukansō 普観想
Fukuhara 福原
Fūshikaden 風姿花伝
futettei 不徹底 (not thorough enough)
gebon geshō 下品下生 (the lowest grade of the lowest class)
Gedatsubō Jōkei 解脱坊貞慶
Genkū shōnin shinikki 源空上人私日記
Genkyū 元久
Genpei seisuiki 源平盛衰記
Genshin 源信
gensō 還相 (return from the Pure Land)
gidan 疑団 (the great doubt)
Gion 祇園
Godan mizuho 五壇御修法
Goe nembutsu 五会念仏
gojisō 護持僧 (a monk who is hired to hold religious services)
Gotoba 後鳥羽
gu 愚 (ignorance, stupidity)
gudon-nembutsu 愚鈍念仏 (*nembutsu* for the ignorant)

Gukanshō 愚管抄

Gutoku hitan jikkai 愚禿悲嘆述懐

Gyakushū seppō 逆修説法

Gyōgen 行玄

Gyokuyō 玉葉

Gyōnen 凝念

Hagakure 葉隠

hakkudoku suisōkan 八功徳水想観

hana 花 (flower)

Hanju zanmaikyō 般舟三昧経 (Skt. Pratyutpannasamādhi Sūtra)

Hata 秦

Heian 平安

Heiankyō 平安京

Heiji 平治

Heijyōkyō 平城京

henjō nanshi 変成男子 (transforming a woman into a man)

henkan issai shikishinsō 遍観一切色身想

Hie 日吉

Hiei 比叡

Higashiyama 東山

Hino 日野

Hi-no-kimi 火君

Hōgen monogatari 保元物語

Hōjōki 方丈記

Hōjō Masako 北条政子

Honchō shinsenden 本朝神仙伝

Hōnenbō Genkū 法然坊源空

Hōnen shōninden 法然上人伝

Hōnen shōnin gyōjō ezu 法然上人行状絵図

Hōnen to Shinran no shinkō 法然と親鸞の信仰

hongan 本願 (Amida's Eighteenth Vow: "If, after I have attained Buddhahood, all sentient beings of sincere mind and serene faith who wish to be born in my country cannot do so even after ten *nembutsu* recitations, may I not attain perfect enlightenment—excepted are those who commit the five deadly sins and abuse the true law.")

hōni dōri 法爾道理 (the reality of Dharma-nature)

honji-suijaku 本地垂迹 (incarnations of Buddhas and bodhisattvas as Shinto gods)

honzon 本尊 (the main Buddha)

Hotsu mujōshin 発無上心 (Awakening the highest mind)

Hōzō 法蔵

ichijō 一乗 (the one vehicle: the single path to enlightenment to be taken by all living beings)

Ichimai kishōmon 一枚起請文

Ichinengi chōji kishōmon 一念義停止起請文

igyō ōjō 易行往生 (rebirth by an easy practice)

Ikkō 一向

Ippyaku shijūgo kajō mondō 一百四十五箇条問答

Issaikyō 一切経

Iwashimizu hachiman 岩清水八幡

Izumi shikibushū 和泉式部集

Jien 慈円

jigoku hitsujō 地獄必定 (doomed to hell)

jigoku ni hotoke 地獄に仏 (encountering the Buddha in the midst of hell)

jihi 慈悲 (compassion)

Jikkaishō 述懐鈔

jinen hōni 自然法爾 (naturalness and Dharma-nature)

jiriki 自力 (self power)

Jishō 治承

jisōkan 地想観

jissō-nembutsu 実相念仏 (*nembutsu* in contemplation of the truth)

jizō 地蔵 (Skt. Ksitigarbha, a bodhisattva who saves suffering beings in the evil realms; especially popular as the savior of the souls of dead children)

Jōdo 浄土 (Pure Land)

Jōgyō zanmai 常行三昧 (one of the four meditative practices of the Tendai sect, it requires walking around a statue of Amida Buddha for ninety days while calling his name and thinking of him)

Jōkyū 承久

Jōzenkan 定善観 (the contemplation on the good defined in the *Kanmuryō-jukyō*)

Jūren 住蓮

juso 呪詛 (curse)

jusōkan 樹想観

Jūun 重雲

kaimyō 戒名 (a posthumous name)

Kaiten 回天

kami 神 (deity)

Kamigamo 上賀茂

Kamikaze 神風 (divine winds)

Kamo 賀茂

Kamo-no-Chōmei 鴨長明

Kan'ami 観阿弥

Kan daiseishi shikishinsō 観大勢至色身想

Kangakue 勧学会

kanjin hijiri 勧進聖 (fund-raising itinerant monks)

Kan kan'non bosatsu shinjitsu shikishinsō 観観音菩薩真実色身想

Kanmuryōjukyō (Kuan wu-liang-shou ching) 観無量寿経

kansatsu 観察 (observation)

kansō 観想（相） (contemplation)

kanzen chōaku 勧善懲悪 (recommending of the good and correcting the evil)

karaoke カラオケ

Karoku 嘉禄

Kasuga Daimyōjin hotsuganmon 春日大明神発願文
katachi 形 (form)
Ken'ei 建永
Kenkyū 建久
kenmitsu 顕密 (exoteric and esoteric Buddhism)
Kenryaku 建暦
kensyō 見性 (Zen experience of enlightenment)
kesa 袈裟 (robe)
kezasō 華座想
kikōhō (qi-gong) 気功法 (a breathing method for enhancing one's internal
    energy)
Kinpu 金峯
Kishū 紀州 (current Wakayama prefecture)
Kiso Yoshinaka 木曾義仲
Kisshōten 吉祥天
Kitadani 北谷
Kita-no-Mandokoro 北政所
Kitano tenjin engi 北野天神縁起
Kiyomizudera 清水寺
Kōchi 高知
koe 声 (voice)
Kōfukuji sōjō 興福寺奏上
Kōkei 康慶
Kokin chomonjū 古今著聞集
kokoro 心 (mind)
Kokuzō gumonji no hō 虚空蔵求聞持法
Kōmyō shingon dosha kaji 光明真言土砂加持
Konjaku monogatari 今昔物語
Konkai Kōmyōji 金戒光明寺
Kōsai 幸西
Kose Hirotaka 巨勢広高
Kōsō wasan 高僧和讃
koto 琴 (a Japanese harp)
kotodama 言霊 (the spirit in words)
Kōzen gokokuron 興禅護国論
Kuan ching shu (Kangyōsho) 観経疏
kugyōshū 恭敬修 (pious *nembutsu* practice)
kuhon 九品 (the nine grades of aspirants to Amida)
Kujō Kanezane 九条兼実
Kumagai Naozane 熊谷直実
Kumano 熊野
Kurikara 倶利伽羅
Kurodani 黒谷
Kusharon (Abhidharma-kosa-bhāsya) 倶舎論
Kyōgyōshinshō 教行信証
Kyōkai 景戒

kyōkan jigoku 叫喚地獄 (the hell of agonizing shrieks)

Kyōtai 教待

makyō 魔境 (a psychological stage in which a Zen practitioner experiences demonic illusions)

Mappō tōmyōki 末法灯明記

Mattōshō 末燈鈔

Minamoto Shigezane 源重実

Minamoto Tameyoshi 源為義

Minamoto Yoritomo 源頼朝

Minō 箕面

Miroku 弥勒 (Maitreya)

Mondōhen 問答篇

mono もの (an entity or a spirit)

monogatari 物語 (stories)

monogurui 物狂 (madness)

Mononobe 物部

mononoke 物怪 (evil spirits)

Monshoshū 聞書集

Motoori Norinaga 本居宣長

Mugen Noh 夢幻能 (plays of dreams and phantasms)

Mujōin 無常院

Mujū 無住

mukenshū 無間修 (poseless *nembutsu* practice)

mumyō 無明 (ignorance)

Murasaki-no-ue 紫の上

muyoshū 無余修 (unmixed *nembutsu* practice)

Myōe Kōben 明恵高弁

Myōjō raieisu 明星来影す (Venus enters into oneself)

myōkōnin 妙好人

myōsō 明相 (a sign of luminosity)

Myōzen Hōin 明禅法印

Nagaokakyō 長岡京

namu Amida butsu 南無阿弥陀仏

namu saihō gokuraku sekai, mimyō jōdodaiji daihi, Amida, Kan'non, Seishi, shobosatsu, shōjō daikaishū 南無西方極楽世界、微妙浄土大慈大悲阿蔓陀観音勢至諸菩薩清浄大海衆

nanto-hokurei 南都北嶺 (the capital in the south and the mountain in the north; Buddhist temples in Nara and Mount Hiei)

nembutsu hijiri 念仏聖 (unofficial monks who specialize in *nembutsu* practice)

nembutsu zanmai 念仏三昧 (concentration on *nembutsu*)

Nembutsu ōjōyōgishō 念仏往生要義抄

Nembutsu ōjōgi 念仏往生義

nen 念 (an idea)

Nenchū gyōji emaki 年中行事絵巻

Nichiren 日蓮

Nihon-koku genpō zen-aku ryōiki 日本国現報善悪霊異記

Nihon ōjō gokurakuki 日本往生極楽記

Nihon ryōiki 日本霊異記

Nihon shoki 日本書紀 (the Chronicle of Japan)

Nijūgo zanmaie 二十五三昧会

Ninshō 忍性

Nishiyama 西山

nishu ekō 二種廻向 (two kinds of blessings, propulsion to the Pure Land and therefrom)

Niso taimen 二祖対面 (the encounter of two patriarchs, namely, Shan-tao and Hōnen)

nissōkan 日想観 (the contemplation of the setting sun)

Nomori kagami 野守鏡

nyoraizō (tathāgata-garbha) 如来蔵 (the Buddhahood contained in a sentient being)

nyosōnen 如想念 (freely willed contemplation)

Ōhara 大原

Ojiba 御磁場

Ōjō jōdo yōjinshū 往生浄土用心集

Ōjō raisan 往生礼賛

Ōjōyōshū 往生要集

Ōkagami 大鏡

Ōmi 近江

Onjyōji 圓城寺

onmyōdō 陰陽道 (divinations based on the Taoist religious idea that the opposing or complementary forces of the universe must be harmonized)

onmyōshi 陰陽師

Onna Sannomiya 女三の宮

onri edo, gongu jōdo 厭離穢土、欣求浄土 (to detest the defiled world and to yearn for the Pure Land)

oroka 愚か (silly, absurd)

raigō 来迎 (Amida and bodhisattvas welcoming a *nembutsu* practitioner)

rikudōe 六道絵 (the picture depicting the six paths of hell, hungry spirits, animals, *asuras*, men, and heavenly beings)

rinjū shōnen 臨終正念 (right thoughts on one's deathbed, thinking rebirth in Pure Land)

Rinzai 臨済

rironteki 理論的 (theoretical)

Risshō ankoku-ron 立正安国論

rokuji raisan 六時礼讃 (hymns in praise of Amida to be chanted at six different hours of the day)

Rokujō Miyasu-dokoro 六条御息所

ropparamitsu (rokuharamitsu) 六波羅密 (the six kinds of practice by which a bodhisattva attains Buddhahood: charity, observing precepts, perseverance, energy, meditation, and wisdom)

Ryōben 良弁

Ryōnin 良忍
Ryūkan 隆寛
Saga Seiryōji 嵯峨青龍寺
Saichō 最澄
Saigyō 西行
Saihō shinanshō 西方指南抄
Saitō 西塔
Sangō shīki 三教指帰
sanji sanbō-rai 三時三宝礼 (worshiping the Three Treasures, Buddha, Dharma, and priests, three times a day)
Sankaiki 山槐記
Sankyō gisho 三経義疏
sanmitsu 三密 (the bodily, verbal, and mental mystic practices)
Sanshin ryōken oyobi gohōji 三心料簡及び御法事
Sanuki 讃岐 (current Kagawa prefecture)
Sanzu 三途 (the three lowest states of existence: the realms of fire, blood, and the sword)
Seikō 聖光
Seishi bosatsu (Mahāthāmaprāpta) 勢至菩薩
Seishi-maru 勢至丸
Sei Shōnagon 清少納言
senchaku hairyū 選択廃立 (option and exclusion)
Senchaku hongan nembutsushū 選択本願念仏集
senju-nembutsu 専修念仏 (exclusive-*nembutsu*)
Sen no Rikyū 千利休
Sesshu-fusha mandara 摂取不捨曼荼羅
Settsu Katsuoji 摂津勝尾寺
Shantao 善導
Shasekishū 沙石集
Shichikajō seikai (kishōmon) 七箇条制誡 (起請文)
shidosō 私度僧 (privately ordained monks)
Shiga 滋賀
Shijū hakkanden 四十八巻伝
Shiju in'nen-shū 私聚因縁集
Shimogamo 下賀茂
shin 信 (faith)
shinbutsu shūgō 神仏習合 (the combination of Shintoism and Buddhism)
shin'en 親縁 (parental relationships)
shinjin datsuraku 身心脱落 (physical and mental dilapidation)
Shinkū 信空
Shinkū Shōnin densetsu no kotoba 信空上人伝説の詞
Shinran 親鸞
Shinshō 真性
shinwa-ryoku 神話力 (power of myth)
shira 尸羅 (Skt. sīla, precepts)
Shirakawa 白河

shite シテ (the protagonist in Noh plays)

shōbō 正法 (a proper Dharma)

Shōbōgenzō 正法眼蔵

shōdai jōbutsu 唱題成仏 (becoming a Buddha through the recitation of *daimoku*)

shōen 荘園 (estates owned by aristocrats, warriors, and temples)

Shōji 正治

shōji o hanaru 生死を離る (leaving behind the world of life and death)

Shōkū 証空

Shoku nihon kōki 続日本後紀

shōsoku 消息 (correspondences)

Shugendō 修験道 (mountaineering asceticism)

Shugo kokka-ron 守護国家論

shukke 出家 (to be ordained; literally, leave home)

Shunjō 俊乗

Shunki 春記

shura 修羅 (the battlefield of the *asura* against Indra)

Soga 蘇我

sokushin jōbutsu 即身成仏 (becoming a Buddha with one's body)

sōshiki bukkyō 葬式仏教 (funeral Buddhism)

sōsōkan 惣相観 (the contemplation of the whole image of Amida)

suisōkan 水想観 (the contemplation of water)

Sujaku 朱雀

sumie 墨絵 (black-ink paintings)

Sumiyoshi 住吉

Sutoku 崇徳

Tadamori 忠盛

Taira-no-Kiyomori 平清盛

Taira-no-Shigehira 平重衡

Taira-no-Shigehisa 平重久

Taira-no-Shigekuni 平重国

Takao 高雄

tanengi 多念義 (the doctrine that recommends many recitations of *nembutsu*)

T'anluan 曇鸞

Tan'nishō 歎異抄 (*Notes Lamenting Deviations*)

Taoch'o 道綽

tariki 他力 (other power)

Tateyama 立山

Teikyū Daitoku 貞久大徳

Tendai Enton 天台円頓

tengu 天狗 (a long-nosed goblin)

Tenri 天理

Tōdaiji jū-mondō 東大寺十問答

Toga-no-o Myōe shōnin yuikun 栂尾明恵上人遺訓

Tōji 東寺

ton-se 遁世 / 貪世 (retirement from the world/ravenous appetite for the world)

Tosa 土佐 (current Kōchi prefecture)

Toyama 富山

Tsurezure gusa 徒然草 (*Essays in Idleness*)

Uji 宇治

Unkei 運慶

Uruma Tokikuni 漆間時国

Wang-sheng li-tsan chieh (Ōjō raisange) 往生礼讃偈

wasan 和讃 (Buddhist hymns)

Wutai 五台

Yakushiji 薬師寺

Yakushimaru 薬師丸

Yamagoe no Amida 山越阿弥陀

Yamashina dōri 山階道理

yamatoe 大和絵

Yasaka 八坂

yin-yang 陰陽

Yokawa shuryōgon'in nijūgo zanmai kechien kakochō 横川首楞厳院廿五三昧結縁過去帳

Yoshida Kenkō 吉田兼好 (c. 1330, author of *Essays in Idleness*)

Yoshimizu 吉水

Yoshishige-no-Yasutane 慶滋保胤

Yōwa 養和

Yuasa Muneshige 湯浅宗重

Yuikyōgyō 遺教経

Zaijarin shōgonki 摧邪輪荘厳記

zaike 在家 (laypeople; literally, stay-at-home)

zanmai hottoku 三昧発得 (mystic experience due to concentrated meditation)

Zeami 世阿弥 (c. 1364–1443, actor-author who wrote not only Noh plays but also treatises on the theater)

zettai tariki 絶対他力 (absolute other power)

zōaku muge 造悪無礙 (to commit evil acts heedlessly)

zōbō 像法 (semblance Dharma)

zōkan 像観

zōryakukan 雑略観

Bibliography

Ariès, Philippe. *Western Attitudes towards Death: From the Middle Ages to the Present*. London: Johns Hopkins University Press, 1974.

Artaud, Antonin. "Le théâtre et la peste." In *Le Théâtre et son double*. Paris: Gallimard, 1964.

Bachelard, Gaston. *Air and Dreams*. Translated by E. R. Farrell and C. F. Farrell. Dallas: Dallas Institute of Humanities and Culture, 1983.

Barthes, Roland. "The Death of the Author." In *Image, Music, Text*, translated by Stephen Heath. New York: Noonday Press, 1977.

Bataille, Georges. *Erotism: Death and Sensuality*. Translated by Mary Dalwood. San Francisco: City Lights Books, 1986.

Boccaccio, Giovanni. *The Decameron*. Translated by Mark Musa and Peter Bondanella. New York: Norton, 1982.

Brackett, D. W. *Holy Terror: Armageddon in Tokyo*. New York: Weatherhill, 1996.

Chaunu, Pierre. *La mort à Paris*. Paris: Fayard, 1978.

Coates, Harper H., and Ryūgaku Ishizuka. *Hōnen the Buddhist Saint: His Life and Teaching*. Kyoto: Society for the Publication of Sacred Books of the World, 1949.

Collcutt, Martin. Review of *Buddhism and the State in Sixteenth-Century Japan* by Neil McMullin. *Journal of Japanese Studies* 12 (1986): 403–12.

Dante. *The Divine Comedy*. Translated by James Finn Cotter. New York: Amity House, 1987.

DeLillo, Don. *White Noise*. New York: Penguin Books, 1984.

Derrida, Jacques. *Dissemination*. Translated by Barbara Johnson. Chicago: University of Chicago Press, 1981.

————. *Of Grammatology*. Translated by Gayatri Spivak. Baltimore: Johns Hopkins University Press, 1974.

————. *Specters of Marx*. Translated by Peggy Kamuf. New York: Routledge, 1995.

————. *Speech and Phenomena and Other Essays on Husserl's Theory of Signs*. Translated by David B. Allison. Evanston: Northwestern University Press, 1973.

Dobbins, James C. *Jōdo Shinshū: Shin Buddhism in Medieval Japan*. Bloomington: Indiana University Press, 1989.

Dōgen. *Shōbōgenzō*. Translated by Norman Wadell and Abe Masao. *Eastern Buddhist* 5, no. 2 (October 1972): 129–40.

Eliade, Mircea. *The Sacred and the Profane*. Translated by Willard R. Trask. New York: Harcourt Brace Jovanovich, 1959.

————. *Shamanism: Archaic Techniques of Ecstasy.* Princeton: Princeton University Press, 1974.

Faure, Bernard. *The Rhetoric of Immediacy: A Cultural Critique of Chan/Zen Buddhism.* Princeton: Princeton University Press, 1991.

Foucault, Michel. *Dream and Existence.* Translated by Forrest Williams. Atlantic Highlands, N.J.: Humanities Press, 1993.

————. *Language, Countermemory, Practice.* Edited by Donald F. Bouchard. Ithaca: Cornell University Press, 1977.

Freud, Sigmund. *Beyond the Pleasure Principle.* Translated by James Strachey. New York: Norton, 1961.

Fujiwara Sukefusa. *Shunki* [Spring Record]. In *Shiryō Taisei* [The Collection of Historical Documents], vol. 7. Kyoto: Rinsen Shoten, 1974.

Genshin. *Eshin Sōzu Zenshū* [Collected Works of Abbot Eshin (Genshin)], vol. 1. Kyoto: Hieizan Tosho Kankōjo, 1927.

Grapard, Allan G. *The Protocol of the Gods.* Berkeley: University of California Press, 1992.

Gutiérrez, Gustavo. *A Theology of Liberation: History, Politics, and Liberation.* Translated by Sister Caridad Inda and John Eagleson. New York: Orbis Books, 1973.

Hayami Tasuku. *Heian Kizoku Shakai to Bukkyō.* Tokyo: Yoshikawa Kōbunkan, 1975.

————. *Jōdo Shinkō-ron* [Discourse on the Pure Land Belief]. Kyoto: Yūzankaku Shuppan, 1973.

Heidegger, Martin. "The Origin of the Work of Art." In *Poetry, Language, Thought,* translated by Albert Hofstadter. New York: Harper and Row, 1971.

Hirota, Dennis. *Plain Words on the Pure Land Way.* Kyoto: Ryūkoku University, 1989.

Hisano Kyūran. "Bushidō no Shinzui." *Daihōrin* (July 1942).

Hōryū. *Eshin Sōzu Eshiden* [Pictorial Biography of Abbot Eshin], vol. 2. Tokyo: Ryūbunkan, 1989.

Hume, David. *A Treatise of Human Nature.* Edited by L. A. Selby-Bigge, rev. P. H. Nidditch. Oxford: Oxford University Press, 1978.

Hurst, G. Cameron III. *INSEI: Abdicated Sovereigns in the Politics of Late Heian Japan, 1086–1185.* New York: Columbia University Press, 1976.

Ienaga Saburō. *Nihon shisōshi ni okeru hitei no ronri no hattatsu* [The Development of the Logic of Negation in Japanese Intellectual History]. Tokyo: Shinsensha, 1973.

Ishida Mizumaro, ed. *Shinran zenshū.* Tokyo: Shunjūsha, 1986.

Ishii Kyōdō. *Shōwa shinshū Hōnen shōnin zenshū* [The Collected Works of Master Hōnen]. Kyoto: Heirakuji shoten, 1955.

Itō Yoshio, ed. *Saigyō Hōshi Zenkashū.* Tokyo: Daiichi Shobō, 1987.

James, William. *The Varieties of Religious Experience.* New York: Macmillan, 1976.

Jung, Carl G. *Psychology and Alchemy.* Translated by R. F. C. Hull. Princeton: Princeton University Press, 1968.

————. *Psychology and Religion: West and East.* Translated by R. F. C. Hull. Princeton: Princeton University Press, 1973.

————. *The Spirit in Man, Art, and Literature.* Translated by R. F. C. Hull. Princeton: Princeton University Press, 1972.

Kamata Shigeo. *Ippen.* Tokyo: Shūeisha, 1987.

Kanda Chisato. *Ikkō Ikki to Shinshū shinko.* Tokyo: Yoshikawa Kōbunkan, 1991.

Kanze Hideo. *Noh.* Tokyo: Sakuhinsha, 1990.

Katō Seishin. "Daijō Bukkyō no Sensōkan" [The Mahāyāna Buddhist View of War]. *Daihōrin* (August 1938).

Katō Shūichi. "Jūsan-seiki no Shisō" [Thought in the Thirteenth Century]. In *Katō Shūichi Chosakushū,* vol. 3. Tokyo: Heibonsha, 1978.

Kierkegaard, Søren. *The Sickness unto Death.* Translated by Howard V. Hong. Princeton: Princeton University Press, 1980.

Kozol, Jonathan. *Amazing Grace: The Lives of Children and the Conscience of a Nation.* New York: Crown Publishers, 1985.

Kujō Kanezane. *Gyokuyō,* vols. 2 and 3. Edited by Ichikawa Kenkichi. Tokyo: Kokusho Kankōkai, 1907.

Kurata Hyakuzō. *Kurata Hyakuzō Senshū,* vol. 7. Tokyo: Daitō Shuppansha, 1948.

Kuroda Toshio. *Kuroda Toshio Chosakushū,* vol. 2. Kyoto: Hōzōkan, 1994.

Loewenich, Walther von. *Martin Luther: The Man and His Work.* Translated by L. W. Denef. Minneapolis: Augsburg Publishing House, 1982.

Lukács, Georg. *History and Class Consciousness: Studies in Marxist Dialectics.* Translated by Rodney Livingstone. Cambridge, Mass.: MIT Press, 1972.

Luther, Martin. *D. Martin Luthers Werke: Kritische Gesamtausgabe.* Weimar: Bohlau, 1883.

————. *Works of Martin Luther,* vol. 2. Philadelphia: Muhlenberg Press, 1943.

Marx, Karl. *Early Writings.* Translated by Rodney Livingstone and Gregor Benton. New York: Penguin Books, 1974.

Matsubara Taidō. *Dōgen.* Tokyo: Shūeisha, 1987.

McCullough, Helen, trans. *The Tale of the Heike.* Stanford: Stanford University Press, 1988.

McMullin, Neil. *Buddhism and the State in Sixteenth-Century Japan.* Princeton: Princeton University Press, 1984.

————. "Historical and Historiographical Issues in the Study of Pre-Modern Japanese Religion." *Japanese Journal of Religious Studies* 16, no. 1 (1989): 3–40.

McNeill, William H. *Plagues and Peoples.* Garden City, N.Y.: Anchor Press, 1976.

Mita Zenshin. *Seiritsushiteki Hōnen shōnin shoden no kenkyū* [The Study of the Development of Hōnen's Historical Biographies]. Kyoto: Kōnenji, 1966.

Morrell, Robert E. *Early Kamakura Buddhism.* Berkeley: Asian Humanities Press, 1987.

Morris, Ivan, trans. *The Pillow Book of Sei Shōnagon.* New York: Columbia University Press, 1991.

Nakamura Hajime. *Ways of Thinking of Eastern Peoples.* Honolulu: University of Hawaii Press, 1985.

Nakanishi Susumu. *Shinwaryoku* [The Power of Myth]. Tokyo: Ōfūsha, 1991.
Nihon bungaku taikei [Collection of Japanese Literature], vol. 15. Tokyo: Kokumin Tosho, 1925.
Nishida Kitarō. *Last Writings.* Translated by David A. Dilworth. Honolulu: University of Hawaii Press, 1966.
―――. *Nishida Kitarō Zenshū* [The Collected Works of Nishida Kitarō]. 19 vols. Tokyo: Iwanami Shoten, 1953–.
Nomori Kagami. In *Shinkō Gunsho Ruijū* [Newly Edited Collection of Miscellaneous Materials], vol. 21. Tokyo: Naigai Shoseki, 1930.
Ōe Kenzaburō. "Geppō [Monthly Newsletter]," September 1970, *Nihon shisō taikei,* vol. 6. Tokyo: Iwanami shoten, 1970.
Plato. *The Symposium.* Translated by Walter Hamilton. New York: Penguin Books, 1980.
Ryūkoku Translation Center, trans. *The Kyō Gyō Shin Shō* [Teaching, Practice, Faith, and Enlightenment]. Kyoto: Ryūkoku University, 1966.
Saichō. *Dengyō Daishi Zenshū* [The Collected Works of Master Dengyō], vol. 1. Tokyo: Sekai Seiten Kankō Kyōkai, 1989.
Sansom, George. *A History of Japan to 1334.* London: Cresset Press, 1958.
Seidensticker, Edward G. trans. *The Tale of Genji.* New York: Alfred Knopf, 1992.
Sekine, Masaru. *Ze-Ami and His Theories of Noh Drama.* Buckinghamshire: Colin Smythe, 1985.
Shigematsu Nobuhiro. *Genji Monogatari no Bukkyō Shisō* [Buddhist Thought in the Tale of Genji]. Kyoto: Heirakuji Shoten, 1967.
Shinran. *Tan'nishō* [Notes Lamenting Deviations]. Tokyo: Iwanami Shoten, 1969.
Stone, Jacqueline. "Rebuking the Enemies of the Lotus: Nichirenist Exclusivism in Historical Perspective." Parts 1 and 2. *Japanese Journal of Religious Studies* 21, nos. 2–3 (1994): 231–59.
Sueki Fumihiko. *Nihon bukkyōshi* [The History of Japanese Buddhism]. Tokyo: Shinchōsha, 1992.
―――. *Nihon bukkyō shisōshi ronkō* [The Discourse on the Intellectual History of Japanese Buddhism]. Tokyo: Daizō Shuppan, 1993.
Sueki Fumihiko and Kajiyama Yuichi, eds., *Jōdo bukkyō no shisō,* vol. 2. Tokyo: Kōdansha, 1992.
Suzuki, Daisetz. *Japanese Spirituality.* New York: Greenwood Press, 1988.
Taira Masayuki. *Nihon chūsei no shakai to bukkyō.* Tokyo: Haniwa Shobō, 1992.
Takagi Yukio. *Saichi Dōgyō.* Kyoto: Nagata Bunshōdō, 1991.
Takayama Tetsuo. *Nishida Tetsugaku* [The Philosophy of Nishida]. Tokyo: Iwanami Bunko, 1975.
Tamura, Enchō. *Hōnen.* Tokyo: Yoshikawa Kōbun-kan, 1988.
―――. *Hōnen shōnin-den no kenkyū* [A Study of Biographies of Master Hōnen]. Kyoto: Hōzō-kan, 1972.
―――. *Hōnen to sono jidai* [Hōnen and His Times]. Kyoto: Hōzō-kan, 1982.
Tanabe, George. *The Dreamkeeper: Fantasy and Knowledge in Early Kamakura Buddhism.* Cambridge, Mass.: Council on East Asian Studies, Harvard University, 1992.

Tōdō Kyōshun, et al. "Hōnen shōnin shippitsu ruijū kaisetsu" [Commentary on Hōnen's Hand-written Materials]. In *Hōnen shōnin kenkyū* [A Study of Master Hōnen], edited by Bukkyō daigaku Hōnen shōnin kenkyū-kai. Tokyo: Ryūbun-kan, 1975.

Tsuji Zen'nosuke. *Bukkyōshi: Jōsei-hen* [The History of Buddhism: Ancient]. Tokyo: Iwanami, 1944.

Umehara Takeshi. "Hōnen." *Chūgai Nippō* [Chūgai Daily Times (Kyoto)], February 1, 1994.

Villon, François. *The Poems of François Villon.* Translated by Galway Kinnell. Boston: Houghton Mifflin, 1977.

Watsuji Tetsurō. *Watsuji Tetsurō Zenshū.* Tokyo: Iwanami Shoten, 1962.

Weber, Max. *The Sociology of Religion.* Boston: Beacon Press, 1964.

Yamaguchi Susumu, ed. *Daijō Butten,* vol. 6. Tokyo: Chūō Kōronsha, 1973.

Yamaori Tetsuo. "Ikki izenno koto." In *Chūsei shakai to Ikkō Ikki.* Tokyo: Yoshikawa Kōbunkan, 1985.

———. *Jigoku to Jōdo* [Hell and the Pure Land]. Tokyo: Shunjūsha, 1993.

Yoshida Kenkō. *Essays in Idleness.* Translated by Donald Keene. New York: Columbia University Press, 1967.

Yuasa Yasuo. *The Body: Toward an Eastern Mind–Body Theory.* Translated by S. Nagatomo et. al. Albany: State University of New York Press, 1987.

———. *Nihon Kodai no Seishin Sekai* [The Spiritual World of Ancient Japan]. Tokyo: Meicho Kankōkai, 1990.

———. *Shintai no Uchūsei* [The Cosmic Nature of Corporality]. Tokyo: Iwanami Shoten, 1994.

Žižek, Slavoj. *The Sublime Object of Ideology.* New York: Verso, 1989.

Index

True Vow. *See* Amida Buddha's True Vow
Tsurezure-gusa (Yoshida Kenkō), 161

Umehara Takeshi, 49
Unconscious, personal versus collective,
75–76, 170n7
Uruma Tokikuni, 48–49

Varieties of Religious Experience (James),
59
Villon, François, 45
Vindictive spirits: appeased by monks,
26, 28, 30–31; and chronicles of salvation, 57; exploitative use of, 35; as
independent of death, 29–30; and
monogurui of Noh, 149–50; Sutoku's
vow to become, 28–29; systematized
in *onmyōdō*, 26–27; warrior class tied
to, 37
Visions: of Amida Buddha, at will, 73;
of hell, 31–32, 71; of Hōnen, during
nembutsu zanmai, 61, 62–63, 66, 67,
169n17; Hōnen's negation of, 72–73
Vocal-*nembutsu*: as choice of Amida, 3,
10, 126, 135; contemplative-*nembutsu*
versus, 15, 61, 72, 165n3; defined, 61;
Hōnen on, as inferior, 165n3; Hōnen
on, as superior, 3, 4, 116; Hōnen's conversion to, 59, 61; Shinran's conversion
to, 59–60; as *tariki* practice, 52; voice/
corporality of, 91–93, 98; without
Lotus Sūtra, 61. *See also* Exclusive-
*nembutsu; Nembutsu, Practitioners of
nembutsu*
Voice *(koe)*: as hierophany, 100; mind/
spirit's relationship with, 92–93; *nen's*
unity with, 98–99, 108; of Noh theater,
150–51; to transform consciousness,
91–92. *See also* Vocal-*nembutsu*

Warrior monks: ethic of inversion for,
120–21; Goshirakawa's edict on, 40–
41; *mappō* doctrine of, 37–38; Sanmon
versus Jimon factions of, 39–40; self-

promotion/ambition of, 42–43; wars
between, from 1145–1149, 41–42
Wasan (Shinran), 140
Watsuji Tetsurō, 20, 157
Ways of Thinking of Eastern Peoples
(Nakamura Hajime), 132, 173n1
Weber, Max, 144, 148
"What He Uttered to His Disciples When
He Passed Away," 66
White Noise (DeLillo), 153
Women: Hōnen's interaction with, 12–
13; salvation for, 11–12, 166n17

Yamaori Tetsuo, 8
Yasaka Shrine (Kyoto), 26
Ying and *yang* polarities, 26
Yōgi mondō (Hōnen), 165n4
Yokawa, Genshin's ties to, 51, 169n4
Yokawa shuryōgon'in nijūgo sanmai kishō
(Genshin), 53–54
Yoritomo, Minamoto, 24, 25–26
Yoshida Kenkō, 77, 161
Yoshishige-no-Yasutane, 56
Yōwa, famine of, 24
Yuasa Muneshige, 124
Yuasa Yasuo, 89, 93, 150
Yuikyōgyō (The Last Teaching Sūtra), 124

Zaijarin (Myōe), 124, 125–26, 130, 142,
161
Zaijarin shōgonki (Myōe), 124, 161
Zanmai hottoku. See Mystical experience
"Zanmai Hottoku-ki," 61, 169n17
Zeami, 149–50
Zen Buddhism, 102
Zettai tariki practice, 60. *See also Tariki*
practice
Žižek, Slavoj, 81, 92, 108–9, 171n14
Zōaku muge (licensed evil), 123, 156
Zōbō (counterfeit law), 35–36
Zōkan (eighth stage of *jōzenkan*), 64
Zōryakukan (observation of one of
Amida's countenances), 52, 73
Zōsōkan (last stage of *jōzenkan*), 64–65

Compositors: G&S Typesetters, Inc.
  Birdtrack Press
Text: 10/13 Palatino
Display: Palatino
Printer and binder: Haddon Craftsmen, Inc.